Key Concepts

1

Core Science

Bryan Milner, Jean Martin and Peter Evans

CAMBRIDGE
UNIVERSITY PRESS

Series Editor	Bryan Milner
Biology Editor	Jean Martin
Chemistry editor	Peter Evans
Physics editor	Bryan Milner
Authors	Jenifer Burden
	Paul Butler
	Zoë Crompton
	Sam Ellis
	Peter Evans
	Jean Martin
	Bryan Milner
Consultants	Kate Chaytor
	Nigel Heslop
	Martyn Keeley

PUBLISHED BY THE PRESS SYNDICATE OF THE UNIVERSITY OF CAMBRIDGE
The Pitt Building, Trumpington Street, Cambridge, United Kingdom

CAMBRIDGE UNIVERSITY PRESS
The Edinburgh Building, Cambridge CB2 2RU, UK
40 West 20th Street, New York, NY 10011–4211, USA
477 Williamstown Road, Port Melbourne, VIC 3207, Australia
Ruiz de Alarcón 13, 28014 Madrid, Spain
Dock House, The Waterfront, Cape Town 8001, South Africa

http://www.cambridge.org

© Cambridge University Press 1998

First published 1998
Sixth printing 2003

Produced by Gecko Limited, Bicester, Oxon

Printed in Dubai by Oriental Press

A catalogue record for this book is available from the British Library

ISBN 0 521 58850 2 paperback

Cover photo: Penguins, Images Colour Library

Contents

■ CHEMISTRY

■ Everyday materials

■ Chemical substances

■ Metals and non-metals

■ Chemical reactions

■ Earth chemistry

■ PHYSICS

■ Forces

■ Light and sound

■ Electricity

■ Energy

■ The Earth and beyond

v

■ Acknowledgements

We are grateful to the following for permission to reproduce photographs:

B & C Alexander, pages 42br, 96t; **Allsport UK Ltd**, page 46l (Chris Cole), 196b (Phil Cole), 197c and 248b (Gray Mortimore); **Animal Photography © Sally Anne Thompson**, pages 74t, cb, bl, bc, br, 75tl, b, 75tr (R Willbie); © **John Birdsall Photography**, page 39c; **The Anthony Blake Photo Library**, pages 22, 42t, 44; **Biofoto's** (Jason Venus), pages 95r, 96ct; **Biophoto Associates**, page 64cl; **J Allan Cash Photolibrary**, page 128b, 158c, 197t, b; **Sylvia Cordaiy Picture Library**, pages 16tl (© Paul Kaye), 74ct (© Renee Jasper); **CTC Publicity (courtesy Zeneca Agrochemicals)**, page 91ct; **Lupe Cunha Photography**, pages 27, 76l, 2nd l; *Daily Mail*, 3.1.97, page 35c (John Frost Historical Newspaper Service); © **Ecoscene**, pages 18tl (Mark Caney), 70l, cl (C Gryniewicz), 90t (Williams), 175 (Cooper); **English Heritage Photographic Library**, page 179c; **Environmental Images**, page 196c (© E.P.L./Martin Bond), 240 (Martin Bond), 242t (Stan Gamester), 247 (© John Novis); **Eye Ubiquitous**, page 36 (Larry Bray), 115; **Galaxy Picture Library**, page 138; **Garden Matters**, pages 56, 61, 70cr, r, 85, 88b (© M. Colins), 91t (© M. Colins), 94 (© M. Colins); © **Richard Gardner**, page 181; **GeoScience Features**, pages 10, 12b, 16tr, 19b, 81 (Dr B Booth); **Robert Harding Picture Library**, page 170, 172; **Holt Studios International**, pages 58, 93 (Nigel Catlin), 242c (Primrose Peacock); **Hutchison Library**, page 174cr; **Image Bank**, page 102, 211cr (David Hamilton), 248c; **Andrew Lambert**, page 30, 104, 106, 113, 114, 126, 127, 128t, c, 132t, c, 140, 141, 154c, 159b, 164, 167, 171t, 174t, 176(5), 180b, 214c; **Frank Lane Picture Agency**, page 80b (© David Hosking); **Microscopix Photolibrary**, page 91cb (© Andrew Syred, 1996); **NHM Picture Library**, page 176tr; **Natural History Photographic Agency**, pages 18br (Karl Switak), 19tr (Norbert Wu), 20bl (Jeff Goodman), 79c (© Stephen Dalton), 84 (© Michael Tweedie), 87c (Anthony Bannister), 90c (© G I Bernard), 91br (© Anthony Bannister), 92t (SCRI), 95l (Manfred Danegger), 96cb (Walter Murray); **National Trust Photograph Library**, page 174cl (Vera Collingwood); **Oxford Scientific Films**, pages 6 (Sean Morris, © London Scientific Films), 16cl, cr (© Mantis Wildlife Films), 18tc (Stephen Dalton), c (© Michael Fogden), bl (© Tom Ulrich), 20t (© Peter Parks), 21 (© Rudie Kuiter), 42bl (© Alistair Shay), 78b (© Michael W Richards), 87t (© Philip Devries), 88c and 91bl (Philip Sharpe), 92b (Raymond Blythe), 96b (© Ben Osborne); **Premaphotos Wildlife**, pages 78c and 90b (© K G Preston-Mafham); **PowerStock Ltd**, page 24; **RAF Honnington, Bury St Edmunds**, page 139; **Redferns Music Picture Library**, page 35t and 214br (Mick Hutson), 214t (David Redfern; © **Rhône-Poulenc, Watford**, page 174b; **Salt Union Ltd**, Winsford, page 158t; **Science Photo Library**, pages 12t (Dr Linda Stannard/UCT), 20br (BSIP VEM), 25 (Martin Dohrn), 31 (Manfred Kage), 32t (Matt Meadow, Peter Arnold Inc), cl (Eye of Science), cr (NIBSC), bl (Dr Dari Lounatmaa), br (A B Dowsett), 35b (John Ratcliffe Hospital), 39t (Department of Clinical Radiology, Salisbury District Hospital), 41 (Mike Devlin), 50tl (Mehau Kulyk), tr (Biophoto Associates), c (Department of Clinical Radiology, Salisbury District Hospital), b (CNRI), 52 (Biophoto Associates), 62t (CNRI), 62c (D Phillips), 64ct (C C Studios), 64cr (Petit Format/Nestle), 71tl (Astrid & Hanns Frieder Michler), tr (R B Taylor), b (Andrew Syred), 132cb (Alfred Pasieka), b (Andrew McClenaghan), 154t, 158b (Andrew Syred), 171c (Tony Craddock), 176tl (George Bernard), 258 (US Geological Survey), 265l (NRSC Ltd), r (NASA); **Courtesy of the South London Natural Health Centre**, page 159t (Tony Isbitt); **Still Pictures**, pages 42c, 43 and 173b (Mark Edwards), 155, 180c; **Telegraph Colour Library**, pages 42bc, 46r, 64t; **Department of Transport**, page 34, the poster was produced by the Department of Transport to support its Christmas 1992 Drink Driving Campaign; © **John Walmsley Photo Library**, page 76 (4), 211cl, 214bl; **The Wellcome Trust Medical Photographic Library**, 48; **Janine Wiedel Photo Library**, page 64b, 179t; **Windrush Photos**, pages 19tl (Chris Schenk), 19tc (J Hollis), 79t (Dennis Green), 79b (Frank V Blackburn), 80c (© Richard Revels); **Reproduced by kind permission of the Dean & Chapter of York**, page 173.

Picture research: Maureen Cowdroy

Core Science

1.1 What can living things do?

Suzy and her dog do not look the same. But they do have a lot in common. This is because they are both <u>living things</u>.

1 Look at the pictures. Then write down <u>three</u> things that are the same about Suzy and her dog.

Suzy and her dog can see, hear, feel and smell. We say that they can **sense** *things.*

Suzy and her dog both **move** *about.*

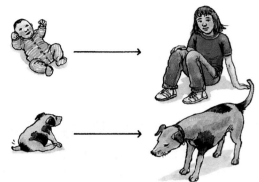

Suzy and her dog were once much smaller. They both **grow**.

■ What do living things need?

Suzy's brother David has a cat. To stay alive David and his cat need to feed and to breathe.

2 Write down <u>two</u> reasons why David and his cat need food.

3 Copy and complete the sentence:

To get energy from food, David and his cat also need _____ .

David and his cat both eat **food**. *They need this to grow and to move.*

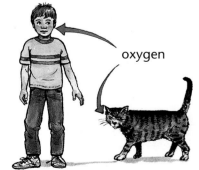

oxygen

To get energy from food, David and his cat both need **oxygen** *from the air.*

■ **Getting rid of waste**

The children and their pets need to get rid of **waste** from their bodies. If they don't get rid of this waste, it will poison them.

4 Write down <u>two</u> kinds of waste they must get rid of.

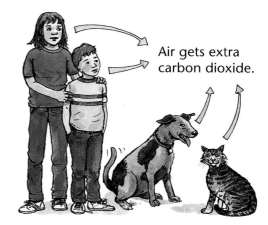

Air gets extra carbon dioxide.

The children and their pets get rid of carbon dioxide. They also get rid of waste in their urine.

■ **What else must living things do?**

David's cat has had kittens. These will still be alive when his cat gets old and dies.

David may become a father when he grows up, and Suzy might have children too.

5 Copy and complete the sentences.

All living things eventually _____.
So some of each kind have to produce young.
We say that they _____.

All animals are alive. They all do the same things as the children and their pets.

We call these things **life processes**.

Plants are alive too. You can read about their life processes on pages 6–7.

*Living things produce young like themselves. We say that they **reproduce**.*

WHAT YOU SHOULD KNOW (Copy and complete using the **key words**)

What can living things do?

All animals:
- _____, _____ and _____;
- take in _____ and _____;
- get rid of _____;
- and _____.

We call these things _____ _____.

1.2 Is it alive?

To see if something is **alive**, we look at what it does.

- If we can find **all** of the life processes, then it's alive.

- If we can't find all the life processes, then it's not alive. We say that it is **non-living**.

1 Copy and complete the sentence.

Things that are alive show _____ of the life processes.

■ Stones and stonechats

Stonechats are small birds. They perch on stone walls, bushes and telephone wires in the countryside.

2 (a) Copy and complete the table.

Does it ... ?	Stonechat	Stone
sense	yes	no
move		
grow		
take in food		
take in oxygen		
get rid of waste		
reproduce		

(b) Is the stone alive? Give reasons for your answer.

3 (a) Make a similar table for a horse and a rocking horse.

(b) Is the rocking horse alive? Give reasons for your answer.

male stonechat

female stonechat

■ Aeroplanes and birds

Aeroplanes look much more alive than stones or rocking horses, and pilots often talk to them as if they were alive.

The plane gives out waste gases.

Lights go on automatically when its dark.

The plane needs fuel and oxygen to provide energy.

The plane moves through the air.

4 (a) Look at the diagram. Then copy and complete the table.

Does it ... ?	Bird	Aeroplane
sense	yes	
move	yes	
grow	yes	no, they are full size when we first make them
take in food	yes	in a way; fuel is like food, but we have to put the fuel in
take in oxygen	yes	
get rid of waste	yes	
reproduce	yes	

(b) Is the plane alive? Give reasons for your answers.

■ Robots

This robot can find items in the warehouse that people need. So can the warehouse person.

The robot uses sensors to find its way around and to find what it has been sent to get.

When you watch the robot, you'd think it was alive.

5 (a) What <u>two</u> life processes does the robot show?

(b) What life processes are <u>not</u> shown by the robot?

WHAT YOU SHOULD KNOW (Copy and complete using the **key words**)

Is it alive?

Some things have never been _____. We say they are _____.

They sometimes show some of the life processes, but they don't show _____ of them.

1.3 Plants are alive

It isn't just animals that are alive.

Plants are alive too. We can tell this by looking at what plants do.

1 Look at the pictures. Then write down <u>five</u> things that plants can do which animals do too.

*Plants **reproduce**. Seeds **grow** into new plants.*

*Plants can **sense** where the light is. They can grow or **move** to face the light.*

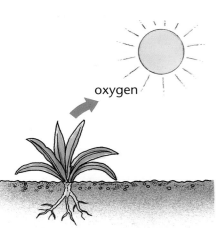

*Plants get rid of **waste**.*

■ Plants can move

Plants can't move about like animals can.

But parts of plants can move, for example to face the Sun. Other parts of some plants can also move.

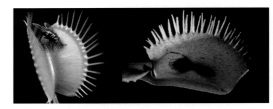

Venus fly trap.

2 Look at the photos of the Venus fly trap.

  (a) Which part of the plant moves?

  (b) When does this happen?

  (c) The Venus fly trap, like other plants, can't move about. Why not?

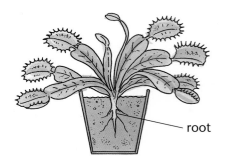

root

Plants can make food

Plants are different from animals because they can make their own food.

The diagrams show what they need to do this.

3 Copy and complete the table.

What the plant needs to make food	Where the plant gets it from

The substances a plant needs to make food are called **nutrients**.

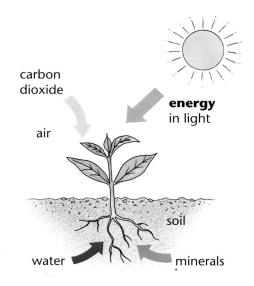

What a plant needs to make food.

Important parts of plants

The different parts of plants do different **jobs**.

4 Look at the diagram. Then copy and complete the table.

Part of plant	What is its job?
flower	
stem	
leaf	
root	
bud	

The different parts of a plant are called **organs**.

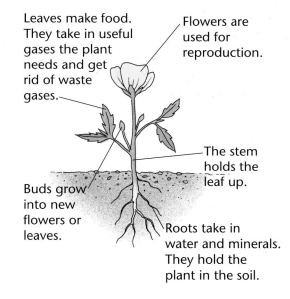

WHAT YOU SHOULD KNOW (Copy and complete using the **key words**)

Plants are alive

Plants, like animals, are living things.
They _____, _____, _____, _____ and get rid of _____.

Plants make their own food using _____ from sunlight and _____ from the soil and air.

Different parts of a plant do different _____.
The different parts of a plant are called _____.

1.4 Important parts of your body

Like plants, your body has many different parts called **organs**. Different organs of your body do different jobs.

For example, your stomach helps your body break down your food. But your stomach does not do this on its own!

Several organs work together to break down your food. Because they digest your food, we call them your **digestive** system.

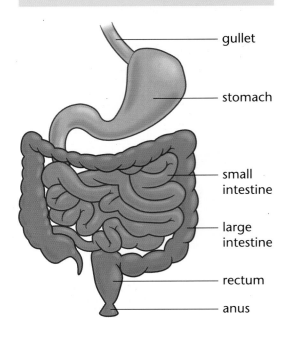

The digestive system.

■ **Your digestive system**

The diagram shows some of the organs in your digestive system.

1 Copy and complete the sentence.

Organs in the digestive system include the _____, stomach, small _____, _____ intestine, _____ and anus.

■ **Your nervous system**

There are other groups of organs in your body. We call one group the **nervous** system.

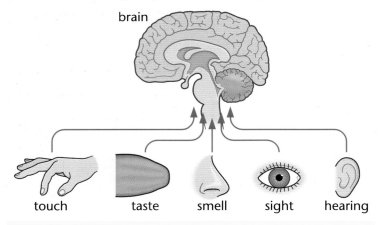

2 List <u>three</u> organs in the nervous system.

3 What life process does the nervous system carry out?

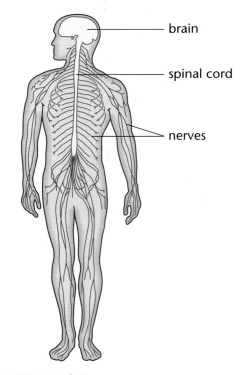

The nervous system.

Your circulatory system

All the organs in your body need food and oxygen.

They all produce waste which needs to be taken away.

Your **circulatory** system carries food, oxygen and wastes around your body.

4   Write down the names of <u>three</u> parts of the circulatory system.

5   Copy and complete the sentences.

The circulatory system carries _____ and _____ to all parts of the body.

It also carries _____ from all parts of the body.

Your body has many other organs. These organs work together in what we call organ **systems**.

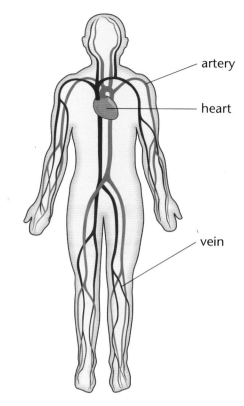

artery

heart

vein

The circulatory system.

WHAT YOU SHOULD KNOW (Copy and complete using the **key words**)

Important parts of your body

The different parts of your body are called _____. These work together in groups called organ _____.

Some organ systems in your body

Organ system	What it does
_____ system	carries food, oxygen and wastes around your body
_____ system	tells you what's happening around you
_____ system	breaks down food so your body can use it

You should also be able to name the organs belonging to each organ system in the table.

1.5 The smallest parts of animals and plants

Animals and plants are made up of parts called organs. These organs are made up of lots of even smaller bits called **cells**.

■ Cells from your cheek

Emma has scraped off a tiny piece from the inside of her cheek. You can see what her cheek lining looks like using a <u>microscope</u>.

Microscopes make small things look a lot bigger. We say that they <u>magnify</u> them.

1 Look at the photograph of the magnified cheek lining. Describe what it looks like.

2 What do we call each small bit of the cheek lining?

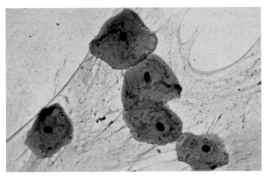

These cheek cells have been stained so they show up easily.

■ How big are cells?

Cells are very small.

Big animals and plants are made up of millions and millions of cells. The bigger an animal or plant is, the more cells it has.

3 Look at the diagram of a cheek cell. How many cheek cells would fit end to end in a space of 1 millimetre?

4 Look at the animals in the pictures. Write down their names in order of how many cells they have. Start with the animal that has the <u>most</u> cells.

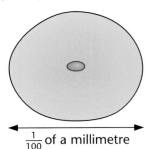

$\frac{1}{100}$ of a millimetre

‖ The space between these lines is 1 millimetre.

Cheek cell.

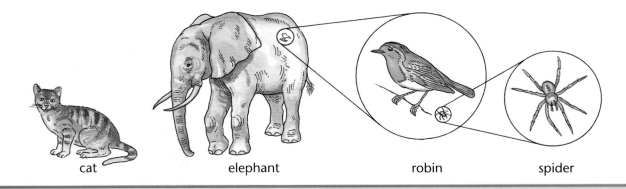

cat   elephant   robin   spider

■ Each part of a cell has a different job

Most animal cells have the same basic parts. The diagram shows what these parts are.

5 Copy and complete the table to show what different parts of a cell do.

Cell part	What it does
nucleus	
cell membrane	
cytoplasm	

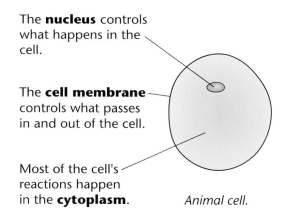

The **nucleus** controls what happens in the cell.

The **cell membrane** controls what passes in and out of the cell.

Most of the cell's reactions happen in the **cytoplasm**.

Animal cell.

■ Plant cells

Plant cells have the same parts as animal cells. They also have some parts that animal cells do not have.

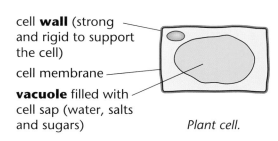

cell **wall** (strong and rigid to support the cell)

cell membrane

vacuole filled with cell sap (water, salts and sugars)

Plant cell.

6 Copy the diagram of a plant cell. Label the nucleus, cytoplasm and cell membrane.

7 What parts does a plant cell have that an animal cell doesn't?

8 Look at the four different kinds of cells, A, B, C and D. For each one, say whether it is an animal cell or a plant cell.

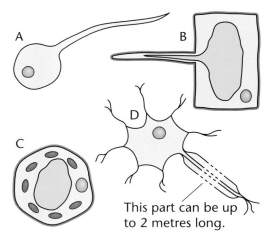

This part can be up to 2 metres long.

WHAT YOU SHOULD KNOW (Copy and complete using the **key words**)

The smallest parts of animals and plants

All plants and animals are made up of tiny bits called _____.

All cells have:
- a _____ which controls what happens in a cell;
- _____ where most chemical reactions take place;
- a _____ _____ which controls what goes in and out of a cell.

Plant cells also have a cell _____ and a _____.

1.6 Microbes

All living things are made from very tiny cells. Large animals and plants are made from lots and lots of cells. The smallest living things are made from just one cell.

The photo shows a living thing which has only one cell. It is very **small**.

You can only see it using a **microscope**, so we call it a microbe or micro-organism.

1 Why can a microscope help us to see this microbe?

2 Copy and complete the table.

Word	What does it mean?
micro_____	This magnifies what you are looking at.
micro-_____ or microbe	You cannot see these organisms with your eyes alone.

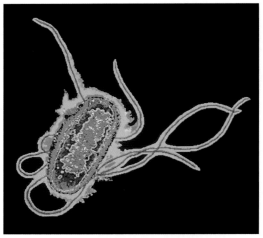

This is an E. coli bacterium. It is magnified 4000 times.

■ Where are microbes?

Microbes are all around us. They are in our air, food, water and our bodies!

Bacteria are one kind of microbe. This student is trying to find out if there are any bacteria in river water.

3 Why can't we see the bacteria in water?

4 Why can we see the bacteria from the water sample after two days?

This colony has millions of bacteria in it.

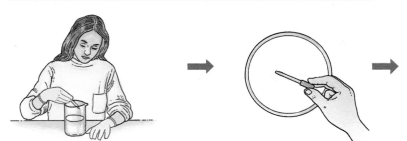

This water is from a river.

The jelly in this dish is food for microbes.

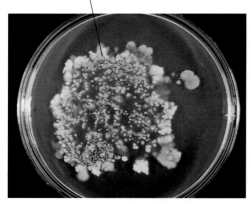

After 2 days in a warm place, the microbes have reproduced lots of times.

Some microbes are harmful

Gary is not feeling very well. He has a bad cold.

Colds are caused by microbes even smaller than bacteria. These microbes are called <u>viruses</u>.

Different viruses and some bacteria can cause other **diseases**.

The diagram shows what happens when Gary catches the cold then gets better again.

5 Write down the following sentences in order to tell the story of Gary's cold.

- He gets better.
- He feels ill.
- A few cold viruses get into his body.
- His body destroys the viruses.
- The viruses reproduce very fast inside his cells.

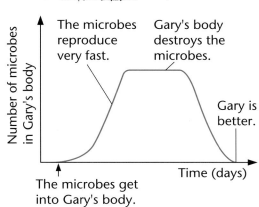

Some microbes are useful

Some microbes are very useful. The pictures show some places microbes are needed.

6 Copy and complete the table.

Where microbes are needed	What the microbes do
in a bakery	
in a sewage treatment plant	
in a dairy	
in a cow's stomach	

Yeast is a microbe that makes bread rise.

Microbes in the cow's stomach help it to digest grass.

Microbes feed on sewage. They break it down into harmless substances.

Microbes turn milk into yogurt and cheese

WHAT YOU SHOULD KNOW (Copy and complete using the **key words**)

Microbes

Microbes are everywhere. They are so _____ we need a_____ to see them.

Some microbes are useful. For example, they can break down _____.

Other microbes are harmful. They can cause _____ in animals and plants.

1.7 Sorting out living things

All living things are alike in many ways. But some living things are more alike than others.

1 Write down <u>five</u> ways in which all living things are alike.

2 Look at the pictures. Then write down <u>three</u> ways that a dog, a cat and a mouse are like each other but different from a snail.

There are millions of different kinds of living things.

It is easier for us to study living things if we sort them into **groups** which have lots of things in common.

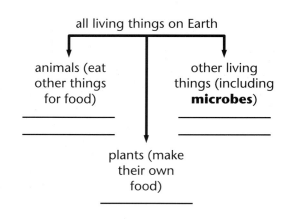

■ Three very big groups

You have already been sorting living things into groups, in pages 2–13.

The diagram shows you what these main groups are.

3 Copy the diagram on the right.

Look at the following pictures of <u>six</u> living things. Then write their names under the correct headings on your diagram.

all living things on Earth

animals (eat other things for food)
_____
_____

other living things (including **microbes**)
_____
_____

plants (make their own food)
_____
_____

lion

dandelion

oak tree

bacterial cell

killer whale

yeast cell

■ Different ways of sorting animals

The three main groups can be sorted into smaller groups. For example, there are many different ways of sorting out animals into smaller groups.

4   Sort the animals on this page into three groups depending on where they live. Give each group a heading:

Live in water	Live on land	Can fly

5   Now use a different way to sort out the animals into groups. (Hint. You might like to try using the number of legs.)

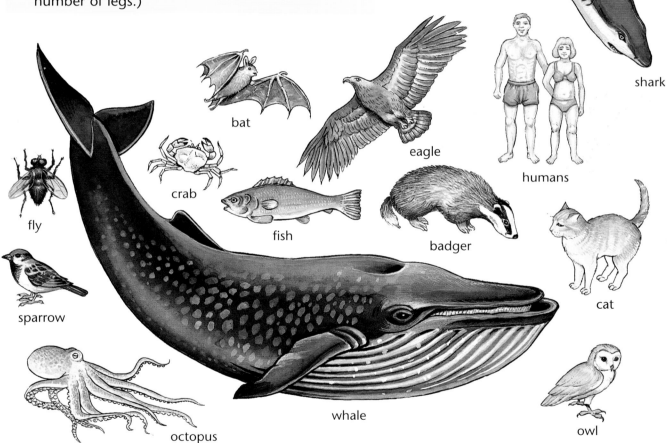

horse

spider

hamster

shark

bat

eagle

humans

crab

fly

fish

badger

cat

sparrow

octopus

whale

owl

WHAT YOU SHOULD KNOW (Copy and complete using the **key words**)

Sorting out living things

We sort out all living things into _____. Plants and animals are two main groups.

Some living things, including _____, do not fit into these two groups.

1.8 What is it?

On pages 14–15, you found out that you can sort living things into groups.

One way of doing this is to use a <u>key</u>.

Cat.

Pine tree.

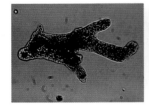
Amoeba. x100

Ant.

■ A simple key

This is how to use a key to find which group the living things in the pictures belong to.

- Go to the start of the key.
- When you come to a branch, choose which way to go.

For example, for the cat you choose these branches:

- made of many cells;
- has no green parts;
- has four legs.

1 Make a copy of the key.

Use the key to find out which group the tree, the ant and the amoeba belong to. Then write their names in the boxes.

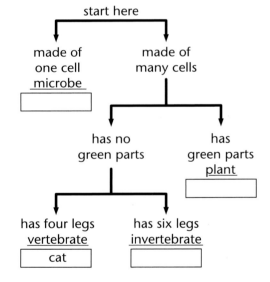

■ Another way of writing this key

A key can also be written as a list of questions.

2 Copy the key below. Then complete the missing parts.

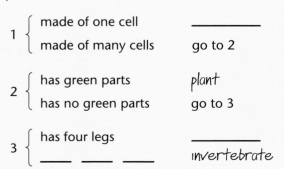

DID YOU KNOW?

Animals can be split into two smaller groups:

- vertebrates (with bones);
- invertebrates (without bones).

You will learn more about these groups on pages 18–21.

■ Keys for smaller groups

All the main groups can be divided into **smaller groups**. You can use a key each time.

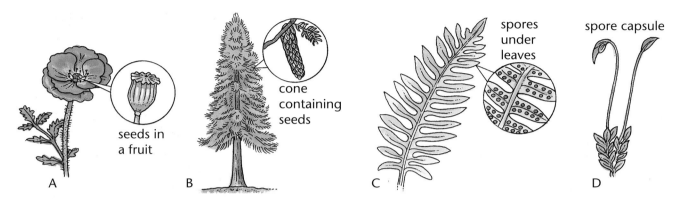

seeds in a fruit

A

cone containing seeds

B

spores under leaves

C

spore capsule

D

3 Copy the table.

Use the key to find out which group each plant belongs to, and complete the table.

Plant	Seeds or spores?	Where seeds or spores are	Plant group
A			
B			
C			
D			

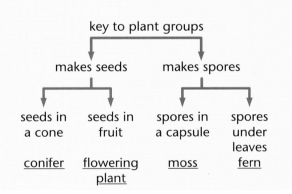

key to plant groups

makes seeds → seeds in a cone / seeds in fruit

makes spores → spores in a capsule / spores under leaves

conifer   flowering plant   moss   fern

■ Special keys for different flowers

Each plant group can be sorted into smaller groups; for example, flowering plants.

There are too many different kinds of flowering plants for one key to cover them all.

We use separate keys for different families of flowers. For example, we can use a **key** just for flowers with four petals.

WHAT YOU SHOULD KNOW (Copy and complete using the **key words**)

What is it?

We can use a key to sort living things into groups and then into _____ _____.

If we want to identify flowering plants, we use a _____ which is just for them.

You need to be able to use a key to identify animals and plants.

1.9 Sorting animals with bones

REMEMBER

all living things

→ animals   → plants   → others (including microbes)

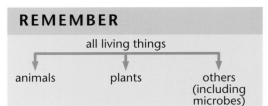

There are many different ways of sorting animals into groups. Scientists have found that some ways of doing this are more useful than others.

Some animals, like you, have bones. Scientists call these animals <u>vertebrates</u>.

We can then split up vertebrates into five smaller groups: **fish**, **amphibians**, **reptiles**, **birds** and **mammals**.

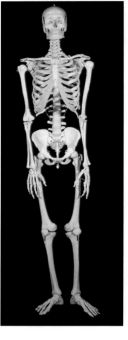

■ Fish

1 Fish do not have lungs. How do they get the oxygen they need?

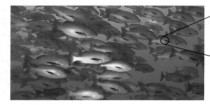

Fish get oxygen from the water through their gills.

Fish have damp scaly skins.

■ Amphibians

2 Why do amphibians have to lay their eggs in water?

Eggs and tadpoles live in water. They would dry up on land.

Amphibians live part of their time in water and part on land.

Amphibians have smooth, moist skin. They do not have scales.

■ Reptiles

3 Write down <u>two</u> differences between amphibians and reptiles.

4 Why can reptiles lay their eggs out of water?

Reptiles have scales, but they are dry. They breathe air into their lungs.

Reptiles lay eggs on land. Their tough leathery shells stop the eggs drying out.

■ Birds

5 What is the difference between reptile and bird eggs?

Birds are covered with feathers.
They have a beak and a pair of wings.

Birds lay eggs with hard shells.   Not all birds can fly!

■ Mammals

6 Mammals have fewer young than other vertebrates because more of them survive. Why do you think this is?

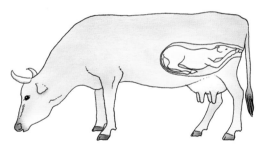

Young mammals develop inside their mother's body and feed on her milk when they are born.

Mammals have hair or fur. They look after their young for a long time.

WHAT YOU SHOULD KNOW (Copy and complete using the **key words**)

Sorting animals with bones

Type of vertebrate	What it is like	Examples
_____	has scales, breathes through gills, lays eggs	cod
_____	moist smooth skin, lives on land and in water, lays eggs	frog
_____	hair covers the body, young feed on mother's milk	cat
_____	dry scaly skin, eggs have tough leathery shell	crocodile
_____	have wings, feathers cover the body, eggs have hard shell	seagull

1.10 Sorting animals that don't have bones

Scientists split up animals into two main groups.

Animals that have bones are called vertebrates.

Most kinds of animals don't have bones. We call them <u>invertebrates</u>.

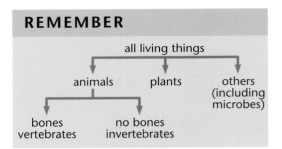
■ Soft-bodied invertebrates

Some invertebrates have completely soft bodies. Examples include **jellyfish**, **flatworms** and **true worms**.

The hydra's mouth is the only opening.

Stinging cells in the tentacles stun the tiny animals it eats.

A tiny jellyfish called a hydra.

All jellyfish live in water.

1 Why should you watch out for jellyfish when you are swimming in the sea?

2 A cat or dog with a tapeworm eats a lot of food but gets thinner. Why is this?

3 Write down <u>two</u> differences between a flatworm (for example, a planarian) and a true worm.

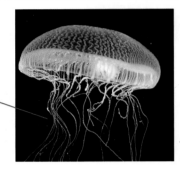

mouth

thin, flat body, no segments

A planarian is a flatworm

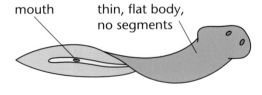

segments

round body

mouth

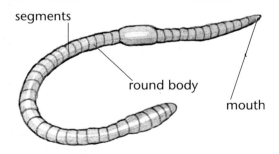

An earthworm is a true worm.

Ragworms are also true worms.

The head of a tapeworm. This kind grows to 4 metres long and lives in human intestines.

4 Copy and complete the table to show the main features of soft-bodied invertebrates.

Soft-bodied invertebrate	Main features
jellyfish	
flatworms	
true worms	

■ Molluscs

Other invertebrates have some hard parts.

shell — tentacle

muscular foot

*A snail is a **mollusc**.*

The squid's shell is inside its body.

5 Most molluscs have shells. Where is a squid's shell?

■ The biggest group of animals on Earth!

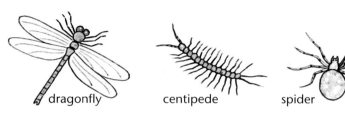

dragonfly   centipede   spider   crab

About three-quarters of all the different kinds of animals on Earth belong to this group of invertebrates. They are called the arthropods.

There are many different kinds of arthropod, so we split them into smaller groups.

But all arthropods do have some things in common:

■ a hard skeleton on the outside of their bodies;

■ jointed legs;

Most arthropods have feelers (antennae).

6 Look at the pictures showing different types of arthropod. Copy and complete the table.

Arthropods

Group	What do they look like?	Examples
crustaceans	two pairs of antennae, five or more pairs of legs	
insects	three pairs of legs, two pairs of wings	
spiders	four pairs of legs, no antennae	
many legs	long body divided into segments, legs on every segment	

WHAT YOU SHOULD KNOW (Copy and complete using the **key words**)

Sorting animals that don't have bones

invertebrates

arthropods   have tentacles and stinging cells   flat body   round body in segments   some hard parts

2 pairs of antennae, 5 or more pairs of legs   3 pairs of legs, 2 pairs of wings   no antennae, 4 pairs of legs   many segments with legs on

2.1 Healthy eating

Our <u>diet</u> is all the food we eat. This food has to be all the things we need, but not too much of any one thing. To stay healthy we mustn't eat too much **fat**, **sugar** or **salt**. Our food must contain **vitamins**, **minerals** and a lot of **fibre**.

■ The traffic-light diet

Here's an easy way to remember the foods to avoid (red ●) and the foods to eat plenty of (green ●).

■ ● Red – stop and think

These foods have a lot of fat or sugar or salt:

sweets, chocolate, cakes, jam, butter, cream, ice cream, fried food, fat on meat, sausages, bacon, chips and crisps.

high fat   high sugar   high salt

Some ● foods.

■ ● Amber – go carefully

Biscuits, red meat, burgers, pies, eggs, cheese, nuts, pasta, pizza, baked beans, samosas; most soft drinks.

Some ● foods.

■ ● Green – go right ahead

Fresh fruit, salad, vegetables, fish, chicken, cottage cheese, yogurt, skimmed milk, bran, bread, rice, lentils; tea (without sugar), water.

1 Name a ● food that has too much salt.

2 Why is cream a ● food?

3 Name a ● food that has a lot of fibre.

Some ● foods.

■ Which meal is healthier?

Working out the traffic-light colour for food can help you decide if a meal is healthy.

4 Copy and complete the table.

Name of food	●	●	●
Meal 1			
rice			*
chicken			
peas			
apple pie			
Meal 2			
fish fingers			
chips	*		
baked beans			
yogurt			

5 Which meal is healthier, meal 1 or meal 2?

meal 1

meal 2

■ Improving Kelly's diet

The picture shows the sort of meal Kelly usually eats.

If Kelly is not more careful all this ● food will make her unhealthy. Doctors have found a link between high fat and high salt diets and heart disease.

6 Draw a picture of a healthy meal for Kelly. Include lots of ● foods.

chocolate pudding

coffee with sugar and cream

sausages and chips

Kelly's meal.

WHAT YOU SHOULD KNOW (Copy and complete using the **key words**)

Healthy eating

To stay healthy we should eat plenty of _____, _____ and _____, but not too much _____, _____ and _____.

2.2 Born to exercise

Thousands of years ago humans had to be very active just to stay alive. So all of us are born with a body ready to move about all day.

But today many people spend their time sitting down – at work, in the car or bus, and in front of the television or computer.

Thousands of years ago humans had to hunt animals for meat and search for fruits and nuts.

1 Why did people thousands of years ago have to be very active?

2 Write down <u>three</u> reasons why many people don't move about very much nowadays.

You can move about because of the muscles in your body. If you don't exercise your muscles, they won't work so well.

Many people who work in offices spend most of the day sitting down.

■ How to exercise your heart muscle

The most important muscle in your body is your <u>heart</u>. Your heart is a bag of muscle that squeezes blood so it moves round your body. Even when you are asleep your heart is busy pumping blood.

When you are resting, your heart beats about 70 times a minute. When you exercise, you can feel your heart beating stronger and faster. It can beat up to twice as fast as it beats at rest. This is good exercise for your heart and keeps it healthy.

3 Where is your heart?

4 About how fast does your heart beat when you exercise?

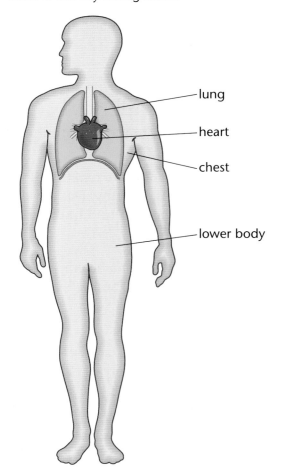

lung

heart

chest

lower body

A close-up of the heart

The picture shows a person's heart during an operation.

Your heart is divided down the middle by a wall of muscle. On each side the blood is squeezed through two spaces (so that is four spaces altogether).

5 Copy and complete these sentences.

Blood comes from your body and goes into the _____ side of your heart. Your heart pumps this blood to your _____ where it gets oxygen. The blood then goes to the _____ side of your heart to be pumped around your _____.

Your heart **pumps** blood by squeezing it out of the **ventricles**. You have **valves** in your heart. These shut when the ventricles squeeze so that blood can't go back the wrong way.

6 (a) What is there between each atrium and ventricle?

(b) What job does this do?

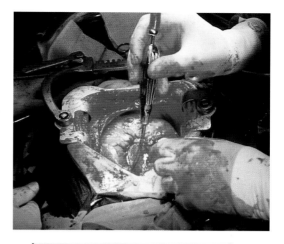

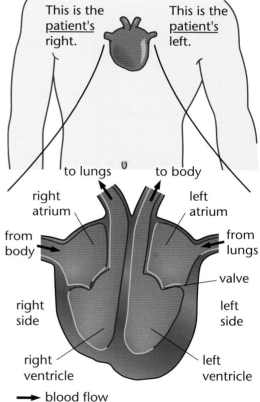

This is the patient's right.   This is the patient's left.

to lungs   to body

right atrium   left atrium

from body   from lungs

valve

right side   left side

right ventricle   left ventricle

➡ blood flow
We always draw the heart this way round.

WHAT YOU SHOULD KNOW (Copy and complete using the **key words**)

Born to exercise

Your heart _____ blood to your lungs and to the rest of your body.
The _____ do this by squeezing the blood.
Your heart has _____ to stop the blood flowing the wrong way.

You need to be able to add these labels to a drawing of the heart: right* atrium, left* atrium, right* ventricle, left* ventricle, valve.   (*Remember – the person's right and left.)

2.3 Where does blood travel?

Blood travels around your body in tubes. There are three kinds of tube: arteries, capillaries and veins.

Your heart pumps blood into the **arteries** which carry blood to all parts of your body.

1 Copy and complete these sentences.

Arteries split into smaller tubes called _____ that reach every part of your body. Capillaries join back together into _____ which carry blood back to your _____ .

■ **Looking at arteries, capillaries and veins**

The diagram shows some of the differences between arteries, capillaries and **veins**.

2 Why do arteries have thick walls?

3 Why do veins have valves?

Capillaries are very thin blood vessels all over your body. Capillary walls are very thin so that substances can move in and out of the blood easily.

4 Copy and complete this table to show what moves in and out of capillaries.

To cells	To blood
oxygen	

REMEMBER

Your heart pumps blood around your body.

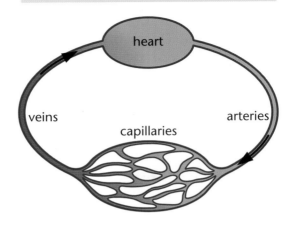

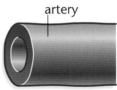

Arteries have thick strong walls because blood is at high pressure after being pumped by the heart.

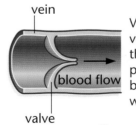

Vein walls are not very thick because the blood is at low pressure. Valves stop blood going the wrong way.

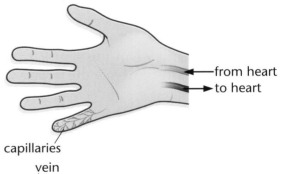

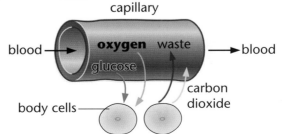

Your body is made of lots of tiny cells. No cell is far from a capillary.

Your pulse

When your heart squeezes the blood into arteries, they stretch bigger for a moment. If an artery is close to your skin, like on your wrist or neck, you can feel the artery stretching. This is your <u>pulse</u>. Each pulse you count is a heart beat.

Your pulse is faster when you exercise. More blood gets to the cells of your muscles so that they can get the things they need to work hard.

5   What <u>two</u> things does the blood carry that the muscle cells need?
(Hint: Look at the diagram at the bottom of p 26.)

How to take a pulse.

How fit are you?

You can tell how fit you are by timing how long it takes for your pulse to go back to normal after exercise. We call this your <u>recovery</u> <u>time</u>.

6   (a)   Look at the graph. What is Asad's pulse rate when he is resting?

(b)   How high does Asad's pulse go when he exercises?

(c)   How long does it take for Asad's pulse to go back to normal after he has stopped exercising?

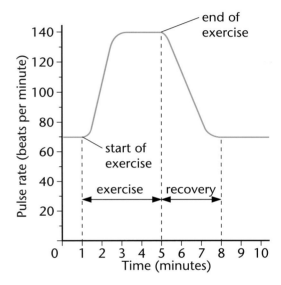

Asad's pulse rate.

WHAT YOU SHOULD KNOW (Copy and complete using the **key words**)

Where does blood travel?

Blood circulates around your body, from the heart to the _____ to the capillaries to the _____ and back to the heart.

Blood carries substances such as glucose and _____ to all the cells of your body.

2.4 Your lungs

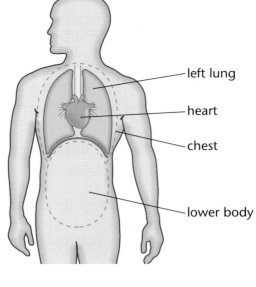

left lung

heart

chest

lower body

All the cells of your body need oxygen to stay alive. So you have to **breathe** air into your body. Air goes into your **lungs**.

Look at the diagram.

1 (a) How many lungs do you have?

(b) In what part of your body are they?

■ What is inside your chest

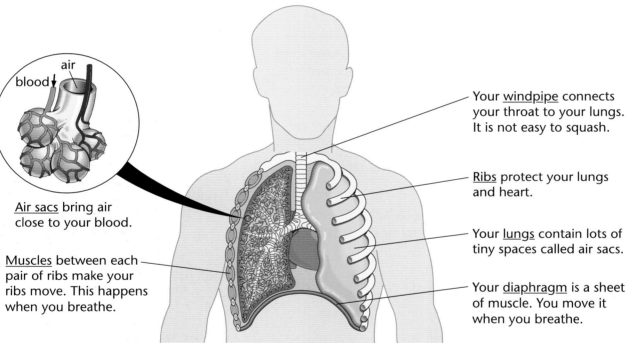

air

blood

Air sacs bring air close to your blood.

Muscles between each pair of ribs make your ribs move. This happens when you breathe.

Your windpipe connects your throat to your lungs. It is not easy to squash.

Ribs protect your lungs and heart.

Your lungs contain lots of tiny spaces called air sacs.

Your diaphragm is a sheet of muscle. You move it when you breathe.

2 Look at the diagram. Then copy and complete the table.

Parts of your body	What jobs they do
rib muscles and diaphragm muscles	
ribs	
windpipe	
air sacs	

You say 'diaphragm' like this: 'die-a-fram'.

◼ How you breathe

When you breathe in:

- ◼ muscles between your ribs move your ribcage up and out;

- ◼ your diaphragm moves down and becomes flatter;

- ◼ the extra space in your lungs fills with air.

When you breathe out:

- ◼ your ribs move down;

- ◼ your diaphragm curves up again;

- ◼ there is less space inside your chest so air is pushed out.

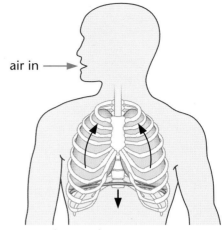

air in →

space inside your lungs:
shallow breath 2000 cm^3
deep breath 4500 cm^3

Breathing in.

3 Copy and complete the table.

	Breathing in	Breathing out
How your ribs move		
What happens to your diaphragm		

4 How much air do you breathe in:

   (a) in a shallow breath;

   (b) in a deep breath?

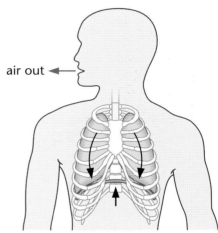

air out ←

space inside your lungs:
1500cm^3
This means that there is 1500 cm^3 of air that you can't breathe out.

Breathing out.

WHAT YOU SHOULD KNOW (Copy and complete using the **key words**)

Your lungs

When you _____, you take air in and out of your _____.

You need to be able to add these labels to a drawing of the breathing system: lungs, windpipe, diaphragm, ribs.

2.5 Breathing and asthma

Saba has asthma. This sometimes affects her lungs. It makes it difficult for her to breathe.

Saba gets wheezy when she runs on a cold day. This also happens when she breathes in smoke or pollution from cars.

1 Copy and complete these sentences.

People with asthma wheeze when the air pipes to their lungs become _____ than normal. This makes it hard for _____ to go in and out of their _____.

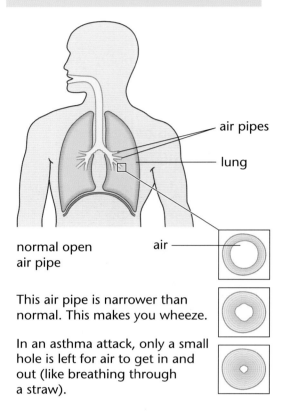

air pipes

lung

normal open air pipe   air

This air pipe is narrower than normal. This makes you wheeze.

In an asthma attack, only a small hole is left for air to get in and out (like breathing through a straw).

What happens in an asthma attack.

■ **Treatment for Saba**

When Saba feels her chest go tight, she uses an inhaler. She breathes in a drug from the inhaler. This drug opens the air pipes in her lungs so she can breathe more easily.

It is important that she stays calm and uses her inhaler straight away. Sometimes her breathing gets very difficult and she has an asthma attack.

2 How does an inhaler help Saba?

Using an inhaler.

A close-up of your lungs

The air you breathe in is not the same as the air you breathe out. In your lungs **oxygen** goes from the air into your blood and **carbon dioxide** goes from your blood into the air. This process is called **gas exchange**.

3 Copy and complete the table using the words <u>more</u> or <u>less</u>.

Air you breathe in	Air you breathe out
more oxygen	_____ oxygen
_____ carbon dioxide	_____ carbon dioxide

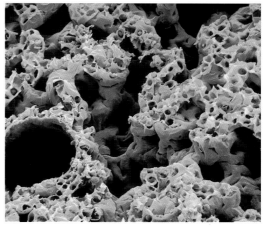

Inside the lungs are lots of tiny spaces called air sacs.

You breathe for your cells

Your blood carries the oxygen round your body. Your cells use the oxygen to get energy. Carbon dioxide is made by cells and needs to be got rid of. So your blood carries it to your lungs so that you can breathe it out.

4 When Saba has an asthma attack, what gas does she not get enough of?

5 Why does Saba feel weak when she has an asthma attack?

Our cells need more oxygen when we exercise so we breathe faster.

6 Why does Saba have more problems when she runs?

7 Saba told her new PE teacher that she had asthma. Why did she do this?

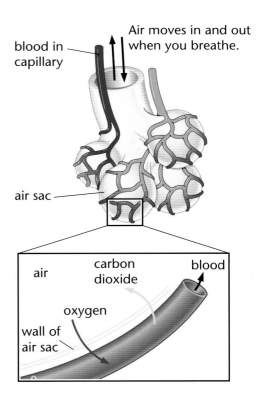

blood in capillary

Air moves in and out when you breathe.

air sac

air   carbon dioxide   blood

oxygen

wall of air sac

WHAT YOU SHOULD KNOW (Copy and complete using the **key words**)

Breathing and asthma

In your lungs, _____ passes into your blood and _____ _____ passes into the air. We call this _____ _____.

2.6 How do we catch diseases?

■ Influenza

Flu (influenza) is an easy disease to catch. All you need to do is to find someone who has flu. Then let them breathe on you, or cough or sneeze near you. Tiny drops that contain microbes can travel through the air for you to breathe in. This is because the microbe that causes flu is very tiny.

1 What causes influenza?

2 Why is flu so easy to catch?

3 Why should you cough or sneeze into a tissue?

A sneeze spreads tiny drops into the air. These drops contain all sorts of microbes.

■ Viruses

The microbe that causes flu is a virus. There are many other **viruses**. Each type of virus causes a different disease. Some diseases are easier to catch than others. There are some diseases that you don't usually catch again after you have had them once.

4 Write down the names of three diseases caused by viruses.

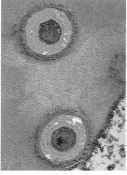 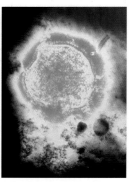

Chicken pox viruses. × 90,000   *Measles virus. × 100,000*

■ Bacteria

Bacteria are also microbes. Some bacteria cause disease.

5 Write down the names of two diseases caused by bacteria.

Microbes are tiny. These photos of viruses and bacteria are magnified enormously.

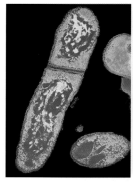 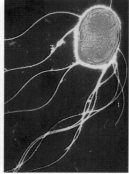

TB (tuberculosis) bacteria.   *Salmonella bacterium. It causes food poisoning.*

■ The frozen chicken story

6 Why did the family decide it was the chicken that caused the food poisoning?

7 What sort of microbe is salmonella?

Salmonella bacteria are often found in chickens.

To kill salmonella bacteria, you must make them very hot. We need to see inside the chicken to find out what went wrong.

8 Does freezing kill salmonella?

9 What should the boys have done to cook the chicken properly?

chicken after defrosting for 1 hour

— still frozen

chicken after cooking for 2 hours

cooked, hot (bacteria killed)

not cooked, only warm (bacteria not killed)

WHAT YOU SHOULD KNOW (Copy and complete using the **key words**)

How do we catch diseases?

Some bacteria and viruses can make you ill. Different microbes cause different diseases.
For example, _____ cause tuberculosis (TB) and salmonella food poisoning.
_____ cause influenza and chicken pox.

2.7 Harmful chemicals

There are lots of different chemicals that can **harm** you. Examples are tobacco smoke and alcohol. But many people still choose to take these into their bodies.

■ Smoking

Nicotine in **tobacco** smoke stops the tiny hairs in your lungs from working. It also increases your heart rate. The tar in cigarette smoke can cause cancer.

1 Write down <u>two</u> ways nicotine damages your body.

2 What other dangerous substance is there in cigarette smoke?

■ Drinking alcohol

Alcohol is a drug that changes the way you behave and move. When you drink, your reactions slow down. People who are drunk slur their words and become clumsy. Over a long time alcohol can damage your liver and your brain.

3 Why is it dangerous to drink and drive?

4 Which <u>two</u> organs of the body does alcohol damage?

■ Solvent abuse

This is when people breathe in the fumes from some sort of glue or other substances containing solvents. The effects are similar to being drunk. But these fumes can make your heart stop or make you choke to death.

5 Describe <u>three</u> ways you can tell if someone has been glue sniffing.

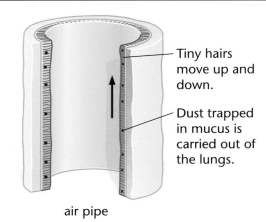

air pipe

Nicotine in tobacco smoke paralyses the tiny hairs which clean dust out of your lungs. So smokers' lungs get dusty. This is why they cough.

Look her in the eye. Then say a quick drink never hurt anybody.

DRINKING AND DRIVING WRECKS LIVES.

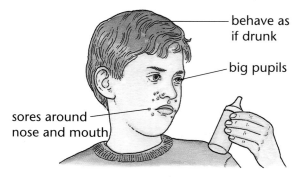

Signs of solvent abuse.

Illegal drugs

People caught with illegal drugs could spend up to 7 years in prison.

<u>LSD (Acid)</u> affects your mind. People who take it see strange things and can feel upset and depressed. This can happen without warning even several years after it is taken.

6 Why is LSD a dangerous drug?

<u>Ecstasy</u> makes your heart beat faster than normal. People use this at raves to help them dance for hours. They get hot and sweat a lot. They need to replace the water and salts they lose. If they don't they can die of heat stroke. Too much water can also kill them.

7 Why do you think some people who take Ecstasy have overheated?

There's only one truth about Ecstasy: it kills

<u>Cannabis</u> is usually smoked and it can cause mouth and throat cancer. People who smoke cannabis feel relaxed.

8 What illness do tobacco and cannabis both cause?

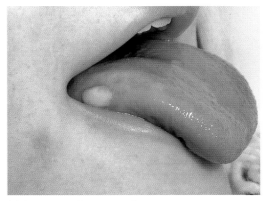

This person has mouth cancer.

WHAT YOU SHOULD KNOW (Copy and complete using the **key words**)

Harmful chemicals

Drugs can _____ you. They affect your mind and body.
Even legal drugs like _____ and _____ are harmful.

2.8 Long-term effects of drugs

■ Addiction

An <u>addict</u> is a person who can't manage without something.

Heroin and cocaine are addictive drugs. So are **nicotine** and **alcohol**. If you stop using them you feel ill. This is why once people start smoking or drinking a lot of alcohol they find it hard to stop.

A lot of ordinary people are addicted to smoking cigarettes or to alcohol. Over the years their bodies will be damaged.

1 Do you think the people in the picture are addicts? Give reasons for your answer.

■ Lung cancer

Look at the graph.

2 (a) How many people (in 10 000) who don't smoke die of lung cancer?

(b) How many people (in 10 000) who smoke 40 cigarettes a day die of lung cancer?

Half the people who have operations to remove lung cancer continue to smoke.

3 Why do you think people who have been made ill by smoking continue to smoke?

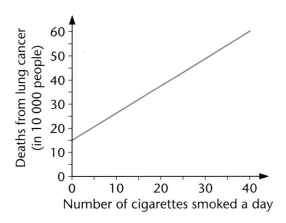

■ Other effects of drugs

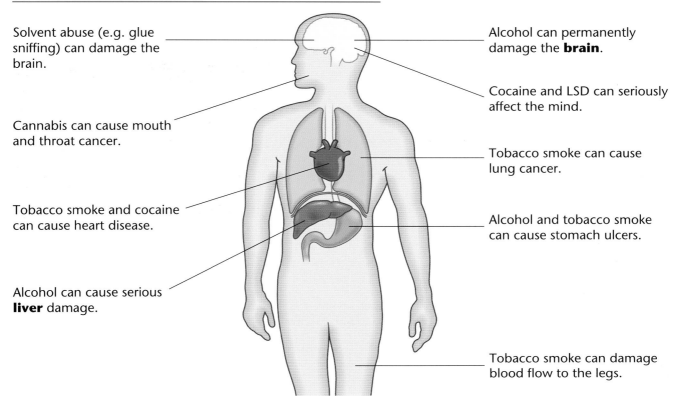

Solvent abuse (e.g. glue sniffing) can damage the brain.

Cannabis can cause mouth and throat cancer.

Tobacco smoke and cocaine can cause heart disease.

Alcohol can cause serious **liver** damage.

Alcohol can permanently damage the **brain**.

Cocaine and LSD can seriously affect the mind.

Tobacco smoke can cause lung cancer.

Alcohol and tobacco smoke can cause stomach ulcers.

Tobacco smoke can damage blood flow to the legs.

4 Which parts of the body does alcohol damage?

5 Copy and complete this table to show how drugs can damage your body.

Effect on the body	Drugs
brain damage	
heart disease and blood flow problems	
lung cancer	
liver damage	
stomach ulcers	

WHAT YOU SHOULD KNOW (Copy and complete using the **key words**)

Long-term effects of drugs

You can become addicted to _____, _____ and other drugs.

Drugs can damage your body.
For example, alcohol damages your _____ and your _____ .

2.9 Your skeleton

You have a skeleton inside your body. It is made of lots of bones all joined together.

Your skeleton holds your body together in the right shape. We say it <u>supports</u> your body.

Your skeleton **protects** some of the softer parts of your body.

You need a skeleton to move about. Bones give **muscles** something to pull on.

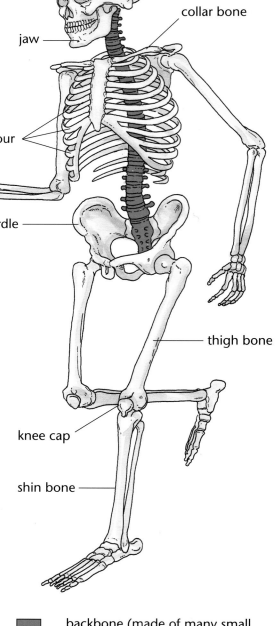

skull (protects your brain)

collar bone

jaw

ribcage (protects your heart and lungs)

pelvic girdle

thigh bone

knee cap

shin bone

█ = backbone (made of many small bones; protects your spinal cord)

1 What is a skeleton?

2 Write down <u>three</u> jobs your skeleton does.

3 Look at the diagram. Then copy and complete the table.

Bone	What it protects
ribcage	
	brain
backbone	

■ Broken bones

Bones are strong but they can break.

Sumera fell off her bike and landed on her arm. At the hospital the doctors X-ray her arm to see which bones are broken.

4 Which bones has Sumera broken?

A broken bone will not heal straight unless the broken ends are held in position.

Bones support your body. If a bone is broken it will not support you.

5 Write down <u>two</u> reasons why Sumera must wear a cast on her broken arm.

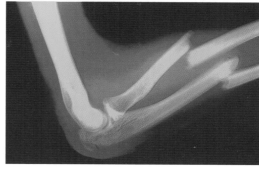

X-ray of Sumera's arm.

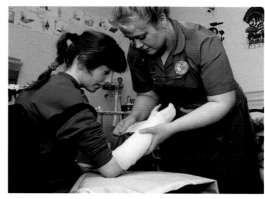

Sumera wears a cast on her arm while the bone mends.

■ Marrow bones

Some bones have a soft **marrow** inside them. Bone marrow makes new blood cells.

6 Look at the diagram. How can bones be light and strong at the same time?

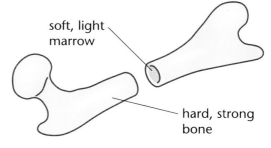

soft, light marrow

hard, strong bone

A tube of bone is a lot lighter than solid bone. It is still very strong.

WHAT YOU SHOULD KNOW (Copy and complete using the **key words**)

Your skeleton

■ supports your body;

■ _____ organs like your brain;

Your bones:

■ give _____ something to pull on;

■ have bone _____ to make new blood cells.

You need to be able to label a drawing of the main parts of your skeleton.

2.10 Joints

The places where your bones are joined together are called **joints**. Muscles are fixed to your bones on each side of a joint. Your muscles pull on the bones to make you move.

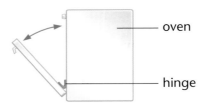

— oven

— hinge

The hinge of an oven door only bends one way, like your elbow joint.

■ Elbow joint

In your elbow the bones fit together so the joint only bends one way. This is like a hinge.

To bend your arm, your biceps muscle shortens or **contracts**. This pulls one bone towards the other.

To straighten your arm, your biceps muscle relaxes and the muscle on the other side of the joint contracts. This pulls the arm straight again.

1 Look at the diagram. Then copy and complete the table.

	Arm straight	Arm bent
Contracting muscle		
Relaxing muscle		

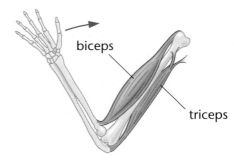

biceps

triceps

The biceps contracts to bend the arm. The triceps relaxes to let this happen.

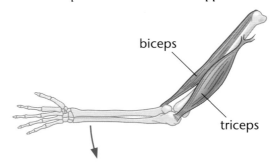

biceps

triceps

The triceps contracts to straighten the arm. The biceps relaxes to let this happen.

■ Hip joint

The end of your thigh bone is round like a ball. It fits into a hollow called a socket. This socket is part of your pelvic girdle. We call this joint a <u>ball and socket</u> joint.

2 (a) Which bone of your hip joint is the ball?

   (b) Which bone of your hip joint is the socket?

   (c) Which way can your hip joint bend?

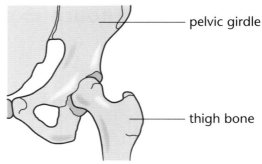

— pelvic girdle

— thigh bone

Your hip joint is a ball and socket joint. It can bend in any direction.

■ Backbone joint

The joints in your backbone hold the bones so they cannot move very much. Inside your backbone is your spinal cord.

3 Why mustn't the bones of your backbone move very much?

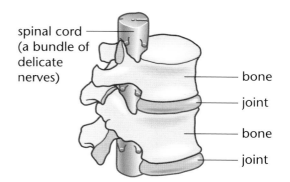

The bones of your backbone protect your spinal cord.

■ Replacing a joint

Marcia's grandfather Jack has had a hip replacement operation. Before the operation he had trouble walking. His hip caused him so much pain he had to stop every few steps. In Jack's hip joint the bones didn't move smoothly against each other, they rubbed and caused pain.

In the hip replacement operation, the joint between Jack's hip bone and leg bone was cut out. Then a plastic and metal joint was put in.

4 (a) What is the ball of the new joint made of?

(b) What is the socket of the new joint made of?

5 How will a hip replacement improve Jack's life?

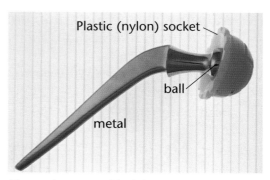

The replacement hip joint.

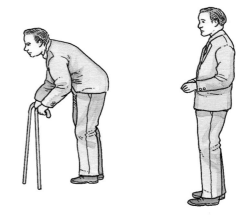

Jack before and after the operation.

WHAT YOU SHOULD KNOW (Copy and complete using the **key words**)

Joints

Bones let you move. Places where two bones meet are called _____.
When a muscle _____, it pulls on a bone and moves it.

3.1 Fuel and energy

We burn fuel to give us energy.

1   Write down <u>two</u> things we use this energy for.

2   Write down the names of <u>two</u> fuels that we burn.

Burning gas gives us heat for cooking.

Burning petrol makes things move.

All plants and animals also need energy. They get this from **food**. Food is their fuel.

3   Humans are animals. Write down <u>three</u> things we use energy for.

 **moving**    **growing**   keeping warm

Different plants and animals need different amounts of food for energy.

What we use energy for.

4   (a)   For each pair of pictures, copy and complete the sentence.

The _____ bee needs more energy than the _____ bee.

The _____ needs more energy than the _____.

(b)   Give reasons for your answers to (a)

Resting    Flying

Briton   Inuit

■ Releasing energy from fuels

fuel ⌐
oxygen ⌐ → energy

food ⌐
oxygen ⌐ → energy

5 Copy and complete the sentence.

Cars and humans need to take in _____ to release energy from _____.

■ Which foods give us energy?

Some of the substances in our food give us energy. These are mainly <u>carbohydrates</u> and <u>fats</u>.

> We measure energy in joules (J) or kilojoules (kJ). 1000 joules make 1 kilojoule.

6 Look at the burger.

   (a) How much energy does it give you?

   (b) Which part of the burger provides most of this energy?

bread (mainly carbohydrate) 650 kJ

chicken (mainly protein) 580 kJ

butter (mainly fat) 150 kJ

■ Why do we need proteins?

7 Look at the diagram, then copy and complete the sentences.

We use proteins mainly for _____ and _____. But if we eat more protein than we need for growing new _____, we use what is left for _____.

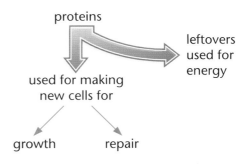

proteins

used for making new cells for

leftovers used for energy

growth   repair

WHAT YOU SHOULD KNOW (Copy and complete using the **key words**)

Fuel and energy

We need energy for _____, _____ and keeping warm.
We get this energy from _____. Food is our fuel.

43

3.2 Food for humans

■ Living off the land

If someone is 'living off the land', it means that they catch animals and collect wild plants for food.

Soldiers learn to do this as part of their training. It is called survival training.

All humans used to get their food this way. Some people still do.

1 Write down <u>three</u> things a person living off the land might eat.

2 People who gather food like this usually need to move from place to place. Why is this?

This fish is a trout.

Blackberries often grow in hedgerows.

■ Farming the land

People living off the land found it hard to find food in the winter. They started to grow food crops like wheat during the summer and saved some for the winter.

They also started to keep animals like sheep and cattle for meat and milk.

3 Copy and complete the sentences.

Farmers may have found it easier to survive the _____ than people who hunted for food because they _____ food.

The meat from a deer is called venison.

When we turn milk into cheese, we can keep it for a long time.

We can store dried grain.

Food in Britain today

Most of us don't grow our own food. A small number of farmers grow it for everybody. Even farmers in other countries grow some of our food.

All of our food comes from **plants** and **animals**. However, it is often hard to tell which ones it came from. This is because it is changed before we get it.

wheat   flour   bread

4 Copy and complete the sentences.

We make bread from _____ which comes from _____.

We make cheese from _____ which comes from _____.

Marmite is made from a microbe called _____.

cow   milk   cheese

Wherever it comes from, our food gives us:

- the **energy** we need to live;

- the **materials** we need to grow and to repair damaged parts.

yeast
(a microbe)   Marmite

How does the energy get into food?

Look at the picture.

5 Copy and complete the diagram.

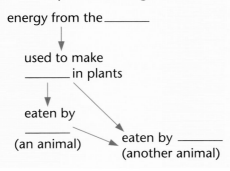

energy from the _____

↓

used to make
_____ in plants

↓

eaten by
_____
(an animal)

eaten by _____
(another animal)

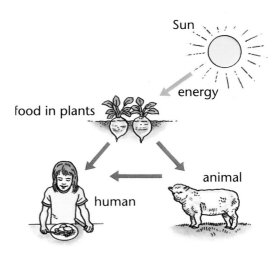

Sun

energy

food in plants

human

animal

WHAT YOU SHOULD KNOW (Copy and complete using the **key words**)

Food for humans

Our food gives us the _____ and the _____ we need to live and to grow.
It comes from _____ or from _____ which ate plants.

3.3 What most of your food is made of

If you eat more food than you need, you store it as fat. If you don't eat enough food, you lose weight and become weak and ill.

It also matters what type of food you eat.

Your <u>diet</u> is everything you eat. You must include carbohydrate, fat, protein and fibre in your diet. Your body needs all of these to keep **healthy**.

> **REMEMBER**
>
> Food is fuel. It gives you energy. You need food for moving about, keeping warm and growing.

These wrestlers wanted to get fat so they ate too much food.

Some people can't get enough food.

■ Energy foods

Carbohydrates and **fats** in your food give you most of your energy.

1 Write down the names of <u>two</u> sorts of food which contain a lot of carbohydrates.

2 Write down the names of <u>two</u> foods which contain a lot of fat.

Eating too much of the foods that give you energy can make you overweight. Being overweight can put a strain on your heart.

3 Write down the names of <u>two</u> sorts of food you should eat less of if you want to lose weight.

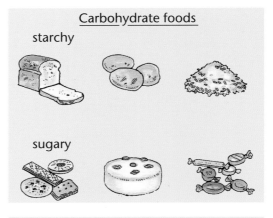

Carbohydrate foods

starchy

sugary

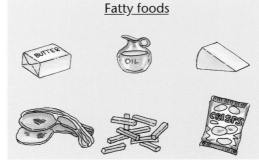

Fatty foods

These foods give us energy.

■ Growth foods

Your body needs **proteins** and some fat to make new cells and repair damaged ones.
Young people need lots of proteins because they are still growing.

4 Write down the names of <u>two</u> foods which contain a lot of protein.

5 Why do children need to eat more protein than adults?

6 What else besides protein do you need to make new cells?

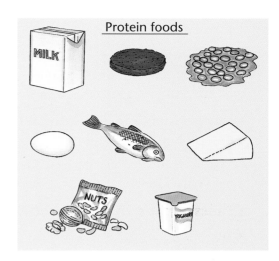

Protein foods

■ Food to keep you regular

When you eat food, the muscles of your intestines push the food along. **Fibre** is the part of food that you cannot digest. It gives the muscles of your intestines something to push on.

7 Write down <u>two</u> foods that could help someone who was constipated to go to the toilet.

Fibrous foods

■ Water

The food we eat contains a lot of water. We also need to drink **water**. Water is important to keep blood flowing and cells working.

8 What percentage of an apple is water?

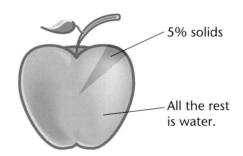

5% solids

All the rest is water.

An apple may not look like a drink, but most of it is water.

WHAT YOU SHOULD KNOW (Copy and complete using the **key words**)

What most of your food is made of

You need the right amount and types of food to stay _____.
You also need to drink _____.

Most food is made of _____, _____, _____, _____ and _____.

3.4 What else must there be in your food?

Adults often say to children: 'Eat your greens. They are good for you.' Have you ever thought why?

Green vegetables contain special substances called **vitamins** that you need to keep you healthy.

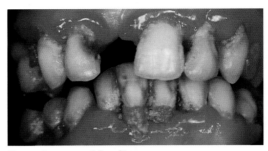

Scurvy causes bleeding gums.

■ Illness caused by an unhealthy diet

Scurvy is a serious disease. Your gums bleed, your teeth become loose and your muscles get weak. Many years ago, sailors on long sea voyages used to get scurvy and some even died.

1 Write down <u>two</u> things that happen to you if you get scurvy.

In 1747, Dr James Lind tried an experiment on 12 men with scurvy. The table shows what happened.

2 What do you think Dr Lind told sailors to do about scurvy?

People get scurvy when there is not enough of a chemical called <u>vitamin C</u> in their diet.

You get most of your vitamin C from eating fresh fruit and vegetables.

3 Why did the men with scurvy who drank cider get a bit better?

As well as vitamin C, you need other vitamins to stay healthy. You also need **minerals** such as iron and calcium.

What Dr Lind gave the men every day	What happened
oranges and lemons	The men got better.
cider (made from apples)	The men got a bit better.
other foods, but no fresh fruit or vegetables	The men didn't get better.

These foods contain vitamin C.

Food for health

Most foods have some vitamins or minerals, but some foods (like most sweets) don't have any.

Each type of vitamin or mineral is needed for a particular job. Each one is important for a healthy body.

Vitamin or mineral	What it is needed for
A	helps you see in dim light, and keeps your lungs healthy
B	helps many of the chemical reactions in your body
C	keeps your skin and gums healthy
D	helps you take in the minerals you need to make bones
iron	makes red blood cells
calcium	for strong bones and teeth

4 Which vitamin do you need to help you see well in dim light?

5 Write down the names of <u>two</u> foods which contain vitamin B.

6 Which mineral do you need for strong teeth?

7 In sunlight you can make vitamin D in your skin, but you still need some from your food. Write down <u>two</u> foods that contain vitamin D.

8 Meena has been told by her doctor to take some iron tablets. What does she need them for?

fish

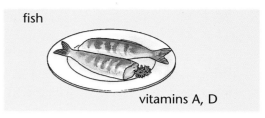

vitamins A, D

milk

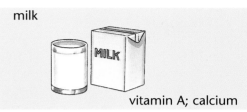

vitamin A; calcium

vegetables

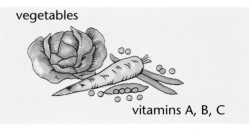

vitamins A, B, C

egg

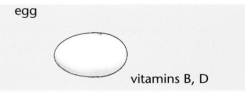

vitamins B, D

liver

vitamins A, D; iron

wholemeal bread

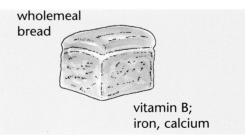

vitamin B; iron, calcium

Examples of vitamins and minerals in different foods.

WHAT YOU SHOULD KNOW (Copy and complete using the **key words**)

What else must there be in your food?

To stay healthy you need to eat foods that contain _____ and _____.

3.5 Where does your food go?

When you swallow your food, it is starting on a long journey. This can last for several days.

■ Cutting food up

You can put a large piece of food in your mouth. It is easier to swallow smaller pieces, so you use your teeth to cut and chew the food.

1 What happens if you try to swallow a very large piece of food?

2 Why is important to take good care of your teeth?

Salivary glands make the saliva in your mouth. Saliva is a **digestive juice**. It also makes your food slippery and easy to swallow.

Once swallowed, muscles in your oesophagus (gullet) push the food into your stomach.

3 Copy and complete these sentences.

Your _____ cut and chew your food.
Saliva wets food so it is easier to _____.

■ What happens after you swallow?

The photographs on this page are of a person who has had a special drink. The drink shows up on X-ray photographs so we can see where food goes.

4 List in order the parts that your food goes through after you swallow.

These parts, and the glands that make digestive juices, work together. They are your <u>digestive system</u>.

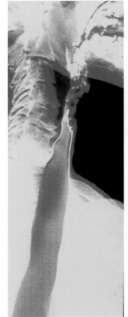 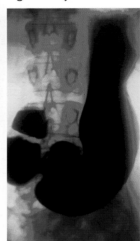

X-ray photographs of a liquid passing through a person's digestive system.

Oesophagus (gullet). Stomach.

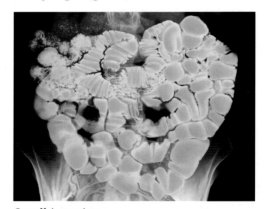

Small intestine.

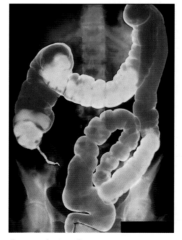

Large intestine.

■ In your stomach

Muscles in the stomach wall churn the food up. Glands in the stomach lining add more digestive juices.

Food can stay in your stomach for 3–4 hours. Liquids leave sooner. Your stomach lets food out a bit at a time into the small intestine.

5   Copy and complete the table.

Part of stomach	What it does
muscles in wall	
glands in lining	
ring of muscle	

■ In the intestines

6   Look at the diagram opposite. How do all your intestines fit in to the lower part of your body?

In the small intestines, more digestive juices are added to your food.

7   What two parts of your body add digestive juices to the food in your small intestine?

Digested food passes into your blood from your small intestine. Blood carries the food to cells that need it.

Your food and drinks also contain a lot of water. Water passes into your blood from the large intestine.

The food that is left contains undigested waste, water and bacteria. We call this waste faeces. This passes through the large intestines and eventually leaves your body.

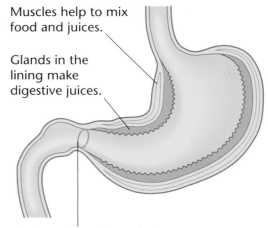

Muscles help to mix food and juices.

Glands in the lining make digestive juices.

A ring of muscle controls what leaves the stomach.

DID YOU KNOW?

There are about 6 metres of intestines inside your body.

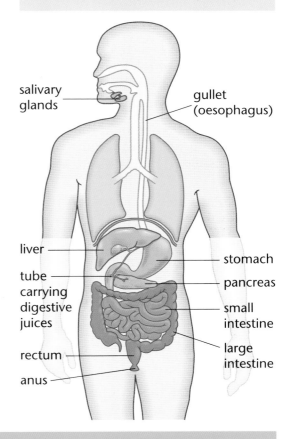

salivary glands

gullet (oesophagus)

liver

tube carrying digestive juices

rectum

anus

stomach

pancreas

small intestine

large intestine

WHAT YOU SHOULD KNOW

Where does your food go?

You must be able to label a diagram of the digestive system like the one above.

3.6 Digesting your food

Food contains large molecules which you cannot absorb into your blood. You need to break these down. Your digestive system does this.

You can't, like the snake, swallow a whole rat, but you still eat your food in large pieces.

■ What happens during digestion?

You put a large piece of food in your mouth.

Chewing your food cuts it into smaller pieces.

But even a small piece of food has large molecules in it.

Parts of the digestive system make digestive juices. The juices contain enzymes which break down large food molecules into **smaller** ones. This is **digestion**.

The chemical links in the molecule are broken. Different types of food are broken down like this:

■ carbohydrates → glucose;

■ fats → fatty acids and glycerol;

■ proteins → amino acids.

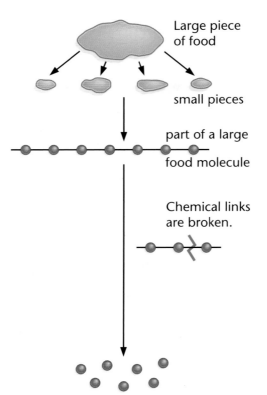

Large piece of food

small pieces

part of a large food molecule

Chemical links are broken.

1 What is digestion?

2 Copy and complete these sentences.

Your teeth cut food into _____ pieces. Even these small pieces can have large _____ in them.

To make the molecules smaller, _____ _____ are added to the food. These break the _____ links in the large food molecules.

The _____ molecules are broken down into _____ ones. Small molecules are soluble. This means that they can dissolve.

■ What happens to the digested food?

All the cells in your body need food.

Digested food passes into the blood from the small intestines. This is **absorption**.

3 Where does food go when it is absorbed?

The digested food molecules can only get across the small intestine wall because they are small and soluble. They dissolve in the **blood**.

4 Write down <u>two</u> reasons why large food molecules must be digested.

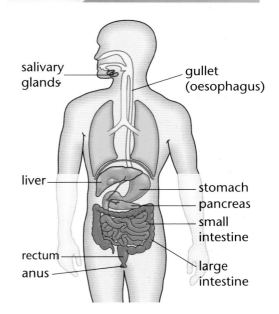

large food molecule in small intestine

blood

digestion

blood

Small, soluble food molecules are absorbed into the blood.

■ What happens to the undigested food?

The food that is left contains undigested waste, water and bacteria. We call this solid waste <u>faeces</u>.

The waste leaves your body through the anus. We say that the waste is <u>egested</u>.

The undigested waste in your faeces is mainly fibre. The muscles in your intestine walls push on fibre to move food along.

5 If you don't eat enough fibre you can become constipated. Why do you think this is?

salivary glands

gullet (oesophagus)

liver

stomach

pancreas

small intestine

rectum

anus

large intestine

■ The complete story of digestion

6 These sentences are in the wrong order. They explain what happens to food in your digestive system. Copy them out in the correct order.

- More digestive juices are added in the small intestine.
- Solid waste leaves the body through the anus.
- Food is chewed and saliva is added.
- In the large intestine water passes into the blood.
- Digested food passes into the blood here too.
- Glands in the stomach add more digestive juices.

WHAT YOU SHOULD KNOW (Copy and complete using the **key words**)

Digesting your food

In your digestive system, you break large food molecules down into _____, soluble molecules. This is called _____.

These small molecules can pass into your _____. This is called _____.

53

3.7 Absorbing and using food

Your blood takes food substances to all your **cells**.

1 Look at the diagram, then copy and complete the sentences.

You _____ food from your _____ system into your blood. Blood _____ it to all parts of your body. It goes into the _____ which need it.

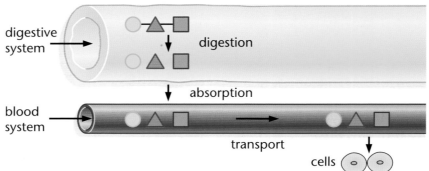

Why do your cells need food?

Your food gives your cells the **energy** and the **materials** they need to live and grow.

Foods for energy
- glucose
- fats
- leftover amino acids

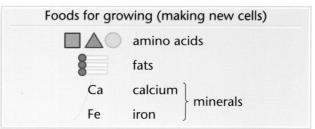

Foods for growing (making new cells)
- amino acids
- fats
- Ca calcium
- Fe iron } minerals

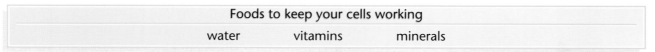

Foods to keep your cells working

water   vitamins   minerals

2 Look at the diagrams, then copy and complete the table.

Food for energy	Food for making new cells

3 Write a list of the foods your cells need to help them to work properly.

■ How do your cells get energy from food?

You take oxygen into your body in your lungs. Like your food, it travels to your cells in your blood.

4 Copy and complete this diagram to show the journey of oxygen.

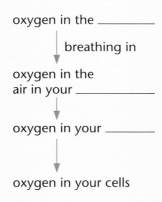

oxygen in the _____

↓ breathing in

oxygen in the air in your _____

↓

oxygen in your _____

↓

oxygen in your cells

In your cells, glucose and oxygen react together to release energy. We say that your cells **respire**.

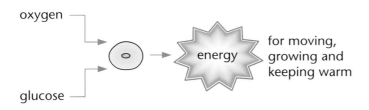

oxygen

glucose

energy → for moving, growing and keeping warm

5 Write down the names of <u>two</u> substances your cells use when they respire.

6 Write down <u>three</u> things your cells need energy for.

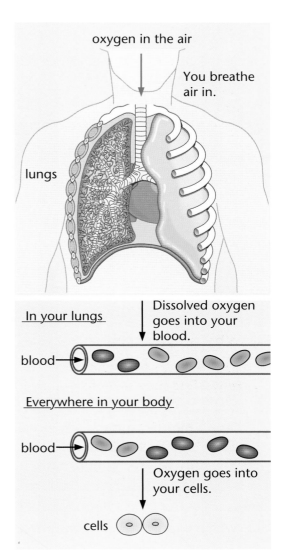

oxygen in the air

You breathe air in.

lungs

In your lungs

Dissolved oxygen goes into your blood.

blood

Everywhere in your body

blood

Oxygen goes into your cells.

cells

WHAT YOU SHOULD KNOW (Copy and complete using the **key words**)

Absorbing and using food

Your _____ transports small molecules of food to your _____.

Your cells use some of these molecules, together with oxygen, to give them _____.
We say they _____.

Your food also gives cells the _____ they need to grow.

3.8 How do plants grow?

New plants often come from seeds. Plants store food in their seeds. But there isn't enough food in a sunflower seed for it to grow into such a big plant.

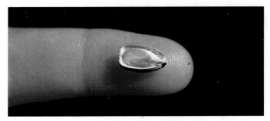

Sunflower plants grow from a seed like this.

1 In the picture, Jenny is 120 cm tall. How tall is the tallest sunflower plant?

■ How a seed starts to grow

Jenny planted some seeds in warm, damp soil. They took in water and started to grow. They do this only when conditions are just right.

Look at the pictures.

2 Which part of the seedling grows first?

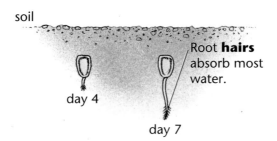

soil

Root **hairs** absorb most water.

day 4

day 7

Like you, plants need food such as glucose and proteins for energy and for growing. The seedling uses stored food from the seed. It also gets bigger because of the water it takes in. The root **hairs** absorb most of this water.

3 Write down <u>one</u> reason why root hairs are important.

■ Soon a shoot starts to grow

4 On which day did the shoot start to come up out of the ground?

The plant has now used up most of the stored food. To keep on growing it needs some way of getting more food.

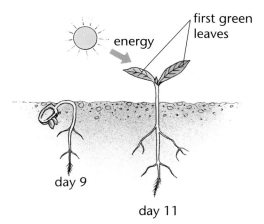

day 9

day 11

energy

first green leaves

■ Making food to grow more

Unlike you, a plant can make food. It makes most of its food in its leaves.

Light makes the leaves turn green. The green substance in leaves is called <u>chlorophyll</u>. This traps light energy for making food.

Plants also use **water** and **carbon dioxide** to make food.

5 On which day did the sunflower start to make food? Give a reason for your answer.

6 Look at the diagram, then copy and complete the table.

What a plant needs to make food	Where it comes from

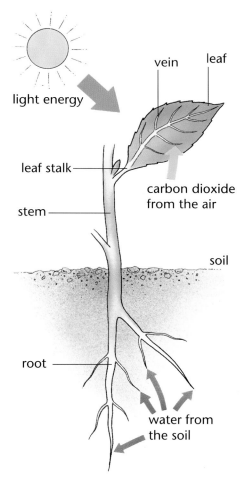

light energy

vein   leaf

leaf stalk

carbon dioxide from the air

stem

soil

root

water from the soil

it

)W   (Copy and complete using the **key words**)

_____ _____ and _____

s _____.

r.

3.9 Minerals for plant growth

Plants use carbon dioxide and water to make their own food. But plants need other chemicals too.

Some people say that they 'feed' their plants. They mean that they give them fertilisers. Fertilisers contain the **minerals** the plants need.

1 Look at the fertiliser label. Write down the three main minerals plants get from this fertiliser.

These minerals contain chemical **elements** that plants need to grow.

2 Look at the table, then copy and complete the sentences.

Nitrates contain the element _____.
Phosphates contain the _____ phosphorus.
_____ is an element.

Element	Mineral
nitrogen (N)	nitrate
phosphorus (P)	phosphate
potassium (K)	potassium salt

■ What happens if plants don't get minerals?

To find out what happens if plants don't get these minerals, we can grow them in water or clean sand. We can then add different minerals to see how well they grow.

3 Why do we grow the plants in clean sand or water instead of soil in this experiment?

Apart from giving them different minerals, we need to grow the plants in <u>identical conditions</u>.

4 **(a)** Why must we grow the plants in identical conditions?

(b) Write down <u>three</u> things which need to be the same.

At the start of the experiment the plants are very similar. We make sure that all the plants get the same amount of water, heat and light.

■ **An example – nitrates**

Look at the pictures.

5 (a) Write down <u>two</u> differences between plants
    A and B.

(b) Write down what these differences tell us
about plants and nitrates.

A This plant has all the minerals it needs.

B This plant didn't get any nitrates.

■ **What do plants use nitrates for?**

Look at the diagram.

6 Copy and complete the sentences.

Like you, plants need proteins for _____.
They need _____ and minerals such as
_____ for making these proteins.

7 Explain, as fully as you can, why you think plants
A and B are different.

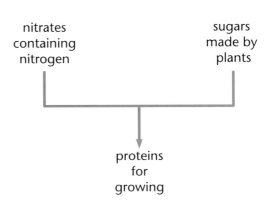

WHAT YOU SHOULD KNOW (Copy and complete using the **key words**)

Minerals for plant growth

Plants need chemical _____ such as nitrogen for growth.
They take them in as _____ such as nitrates.

3.10 How plants take in what they need

■ Leaves take in sunlight and carbon dioxide

Leaves are **thin** and **flat**.

They are only a few cells thick so that light and carbon dioxide can reach the cells inside.

1 Copy and complete the sentences.

   Leaves look green because their cells contain lots of tiny _____.
   These have a green substance called _____ inside them.

2 Where does a plant take in carbon dioxide?

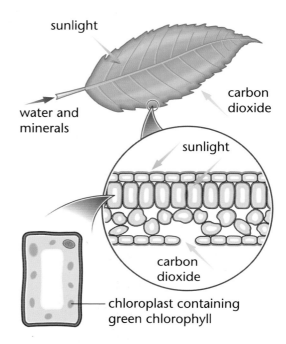

■ Roots take in water and minerals

Roots take in the minerals and the water which plants need. Most of these go in through the **root hairs**. We say root hairs <u>absorb</u> them.

3 Look at the drawing. Describe, as fully as you can, where the root hairs are.

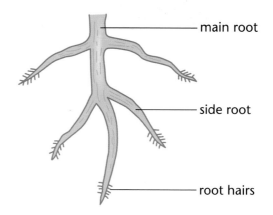

Where do the water and minerals go?

Look at the diagram.

4 Copy and complete the sentences.

Root hairs take in _____ and _____.
The water and minerals then pass into special
tubes. These tubes are long and very thin, and go
from the roots to the _____ and all the way
up to the _____. They are made of many
_____.

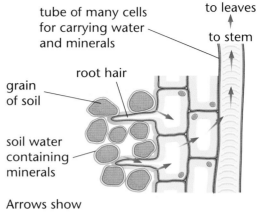

tube of many cells
for carrying water
and minerals

to leaves

to stem

root hair

grain
of soil

soil water
containing
minerals

Arrows show
where the water and minerals go.

What else do roots do?

Plant roots are not just for taking in water and
minerals. They have another job too.

Roots hold plants in the soil so that they don't
come out of the soil easily. We say they **anchor**
plants so that they don't get uprooted.

5 Write down <u>two</u> things which could uproot a plant.

The wind uprooted this tree.

A badger dug up these bluebell bulbs.

WHAT YOU SHOULD KNOW (Copy and complete using the **key words**)

How plants take in what they need

Plant leaves make _____.

Leaves which are _____ and _____ are best for taking in the sunlight and
carbon dioxide the plant needs.

The water and minerals a plant needs go into it through its _____ _____.
They pass in special tubes through the root and stem to the leaves.

Roots also _____ plants in the soil.

4.1 Making babies

To make a baby we need two special cells. They are called <u>sex cells</u>. One of these cells comes from the father. The other comes from the mother.

1 What are the mother's sex cells called?

2 What are the father's sex cells called?

3 Why do humans make sex cells?

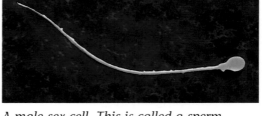

A male sex cell. This is called a sperm.

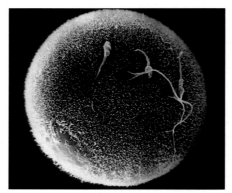

*This female sex cell is much bigger than the male sex cells around it. Female sex cells are called eggs or **ova**.*

■ Where sex cells are made

Sex cells are made in special places in your body. Making babies is called <u>reproduction</u>. So we call the places where sex cells are made the <u>reproductive organs</u>.

A woman has two **ovaries** that make the eggs. She also has a **uterus** (also called a womb) inside which a baby can grow.

A man has two **testes** where **sperm** are made. He also has a **penis**.

4 Copy and complete the sentences

Eggs are made in a woman's _____.
Sperm are made in a man's _____.

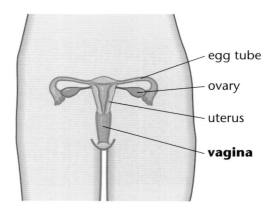

egg tube

ovary

uterus

vagina

Female reproductive organs.

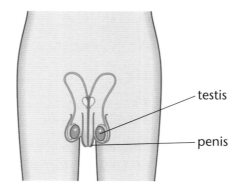

testis

penis

Male reproductive organs.

■ How is a baby started?

Before a new human can start to grow, a sperm and an egg must join up. We call this <u>fertilisation</u>.

For an egg to be fertilised, a man must put sperm inside a woman's body. This happens when they have sex.

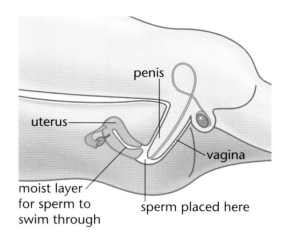

5 Look at the diagram. Then copy and complete the sentences.

A man puts sperm inside a woman's body through his _____. The sperm are put into the woman's _____ , at the opening into her _____ .

Eggs are fertilised in the egg tube. The fertilised egg grows inside the mother's uterus. After about 9 months the baby is ready to be born.

6 **(a)** What is fertilisation?

   (b) Where does it usually happen?

7 How do sperm get to the egg tube from the opening of the uterus?

8 How long does it take for the fertilised egg to grow into a baby which is ready to be born?

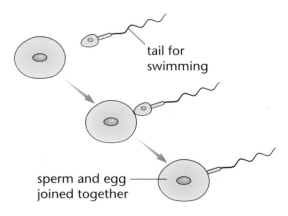

Fertilisation.

WHAT YOU SHOULD KNOW (Copy and complete using the **key words**)

Making babies

	Male	Female
Name of sex cells	_____	_____
Where the sex cells are made	_____	_____
Opening to the outside	a tube through the _____	_____
Other organs	_____ to put the sperm in the woman's vagina	_____ where the baby grows

You need to be able to label diagrams of male and female reproductive organs.

4.2 Growing and changing

Graham has been growing in his mother's womb (uterus) for nearly nine months. In a few weeks' time he will be born.

How did Graham start?

Graham started life as a **fertilised** egg cell.

A fertilised egg starts to develop straight away. The cell splits into two cells. These two cells then split again to make four. This carries on until there is a ball of cells.

After a few weeks you can see how the cells are making different parts of the new person.

1 What features of the new person can be seen at four weeks?

2 What features develop between two weeks and seven weeks?

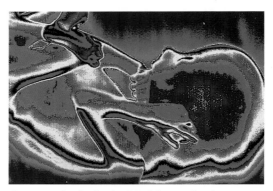

A scan of a baby inside his mother's uterus.

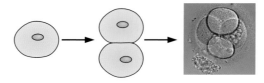

Cells split over and over again.

*Four weeks. The developing baby is called an **embryo**.*

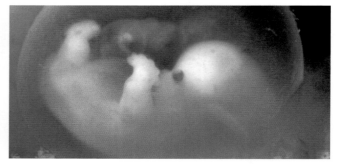

Seven weeks. As the embryo becomes more like a baby, we call it a <u>fetus</u>.

The new baby

Graham is now three months old. He needs his parents to do everything for him. They still have to feed him in the night sometimes.

Three months after birth.

■ Growing up

More changes will happen as Graham gets older.

When a girl is an adolescent her ovaries start to release eggs.

*As a baby Graham grows. He learns to control his body. As a young **child** he walks and uses his hands. He has learnt to talk.*

*When he is an **adolescent** Graham's testes start to make sperm.*

When he is a fully grown adult, Graham may marry and produce children of his own. So we start at the beginning of the cycle again.

3 What will happen to Graham when he is an adolescent?

4 Draw a chart to show the main changes in your life so far.
   Then add what might happen as you get older.

■ Old age

Graham's grandfather spends time playing with Graham. He helps to look after him.

Graham's grandfather has a lot of knowledge and experience of life. He can pass this on to Graham to help him as he grows up.

5 Write down <u>three</u> ways a grandparent can help a child.

WHAT YOU SHOULD KNOW (Copy and complete using the **key words**)

Growing and changing

Copy and complete the diagram to show all the stages in a human life cycle.

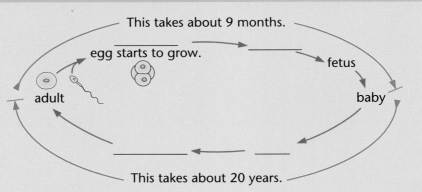

This takes about 9 months.

egg starts to grow.

fetus

adult

baby

This takes about 20 years.

4.3 Growing pains

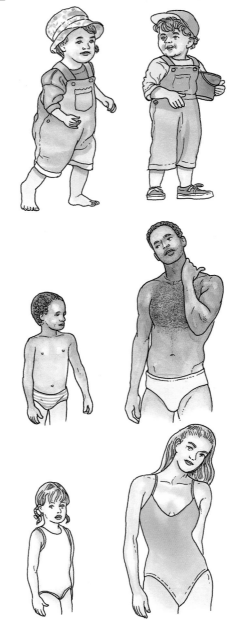

When they are very small, girls and boys look quite similar. Their bodies are the same shape.

But as children grow up, their bodies **change**. They start to look more like adult women and men. The time when these changes happen is called **puberty**.

1 Copy and complete the sentence.

Puberty is the time when girls start to change into _____ and _____ start to change into men.

■ How do people's bodies change?

The pictures show some of the differences between the bodies of adults and children.

2 Write down <u>three</u> differences you can see between:

(a) the man's body and the boy's body;

(b) the woman's body and the girl's body.

The table shows some of the other changes that happen at puberty.

3 (a) Write down <u>two</u> changes that are exactly the same for boys and girls.

(b) Write down <u>one</u> change that is different for girls and boys but is the same <u>sort</u> of change.

(c) Write down <u>one</u> change which applies only to boys.

Other changes during puberty	
Girls	**Boys**
hair grows under arms	hair grows under arms
pubic hair grows (around vagina)	pubic hair grows (around penis)
ovaries start to release eggs	testes start to make sperm
monthly periods (of bleeding) begin	penis grows bigger
	voice deepens

A woman's monthly cycle

When a girl changes into a woman, an egg is released each month from one of her ovaries. Her monthly periods also begin.

4   Look at the diagram.

   (a) What is happening during a woman's monthly bleeding period?

   (b) What happens in the uterus in the week after the period of bleeding?

   (c) What happens about halfway through each monthly cycle?

This monthly cycle of events is called the **menstrual cycle**.

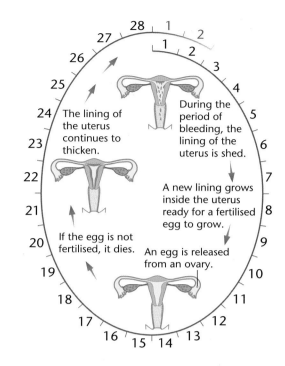

The menstrual cycle.

Labels on diagram:
- During the period of bleeding, the lining of the uterus is shed.
- A new lining grows inside the uterus ready for a fertilised egg to grow.
- An egg is released from an ovary.
- If the egg is not fertilised, it dies.
- The lining of the uterus continues to thicken.

When does puberty occur?

Puberty doesn't happen at the same time for everyone.

Girls can start to change from about the age of 9. Most girls notice a lot of changes in their bodies from age 11 to 14.

Most boys start to change at about 11 years old. Later, at about 16, they start to grow hair on their face and become more muscular.

5   Many teenagers find puberty a difficult time. Write down <u>one</u> reason for this.

6   At 10 Gemma's breasts have started to develop. At 14 Shane's pubic hair has not started to grow.

   (a) Why might Gemma and Shane be worried?

   (b) Why is there no real need to worry?

Some teenagers get spots. This can upset them when they have started to care about how they look. The problem clears up by itself after a few years.

WHAT YOU SHOULD KNOW (Copy and complete using the **key words**)

Growing pains

Our bodies _____ as we grow. Sometimes it is hard to adapt to these changes.

Boys and girls start to make sex cells at the time of _____. Girls start their _____ _____ and they have a period (of bleeding) about once a month.

4.4 A new plant life

Flowering plants grow from seeds.

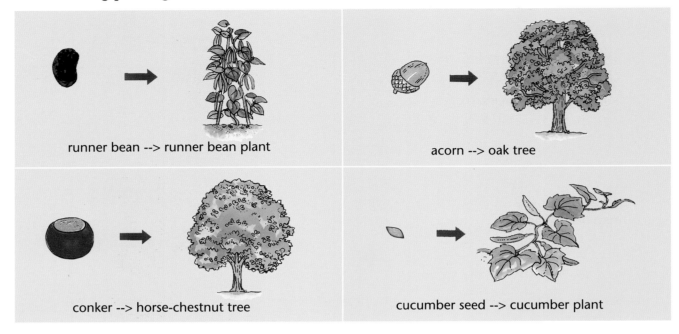

runner bean --> runner bean plant

acorn --> oak tree

conker --> horse-chestnut tree

cucumber seed --> cucumber plant

1 What flowering plant grows from:

(a) an acorn;

(b) a conker?

■ What is in a seed?

Seeds from different plants are different sizes, shapes and colours. But they all have the same basic parts.

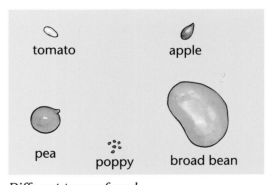

tomato

apple

pea

poppy

broad bean

Different types of seed.

Look at the diagram. It shows a bean seed cut open, right down the middle.

2 A seed contains a very tiny plant. What is this tiny plant called?

3 Why does the seed need a food store?

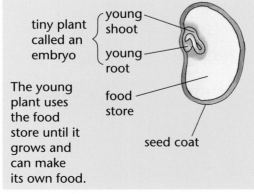

tiny plant called an embryo

young shoot

young root

The young plant uses the food store until it grows and can make its own food.

food store

seed coat

Bean seed cut in half.

■ Starting to grow

If a seed is given the things it needs, it will start to grow. We say that it germinates.

The diagram shows what happens to the seed. This is the plant's life cycle.

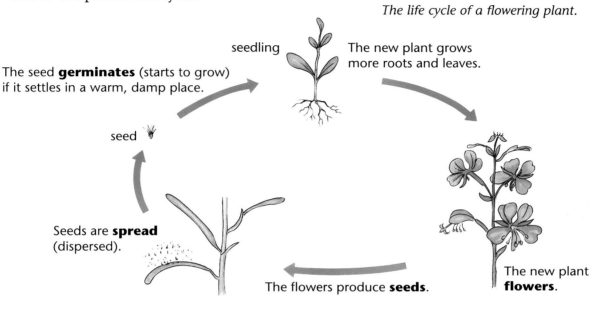

The life cycle of a flowering plant.

seedling

The new plant grows more roots and leaves.

The seed **germinates** (starts to grow) if it settles in a warm, damp place.

seed

Seeds are **spread** (dispersed).

The flowers produce **seeds**.

The new plant **flowers**.

4 What <u>two</u> things do seeds need so they can start to grow?

5 Plants grow roots, stems and leaves. Then they flower. Which of these parts of a plant makes the seeds?

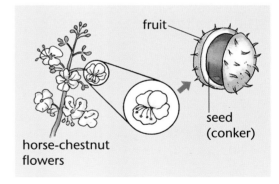

fruit

seed (conker)

horse-chestnut flowers

WHAT YOU SHOULD KNOW (Copy and complete using the **key words**)

A new plant life

The life cycle of a flowering plant.

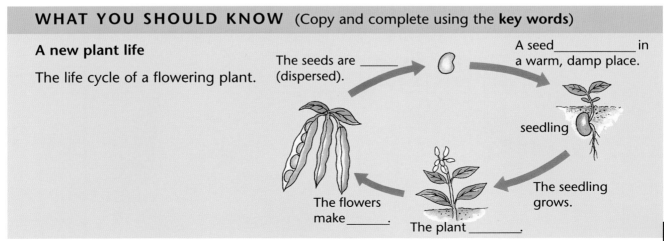

The seeds are _____ (dispersed).

A seed_____ in a warm, damp place.

seedling

The seedling grows.

The plant _____.

The flowers make_____.

69

4.5 Looking at a plant's sex organs

Many plants grow from seeds. Seeds are made by flowers. So flowers are the parts of plants that are used for reproduction.

Flowers have male and female parts. These male and female parts are often on the <u>same</u> flower.

1 (a) What are the female parts of the flower?

  (b) What are the male parts?

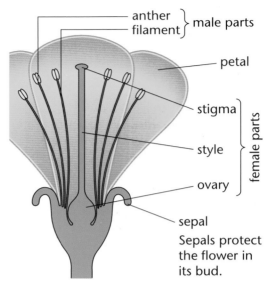

anther } male parts
filament
petal
stigma
style
ovary } female parts
sepal

Sepals protect the flower in its bud.

■ Comparing different flowers

Flowers from different plants look different from each other. But they all have the same basic parts.

Violet   *Hibiscus*   *Daylily*   *Peony*

2 Write down <u>three</u> ways in which flowers can be different from each other.

The diagram shows a primrose flower.

3 On a copy of the primrose flower:

  (a) label the female parts;

  (b) label the male parts.

4 Write down <u>two</u> differences between the primrose flower and the flower at the top of the page.

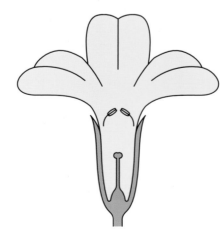

A primrose flower.

■ What do the male parts do?

Inside each pollen grain is a special cell. This is the plant's male sex cell.

5 (a) What are the flower's male sex cells inside?

(b) Where in the flower are these made?

The male parts of a flower.

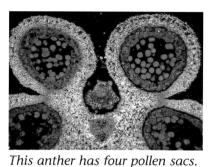

This anther has four pollen sacs.

Pollen sacs have many pollen grains. This shows them magnified 250 times.

■ The female parts of a flower

Each ovule has a female sex cell inside it.

6 Where in the flower are the ovules?

To make a seed, a male sex cell must join with a female sex cell.

7 Where on a flower does pollen land?

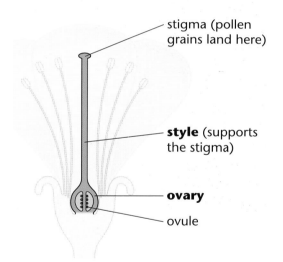

The female parts of a flower.

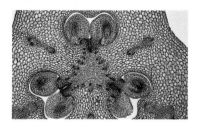

Many ovules can grow inside the ovary. This photograph shows them magnified 60 times.

WHAT YOU SHOULD KNOW (Copy and complete using the key words)

Looking at a plant's sex organs

Flower part	What it does
_____	Pollen is made here.
_____	This supports the anther.
_____	This supports the stigma.
_____	Ovules are made here.

You need to be able to label a diagram of a flower.

4.6 Making seeds

New flowering plants grow from **seeds**.

To make seeds, **pollen** must first travel from the anther to the stigma.

1 Copy and complete the sentences.

Pollen is made in the _____ of a flower.

It _____ to another flower of the same kind.

When pollen lands on the stigma of this other flower we call it _____.

Some plants have flowers which can pollinate themselves.

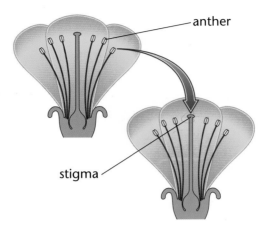

*Pollen travels from an anther to a stigma. This is called **pollination**.*

■ How does the pollen travel?

Some flowers use insects to move their pollen.

The insects get food and the flowers get their pollen carried to other flowers.

2 What <u>three</u> things can attract an insect to a flower?

3 Insects transfer pollen from one plant to another by accident. Explain, as fully as you can, how this happens.

Pollination by insects.

Insects are attracted by the bright colour of petals or by the flower's scent.

anther

Inside, the insect picks up pollen on its body. The pollen is sticky to help this.

This flower has nectar at the bottom. Some insects go into the flower to feed on the nectar.

stigma

The insect goes to another flower. Pollen on its body is transferred to the stigma of this flower.

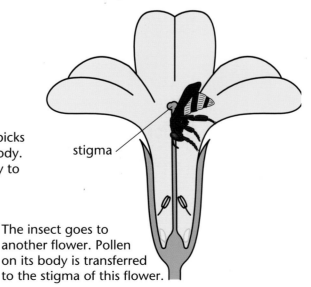

■ Moving pollen by the wind

The diagram shows a flower that does not attract insects. Instead, pollen is carried between these types of flowers by the wind.

4 Write down <u>two</u> ways this flower is adapted for pollination by wind.

5 Why doesn't this flower have brightly coloured petals or a strong scent?

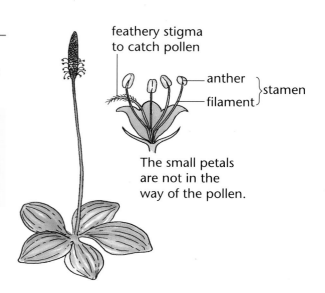

feathery stigma to catch pollen

anther
filament
} stamen

The small petals are not in the way of the pollen.

■ What happens after pollination?

As soon as pollen lands on a stigma, a tube starts to grow from it.

The male sex cell now goes down to the **ovule** and joins with the female sex cell.

The two cells join together to make a single cell. We call this **fertilisation**. It is the beginning of a new seed. Remember, this is how a new animal starts life too.

The diagrams show how all this happens.

6 A plant has just been pollinated. How does fertilisation then happen?

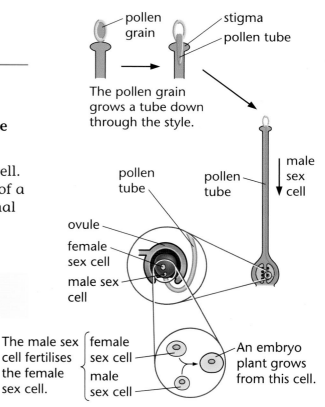

pollen grain
stigma
pollen tube

The pollen grain grows a tube down through the style.

pollen tube
pollen tube
male sex cell

ovule
female sex cell
male sex cell

The male sex cell fertilises the female sex cell.
{ female sex cell
male sex cell

An embryo plant grows from this cell.

WHAT YOU SHOULD KNOW (Copy and complete using the **key words**)

Making seeds

Flowering plants grow from _____. Seeds are made inside the flower.

First, _____ is moved from an anther to a stigma. We call this _____.

The male sex cell nucleus inside the pollen joins with the female sex cell nucleus inside an _____. We call this _____.

4.7 What is a species?

There are many different kinds of plants and animals. We call each different kind a **species**.

Each species of plant or animal must be able to reproduce or it will die out.

Pekinese.

■ Sorting animals into species

The pictures show six animals.

Kris and Sam decide to sort them into groups. This is how they do it.

Kris's table

Black	White	Ginger

Burmese white.

Sam's table

Dogs	Cats

1 Copy and complete the tables for Kris and Sam.

2 (a) Who sorted the animals into their species?

(b) Why is this a more useful way of sorting the animals?

Terrier.

Animals of the same species are similar and do the same sorts of things. They can also mate with each other and produce young.

Labrador.

Ginger tabby.

Persian.

■ Having young

A female cat can mate with a male cat and produce kittens. This is because the female cat and the male cat belong to the same species.

A cat cannot mate with a dog. This is because they belong to different species. We say that cats and dogs cannot **interbreed**.

male wild rabbit

female hare

female Dutch rabbit

3 Look at the pictures.

   (a) Which animal will interbreed with the male wild rabbit?

   (b) Write down <u>one</u> reason for your answer.

■ Are horses and donkeys different species?

Sometimes animals from slightly different species do try to mate. In some cases they are successful.

Horses and donkeys sometimes mate. The young are not horses or donkeys. They are something in between.

horse

donkey

4 Look at the pictures. What do we call the young produced when a horse and a donkey mate?

When young mules grow up they cannot breed. We say that mules are <u>infertile</u>. So we still call horses and donkeys different species because they cannot breed to produce **fertile** offspring.

mule

5 If people want more mules, how do they get them?

WHAT YOU SHOULD KNOW (Copy and complete using the **key words**)

What is a species?

A species is one kind of living thing. It differs from other _____ and it cannot _____ with them to produce _____ offspring.

4.8 We are all different

Humans are different from each other in lots of ways. They **vary** a lot. But they can interbreed so all humans belong to the same **species**.

1 Write down <u>three</u> ways in which some of these girls are different from the others.

The things you have described in your answers are called features or **characteristics**.

■ The identity parade

The owners of a flat saw a girl breaking in. They described her to the police.

2 Look at her picture, then write your own description of her.

The police thought that they knew who the burglar was. Her name is Gail.

The owners of the flat picked out Gail in an identity parade. But the police needed other evidence that she was the right girl.

3 Look at the picture. Write down <u>two</u> pieces of evidence that the police found.

The suspect, Gail.

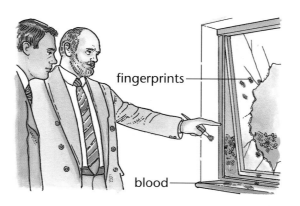

fingerprints

blood

The blood

Everyone fits into one of four blood groups: A, B, AB and O.

4 Look at the chart. Write down the percentage of people in each blood group.

5 (a) Gail's blood is group O. If the blood on the window is also group O, it does not prove that Gail was the burglar. Why is this?

(b) What does it tell the police?

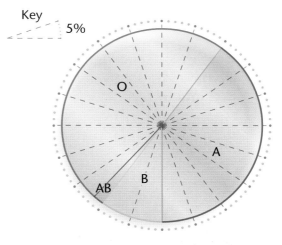

Key
5%

Percentage of people in the UK with each blood group.

The fingerprints

We all have different fingerprints. So, if the police find Gail's fingerprints at the scene of the crime, they will know that she was there.

6 Look at the fingerprints.

(a) Which fingerprint is like Gail's?

(b) Write a sentence about what this tells the police.

7 Write a list of evidence against Gail that the police can use in court.

Fingerprints found on the window.

Gail's fingerprint.

WHAT YOU SHOULD KNOW (Copy and complete using the **key words**)

We are all different

Members of a species can be different in many ways.
We say they _____ or they have different _____.
But they are still members of the same species if they can _____.

All humans belong to the same _____.

5.1 Night-time and day-time animals

You can see some animals, like squirrels, in the daytime. At night you see other animals, such as bats and owls.

The charts show some differences between the day and the night. We call these different <u>conditions</u>.

1 What do we call the time of day when it is:

(a) getting light;

(b) getting dark?

2 At what time of day is it warmest and lightest?

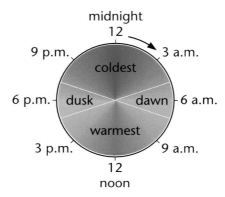

◼ Animals of the night

Foxes often sleep during the day. They hunt for food at night. Foxes love eating earthworms. Earthworms only come up out of the soil when it is **cool** and **dark**.

3 Foxes find lots of earthworms at night. Why is this?

4 Write down <u>two</u> reasons why earthworms are likely to die if they come up during the day.

We call animals that are active at night <u>nocturnal</u> animals.

5 Write down the names of <u>three</u> nocturnal animals.

Earthworms mate above ground at night. They may dry up and die if they come up during the day.

Foxes use their senses of smell, hearing and sight when hunting.

Animals of the day

House sparrows are common in towns. They start feeding as soon as it begins to get light. They shelter at night when it is cold and dark.

Kestrels need good light to hunt for food. One of their favourite foods is sparrows.

6 At what times are sparrows most in danger of being eaten by kestrels?

Kestrels feed when it is light.

Senses for finding food

Animals use their senses for finding food. Some senses are more useful during the day and others at night. Animals' senses are **adapted** to the time of day that they hunt.

7 Copy and complete the table.

Animal	Senses it uses to find food
fox	
bat	
owl	
kestrel	

You can see foxes, owls and kestrels all the year round.

Bats eat insects, so you don't see them in the winter when there are hardly any insects for them to feed on.

Bats hunt by sending out sound and listening for echoes.

Owls hear well and can see in dim light.

WHAT YOU SHOULD KNOW (Copy and complete using the **key words**)

Night-time and day-time animals

Some animals are _____ for feeding during the day.
Other animals feed at night when it is _____ and _____.

5.2 How animals and plants survive the winter

In winter the days are short, and it is often very **cold**. Animals and plants do different things to survive the winter. We say they are **adapted** in different ways.

> **1** The pictures show the same place in winter and summer. Write down <u>three</u> differences you can see.

■ Animals in winter

In winter some British animals, such as bats, go into a deep sleep: they <u>hibernate</u>.

Other animals go to a warmer country: they <u>migrate</u>.

spring	summer	autumn	winter
		robin	
		adder	
		frog	
		swallow	

↑ migrating   ↑ migrating

Key ▭ active in Britain
    ▭ hibernating
    ▭ in a warmer country

We call the different parts of each year **seasons**. We see different animals in different seasons. Look at the diagram.

> **2** Which animal can we see in the UK all the year round?
>
> **3 (a)** During which seasons are adders active?
>
> **(b)** Why can't they hunt in the winter?
>
> **4** Write down the names of <u>two</u> animals which hibernate.
>
> **5** Write down <u>two</u> reasons why swallows migrate to Africa.

Even in summer adders need to sunbathe until they are warm enough to go hunting.

When it is winter in Britain, it is summer in Africa. So it is warm and swallows can find lots of insects to eat.

■ Plants in winter

Plants also do different things in different seasons. Look at the pictures of an apple tree.

6 For each season, write down one sentence about the tree.

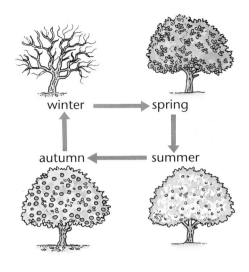

winter ➡ spring

autumn ⬅ summer

Different plants have different ways of surviving the winter.

spring	summer	autumn	winter
apple tree			

poppy

New plants grow from seeds.   Only the seeds survive.

bluebell

The bulb is alive under the ground.

pine tree

☐ has green leaves and makes food
☐ doesn't make food or grow

7 Describe what each of the plants in the diagram does to survive the winter.

Bluebells are adapted to living in woods.

8 When do bluebells finish growing?

9 Why can't bluebells get enough light in the summer?

Plants under trees cannot make enough food when tree leaves block the light.

WHAT YOU SHOULD KNOW (Copy and complete using the **key words**)

How animals and plants survive the winter

The different parts of the year are called _____.

In winter there is less light and it can be very _____.

Plants and animals are _____ in different ways to survive the winter.

5.3 Town and country

Town.

Countryside.

Many people think that wild plants and animals live only in the countryside. But lots of wild plants and animals also live in towns.

Look at the pictures above.

1 For each picture, write down <u>three</u> different places where plants and animals can live.

The place where a plant or animal lives is called its **habitat**. A habitat provides space and shelter.

2 Is the number of different habitats greater in the town picture or the country picture?

3 Copy and complete the sentences.

Where there are lots of different _____ , lots of different plants and _____ can live. So more species live in a square kilometre of a town than in the same area of _____ .

Key
- farm and pet animals
- food waste from kitchens
- wild birds and mammals
- insects
- earthworms
- fruit and vegetables

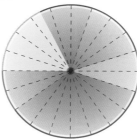

What a country fox eats.

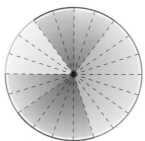

What a town fox eats.

Town fox, country fox

When young foxes grow up, they have to find a habitat which has everything they need. Lots of young foxes moved from the countryside into towns. So foxes are now more common in towns than in the countryside.

The pictures show two ways that a fox can get the **shelter** it needs.

4 Write down <u>two</u> ways in which these shelters are similar.

5 Why must the habitat of a fox contain somewhere to shelter or hide?

A town fox.

A fox's habitat must also supply the **food** it needs to live and grow.

6 Look at the pie charts on page 82.

    (a) Write down the <u>two</u> main types of food which a country fox eats.

    (b) Write down the <u>two</u> main types of food which a town fox eats.

7 Copy and complete the sentences.

Most foxes used to live in the _____. Many foxes now live in _____.

They have learned to find the _____ and _____ that they need.

A fox in the country lives in an <u>earth</u>.

WHAT YOU SHOULD KNOW (Copy and complete using the **key words**)

Town and country

The place where a plant or animal lives is called its _____.
A habitat must provide _____ and a source of _____.

5.4 Different bodies for different habitats

Different animals and plants live in different **habitats**. Their bodies are **adapted** so they can survive in their habitats.

■ Bodies designed for moving

The bodies of animals and plants have **features** suited to where they live and what they do.

Plants don't move from place to place, but animals do.

1 Look at the pictures. Write down <u>three</u> reasons why animals need to move.

2 An earthworm is adapted for burrowing in soil. Explain why its shape is good for burrowing.

A mole is adapted for burrowing in a different way. It has a skeleton, and muscles to pull on the bones. Look at the pictures.

3 Write down <u>two</u> ways the mole's skeleton is adapted for its way of life.

hunting · escaping · finding a mate · finding food

Why animals move.

pointed 'head' end

An earthworm has a long, thin body and a slimy skin.

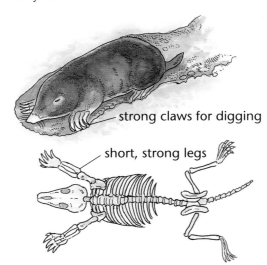

strong claws for digging · short, strong legs

A mole.

Bodies designed for support

A skeleton isn't just for movement. It also holds an animal together in the right shape. We say it supports the animal.

Elephant and whale skeletons drawn to the same scale.

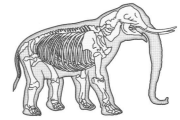

4 Look at the diagrams.

(a) Which animal is bigger, an elephant or a whale?

(b) Why does an elephant need a stronger skeleton than a whale?

Water helps to support the whale's body.

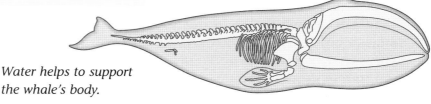

Plants need support too

Water helps to support water plants as well as animals.

5 Look at the pictures. Write down two differences between the land plant and the water plant.

Plants have roots to anchor them in soil or mud. Some plants also have woody stems to make them stronger.

6 Suggest one reason for each of the differences you described in your answer to question 5.

Water plant.   Land plant.

WHAT YOU SHOULD KNOW (Copy and complete using the **key words**)

Different bodies for different habitats

Different plants and animals live in different _____.

Plants and animals have _____ which suit them to the places they live.
We say that they are _____ to their habitats.

5.5 Surviving in a garden

The compost heap in the drawing is just one of the <u>habitats</u> in the garden. Lots of earthworms, woodlice and millipedes live there.

1 Write down <u>three</u> other habitats you can see in the drawing.

Worms, spiders and beetles live in all parts of the garden, but the ones in the pond are different from the ones which live in the flower bed. Their bodies have **features** which suit them to the places they live. We say that each kind is **adapted** to its own habitat.

2 Look at the pictures. Write down <u>two</u> ways the compost worm is different from the earthworm.

■ Ways of getting oxygen

All animals need oxygen.

Some use oxygen from the air. Others use oxygen dissolved in the water.

Earthworms take in oxygen from the air through their damp skins.

Like all beetles, water beetles get their oxygen from the air. Their bodies are adapted to do this under the water.

3 How can water beetles get air under water?

4 Why do water beetles keep coming up to the surface of a pond?

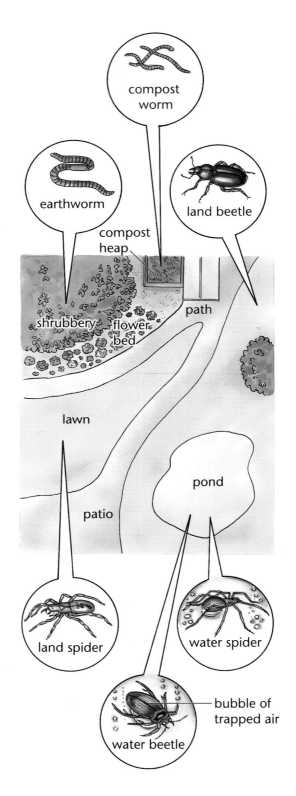

compost worm

earthworm

land beetle

compost heap

path

shrubbery

flower bed

lawn

pond

patio

land spider

water spider

water beetle

bubble of trapped air

Ways of getting food

Beetles and spiders feed on other animals so we call them <u>predators</u>.

Beetles have jaws to cut up their food. Spiders suck the juices from their prey. Their jaws are adapted to these different ways of feeding.

5 Look at the pictures. Which jaws, A or B, belong to the spider? Explain your answer.

Plants make their own food. They take in carbon dioxide, water and minerals to do this.

6 How do plants take in the carbon dioxide, water and minerals they need?

A: these jaws cut up prey.

B: these jaws make a hole in the prey.

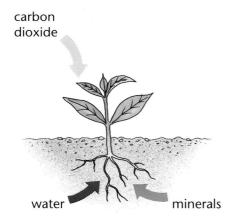

carbon dioxide

water   minerals

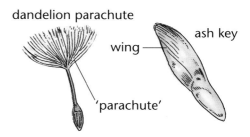

dandelion parachute

wing — ash key

'parachute'

Adapted to be spread by the wind.

How do plants get to different places?

Because they have roots, plants can't move. So, many plants make <u>seeds</u> which can be moved.

7 Write down <u>two</u> ways plant seeds are adapted to reach new places.

burdock   blackberry

hooks

Adapted to be spread by animals.

WHAT YOU SHOULD KNOW (Copy and complete using the **key words**)

Surviving in a garden

Plants and animals have _____ which suit them to the places they live and for what they do. We say they are _____ to their habitats and their way of life.

5.6 Feeding on plants

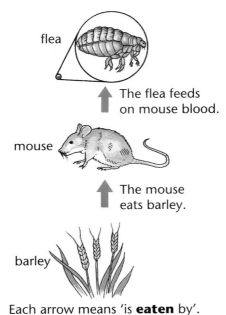

flea

The flea feeds on mouse blood.

mouse

The mouse eats barley.

barley

Each arrow means 'is **eaten** by'.

Only green plants can make food. So all <u>animals</u> depend on green plants to stay alive.

Even a flea which feeds only on mouse blood depends on green plants for its food. The diagram shows why this is.

1 Copy and complete the sentences.

The green plants are eaten by the _____ and the mouse's blood is _____ by the flea. This means that both the _____ and the _____ depend on the green _____ for food.

■ Food chains

A diagram which shows who eats what is called a <u>food chain</u>. You can draw a food chain using words or pictures.

You always start with **green plants**, then show what **animals** eat. The arrows point the same way as the food goes.

2 What does the following food chain tell you?

ladybird
↑
greenfly
↑
leaf

3 Look at the photos. Then write a food chain to show who eats what.

hedgehog

snail

snail   lettuce

■ Food chains everywhere

There are food chains in every habitat.
The diagrams show who eats what in
different habitats.

4 Draw a food chain for each habitat.
Make sure your arrows go in the same
direction as the food.

Seashore.

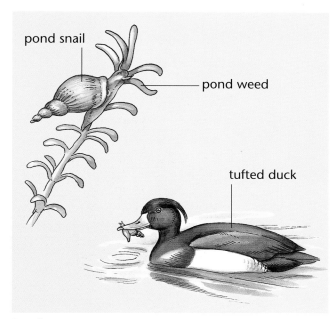

Pond.

Woodland.

5 (a) What kind of living thing is at the <u>start</u>
of each food chain?

(b) Why do all food chains start in this way?

WHAT YOU SHOULD KNOW (Copy and complete using the **key words**)

Feeding on plants

Food chains start with _____ _____. The rest of each food chain shows
what _____ eat.

In a food chain, A → B → C means that A is _____ by B and B is eaten by C.
We use the arrows to show the direction in which the food goes.

5.7 Growing plants for food

Farmers and gardeners work hard to grow food crops. But a lot of food is lost to **pests**, diseases and weeds.

1 Look at the pie chart.

   (a) What percentage of a crop do people harvest in Africa?

   (b) What happens to the rest of a crop?

2 Use the information in the table to draw a similar pie chart for Europe. Start by splitting a circle in 5% segments (each 18° on a protractor).

> **Pesticides**, fungicides and herbicides can harm other living things, including humans.

3 (a) How does the percentage lost in Europe compare with that in Africa?

   (b) Write down <u>two</u> possible reasons for the difference.

4 Write down one good thing and one bad thing about using pesticides.

■ Who's been eating the plants?

Sometimes a gardener find pests eating plants. Look at the pictures.

5 Write down the part of the plant which is eaten by:

   (a) the caterpillar,

   (b) the greenfly.

Key
- lost to pests
- lost to diseases
- lost to weeds
- harvested

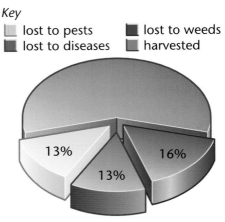

13%   16%   13%

Percentages of crops lost in Africa.

Percentages of crops lost in Europe.

Pests	Diseases	Weeds
5%	13%	7%

Pesticides	Fungicides	Herbicides
kill animals which eat crops	kill fungi	kill weeds

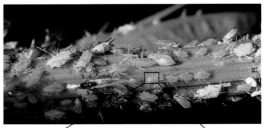

Greenflies suck sap from leaves.

Sometimes the gardener doesn't see what ate the plants. Many pests hide in the soil.

But she does know that different pests feed in different ways. Look at the photographs of the pests and the leaves they were eating.

6 Copy the drawing of the leaf and complete the labels.

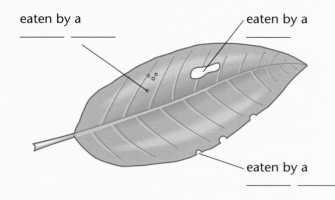

eaten by a
_____ _____

eaten by a
_____

eaten by a
_____ _____

Slugs make large holes in leaves.

Bean weevils eat the edges of leaves.

Flea beetles make small round holes.

■ Other animals eat the pests

Luckily for the gardener, even if she doesn't kill the pests, other animals eat them. We call these other animals **predators**.

7 Copy and complete the sentences.

Snails can do a lot of damage to garden plants. So gardeners like having _____ in their gardens.

Instead of spraying aphids with pesticides, a gardener could bring lots of _____ into the garden.

A hedgehog eating a snail.   *A ladybird eating an aphid.*

WHAT YOU SHOULD KNOW (Copy and complete using the **key words**)

Growing plants for food

Animals which eat the plants we grow for food are called _____.
We can kill them with chemicals called _____.

We can also encourage other animals to eat them. These animals are called _____.

5.8 Predators, harmful and useful

Some animals eat plants. Others eat animals. Animals which kill and eat other animals are called **predators**. The animals which get eaten are called **prey**.

1 Copy the table. Write in the names of two predators which live in gardens. Add the names of their prey.

Predator	Prey

Earthworms make soil more fertile, so plants grow better. Flatworms don't do this.

Plants don't grow well if greenfly are feeding on them.

2 Why don't gardeners want New Zealand flatworms in their gardens?

3 Why are they pleased to have ladybirds?

■ Red spider mites

Red spider mites are pests in greenhouses.

4 Write down one reason why gardeners don't want them.

5 Look at the food chain and write down the name of

(a) the predator;

(b) the prey.

New Zealand flatworms eat earthworms.

New Zealand
flatworm
↑
earthworm
↑
dead leaves

ladybird
↑
greenfly
↑
plant sap

One kind of red spider mite. They do not all look as red as this one.

'Phyto'
↑
red spider mite
↑
cucumber plant

■ Making use of predators

Some students found red spider mites in a greenhouse where they were growing cucumbers.

They didn't want to use chemical pesticides to kill them because pesticides also kill useful animals such as ladybirds.

So they decided to put some predators of the mites into the greenhouse.

6 What would the predators do?

The graph shows how the number of red spider mites and predators **increases** and then **decreases**.

7 How many red spider mites were there when the students put the predators into the greenhouse?

8 On which day was the number of spider mites greatest?

9 The number of spider mites then fell quickly. What happened to them?

10 Copy and complete the sentences.

As the number of _____ _____ mites (prey) goes up, the number of predators also goes _____.
So, the number of red spider mites starts to decrease. Then the number of predators also _____.

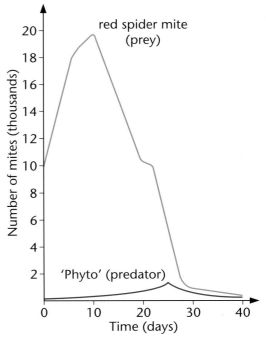

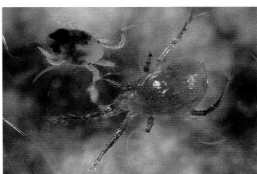

Phyto may be the predator but it is smaller than the red spider mite. The mite is less than a millimetre wide.

WHAT YOU SHOULD KNOW (Copy and complete using the **key words**)

Predators, harmful and useful

Animals which kill and eat other animals are called _____.
The animals they eat are called their _____.

If the number of prey increases, the number of predators also _____.
As the number of predators increases, the number of prey _____.

5.9 Garden food webs

REMEMBER

Food chains begin with green plants.

They show what animals eat.

Different pests often eat the same plant. This means that the plant is at the start of more than one **food chain**.

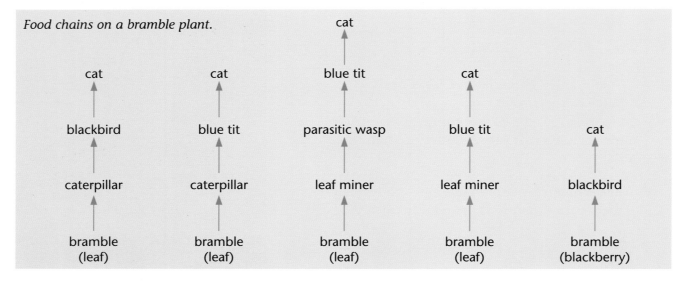

Food chains on a bramble plant.

cat
↑
blackbird
↑
caterpillar
↑
bramble
(leaf)

cat
↑
blue tit
↑
caterpillar
↑
bramble
(leaf)

cat
↑
blue tit
↑
parasitic wasp
↑
leaf miner
↑
bramble
(leaf)

cat
↑
blue tit
↑
leaf miner
↑
bramble
(leaf)

cat
↑
blackbird
↑
bramble
(blackberry)

1 Write down the names of <u>two</u> pests that eat the leaves of a bramble plant.

In fact, most of the plants and animals in a garden belong to more than one food chain.

2 Look at the diagrams. What do all these food chains start with?

3 Write down the name of an animal which belongs to <u>two</u> food chains.

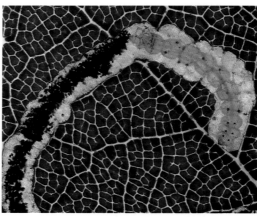

A leaf miner makes a burrow in a leaf. It eats the middle layers.

■ **Making a food web**

We can join these food chains to make a **food web**. This shows more clearly what happens in a particular **habitat** or place.

4 Copy and complete the food web, starting with the bramble plant.

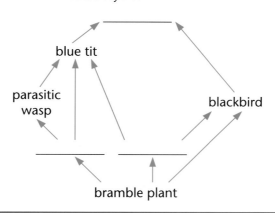

What's eating the pea plants?

A gardener wanted to grow peas so he planted a row of seeds. Mice and sparrows ate some of the seeds before they could even grow.

Look at the picture. It shows some of the other pests which feed on the pea plants.

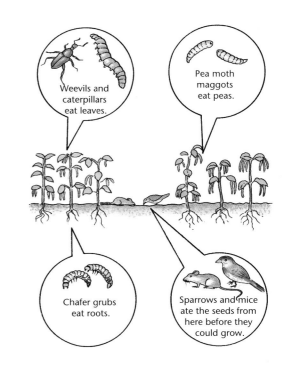

Weevils and caterpillars eat leaves.

Pea moth maggots eat peas.

Chafer grubs eat roots.

Sparrows and mice ate the seeds from here before they could grow.

5 Copy and complete the table.

Pest	Part of the pea plant that it eats
mouse	
sparrow	
pea moth maggot	
weevil	
caterpillar	
chafer grub	

6 Copy the food web.

  (a) Write in the boxes the names of the pests that eat the pea plant.

  (b) Look at the pictures of animals which eat these pests. Add their names to the food web.

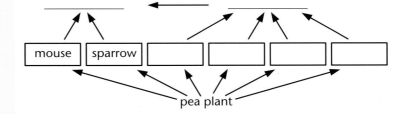

| mouse | sparrow | | | | |

pea plant

7 (a) Write down one of the longest food chains you can find in your food web.

  (b) How many others are the same length?

Cat.

Blackbird.

WHAT YOU SHOULD KNOW (Copy and complete using the **key words**)

Garden food webs

In a habitat, plants and animals belong to more than one _____ _____.
This is why a _____ _____ is better for showing what eats what in a
particular _____.

5.10 Competition

All animals need a place to live. Often they have to **compete** with other animals for **space** and **food**.

Many animals, or groups of animals, have an area of their own. They chase away other animals of their own kind.

1 Look at the pictures. Write down <u>two</u> reasons why animals need space.

The space which an animal defends is called its <u>territory</u>.

2 Penguins feed on fish from the sea. Why do you think they need only a small territory on land?

A pair of robins defends a territory about half the size of a football pitch.

3 Why do such small birds need so much space?

■ How do animals mark their territories?

People often put fences around their homes to show how much space is theirs. Animals need to show other animals too. Different animals do this in different ways.

4 Look at the pictures, then copy and complete the sentences.

Robins _____ at the edges of their territories. Otters and _____ mark their territories with _____ and _____ substances from their bodies.

Penguins defend a small space to keep their eggs and young safe.

Robins sing to keep other robins out of their feeding space.

Groups of rabbits scent-mark their territories with a smelly substance from under their chins. They also use their urine and droppings.

Otters also scent-mark their territory.

■ Competition between plants

Plants also compete with each other for **space** and the other things they need.

5 Look at the diagram, then copy and complete the sentences.

Plants compete for the _____ and _____ in the soil. Above the ground, they _____ for _____ and carbon dioxide.

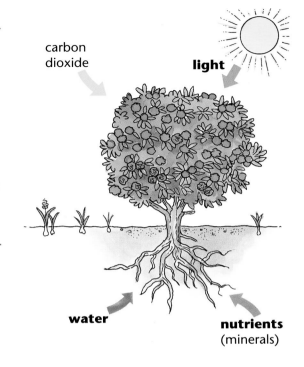

carbon dioxide

light

water

nutrients
(minerals)

■ The problem of rhododendrons

Explorers brought rhododendrons to Britain from Asia many years ago.

They grow so well in Britain that they have spread from people's gardens into woodland. Other plants, such as bluebells, cannot compete with them.

6 Look at the picture.

(a) Write down <u>three</u> things which bluebells and rhododendrons compete for.

(b) What happens to bluebells in woods as rhododendrons spread?

Rhododendrons affect animals too. Few insects eat the tough leaves.

If there are fewer insects in a wood, there are also fewer birds.

7 Ecologists think that we should get rid of all the rhododendrons from our woods. Why is this?

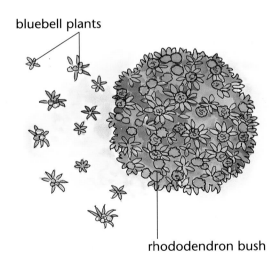

bluebell plants

rhododendron bush

WHAT YOU SHOULD KNOW (Copy and complete using the **key words**)

Competition

Animals _____ with each other for _____ and _____.

Plants compete with each other for _____, _____, _____ and _____.

1.1 The right one for the job

Things like how strong a material is, or if heat passes through it, are called its **properties**. We choose a material for a particular job because it has the right properties for that job.

■ Why use stainless steel for a pan?

Stainless steel is good for making pans.

1 Write down <u>three</u> properties of stainless steel that make it good for this job. Give a reason for each property you choose.

Properties of stainless steel
shiny polished surface
does not rust
hard wearing
not too heavy
does not melt easily
does not catch fire
nice to look at
heat passes through it

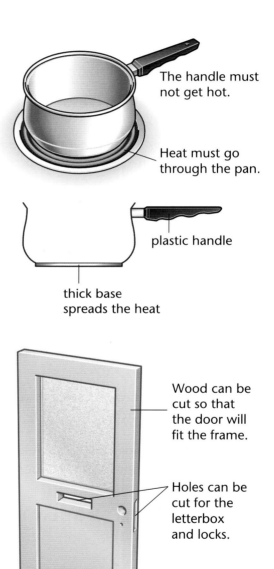

The handle must not get hot.

Heat must go through the pan.

plastic handle

thick base spreads the heat

Wood can be cut so that the door will fit the frame.

Holes can be cut for the letterbox and locks.

Wood is a poor conductor of heat. (It stops heat going in and out.)

■ Properties of wood

Wood is used for doors. You can cut and shape wood easily. It is strong.

2 Write down <u>three</u> properties of wood that make it good for doors.

3 Write down <u>two</u> properties of wood that explain why it is not used to make cooking pans. (Hint. Look back at the table of properties of stainless steel.)

We usually talk about 'heat', but the correct technical term is 'thermal energy'.

Materials we can see through

We need to see through a window. So we make a window out of a **transparent** material.

4 Write down <u>three</u> other important properties for a window. Give a reason for each.

5 Why is glass better than clear plastic for the windows in a house?

6 Why is plastic better than glass for the windows in a child's play house?

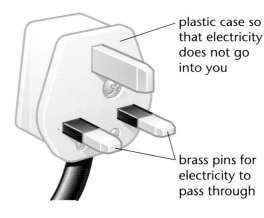

Glass is transparent (it lets light through).

Glass keeps wind and rain out.

Glass does not dissolve in rain.

Glass does not scratch or mark as easily as plastic.

If glass breaks, the pieces are very sharp.

Conductors and insulators of electricity

Materials that let electricity flow through them easily are called **conductors**. All metals conduct electricity.

Materials called **insulators** do not let electricity flow through.

7 Copy and complete the sentences.

The case of a plug is made of _____ because it is an _____.

The pins of a plug are made of _____ because it is a _____.

plastic case so that electricity does not go into you

brass pins for electricity to pass through

WHAT YOU SHOULD KNOW (Copy and complete using the **key words**)

The right one for the job

The things that make a material good for a particular job, like how hard it is, are called its _____.

Materials you can see through are _____.

All metals let electricity pass through them. They are called _____.
Materials that do not let electricity through are called _____.

Note. You must be able to say what properties other materials must have to make them good for various jobs.

1.2 Solid, liquid and gas

Some things are solid, some things are liquid and some things are gas. Solids, liquids and gases have different properties.

For example, gases and liquids will **flow**. Solids do not flow.

1 Water and gas come into people's houses through pipes. Why can they be delivered this way?

2 Look at the pictures. Explain why Sadia cannot pour the milk.

3 Copy and complete the table using the following substances: (They are all shown in the picture.)

snow, glass, pottery, orange juice, plastic, water, steam, steel, wood

Solid	Liquid	Gas

■ Liquids change shape, gases fill space, solids stay the same

Liquids **change** shape to fit what they are in. Lumps of solid keep the same **shape**. A gas will spread out to fill any **space**.

4 Answer the questions. For each question write down why you think the substance is a solid, liquid or gas.

(a) What does the brown substance do when the plate is removed?

(b) What happens to the shape of the meths when the bottle is tilted?

(c) What happens to the shape of the ice cube when the board is tilted?

On a snowy day Sadia gets her milk from the doorstep.

It is cold and the top of the milk is frozen solid.

Sadia cannot pour the milk because the top is frozen.

(a)

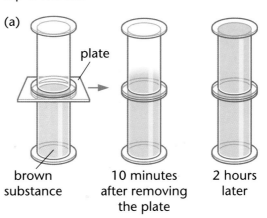

plate

brown substance   10 minutes after removing the plate   2 hours later

(b)

METHS   METHS

(c)   ice cube

Some substances are heavier than others

The table shows how heavy different substances are. To make the table fair, the figures are for one cubic centimetre of each substance. One cubic centimetre is about the size of a small dice.

Solids and liquids are heavier than gases. We say that solids and liquids are **denser** than gases.

Mass of one cubic centimetre.		
Solid	**Liquid**	**Gas**
iron 7 g	water 1 g	air 0.0013 g
gold 18 g	olive oil 0.9 g	steam 0.0006 g
pine 0.5 g	petrol 0.9 g	
cork 0.2 g	Ribena 1.3 g	

5 Which solids are denser than water?

6 Which solids are less dense than water?

A suitcase full of air is a lot lighter than one full of gold!

Floating and sinking

Cork floats on water because it is a **less dense** substance than water. A lump of iron **sinks** in water because it is a denser substance than water.

7 Look at the table again. Which solids will float on water?

8 Copy the diagram of oil and water.

Underneath the diagram, copy and complete this sentence:

The oil floats on the water because it is less _____ than the water.

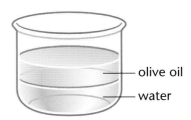

olive oil

water

WHAT YOU SHOULD KNOW (Copy and complete using the **key words**)

Solid, liquid and gas

Solids have their own _____. Liquids and gases can _____ shape. A gas spreads out to fill any _____.

Gases and liquids will _____ through pipes.

Solids and liquids are heavier substances than gases; we say they are _____.

Something floats on a liquid if it is _____ _____ than the liquid. A lump of iron _____ in water because it is a denser substance than water.

1.3 Explaining the way things are

A lot of cars have airbags in them. An airbag can save a driver in a crash.

When the bag fills with air, it makes a cushion. This stops the driver hitting the wheel. Air works because it is a gas. You can squash a gas and it will spring back.

Look at the pictures.

1 (a) What happens to the air in the tube when the weight is put on the top?

   (b) What happens to the air in the tube when the weight is taken away?

2 What happens when you do the same test with a tube of liquid?

3 What happens when you do the same test with a block of solid?

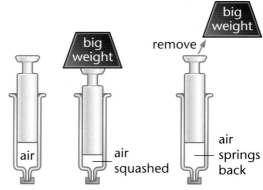

Air squashes and springs back.

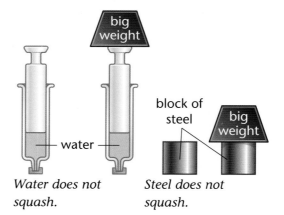

Water does not squash.

Steel does not squash.

■ Why can a gas be squashed?

Gases are made up of tiny **particles** that **move** about at high speed.

The particles are **far apart**. They do not hold each other together.

4 What is a gas made up of?

5 What do gas particles do when they hit each other?

6 Why can you squash a gas?

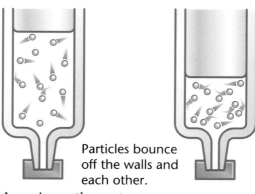

Particles bounce off the walls and each other.

A gas is mostly empty space, so you can squeeze the particles into a smaller space.

■ How are the particles arranged in a liquid?

The particles are very close together in a liquid. There is not very much space between the particles.

Though the particles in a liquid stay close together they are always moving about. They **change places** with each other all the time.

7 Why is it hard to squash a liquid?

8 You can pour a liquid into a container with a different shape. Explain why you can do this.

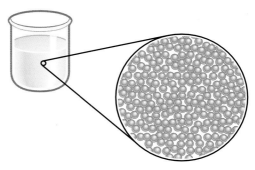

The particles in a liquid move around each other. There is no pattern.

■ What about solids?

The particles in a solid hold each other together **strongly**. They are packed **close together**.

The particles can jiggle about or **vibrate**, but they do not change places.

Particles in a solid are usually fixed in a pattern.

9 How are the particles arranged in a solid?

10 Why is it hard to squash a solid?

*You can **pour** a liquid.*

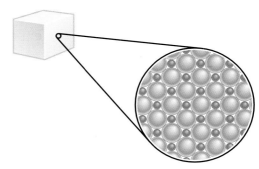

Particles in a solid are fixed in a pattern.

WHAT YOU SHOULD KNOW (Copy and complete using the **key words**)

Explaining the way things are

Solids, liquids and gases are all made of _____.

In solids, the particles hold each other together _____. They cannot change places, but they can _____.

In liquids, the particles stay close together but they can _____ _____ with each other. This means you can _____ a liquid.

In a gas there is a lot of space between the particles. The particles _____ around at high speed.

You can squash a gas because the particles are _____ _____.
It is hard to squash a liquid or a solid because the particles are _____ _____.

1.4 Mixing solids and liquids

To make drinks sweet you add sugar. When you add sugar to water and stir for a time you can't see the sugar any more. But it is still there in the water. The sugar <u>dissolves</u> in the water and produces a **solution**.

Just mix with water …

1 Write down <u>four</u> solids which dissolve in water and are commonly used in the kitchen.

■ Making solutions sweeter

Vicky added spoonfuls of sugar to two beakers of water. She stirred the water 10 times after adding each spoonful to see if all the sugar would dissolve.

Look at the diagram of the experiment.

2 Why can beaker B dissolve more sugar than beaker A?

3 Write down how this investigation was made fair.

More sugar dissolves in **hot** water than cold. The sugar is more <u>soluble</u> in hot water.

4 How could you dissolve more spoonfuls of sugar in the water in beaker A?

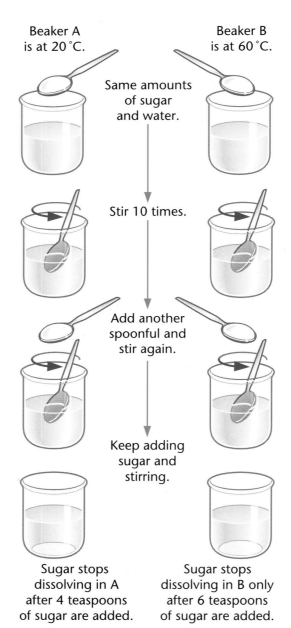

Beaker A is at 20 °C.
Beaker B is at 60 °C.

Same amounts of sugar and water.

Stir 10 times.

Add another spoonful and stir again.

Keep adding sugar and stirring.

Sugar stops dissolving in A after 4 teaspoons of sugar are added.

Sugar stops dissolving in B only after 6 teaspoons of sugar are added.

Cleaning the mess!

Graffiti on desks or a wall is a nuisance. Water will not always clean the coloured dye from ink or marker pens. To remove graffiti we need a liquid which dissolves the dye. This liquid is called a **solvent**.

5 (a) Which liquid removes the dye in the picture?

(b) Does the dye dissolve in water?

(c) Which liquid is a good solvent for dye?

The dye which dissolves in the solvent is called the **solute**.

6 Copy the table of words. Then copy the correct definition or example next to each word.

Word	Definition or example
dissolve	
solvent	
solution	
solute	

Definitions or examples

- The name for a solid which dissolves in a liquid.

- A liquid which contains sugar or salt.

- A liquid which will dissolve a dye.

- This is what happens when a solid disappears into a liquid.

WHAT YOU SHOULD KNOW (Copy and complete using the **key words**)

Mixing solids and liquids

When a solid dissolves in a liquid we get a _____.

Solids often dissolve better when the liquid is _____.

The liquid that the solid goes into is called the _____. The solid is called the _____.

1.5 Melting and boiling

Many solids melt when they are heated. They change into a liquid. This happens at a temperature called its **melting point**.

If you make a liquid hot enough, it will boil. The temperature at which this happens is called its **boiling point**. As a liquid boils it changes into a **gas**.

All these substances are at room temperature (20 °C).

■ Comparing melting points and boiling points

The table shows temperatures of melting and boiling for some substances.

For each substance, the temperature of the boiling point is always **higher** than that of the melting point.

1 Which substances in the table are solids at 20°C?

2 Which substance in the table is a liquid at 20°C?

3 Why do you need a very hot furnace to turn iron metal into a liquid?

Substance	Melting point (°C)	Boiling point (°C)
aluminium	666	2470
water	0	100
iron	1535	2750
sulphur	113	445

■ Making ice lollies

To change a liquid to a solid you must cool it down to below its melting point. So to change water to ice you must cool it to below 0°C.

Arthur tried to make ice lollies. He put one lolly tray into the main part of the fridge. He put the other tray into the freezer section.

4 Which tray will contain the best lollies after a day? Explain your answer.

To get the lollies out of the tray, Arthur put the tray in hot water for a few seconds.

5 Explain why this works.

fridge at 2 °C

freezer at −18 °C

Making the tea

Arthur was disappointed with his efforts to make lollies. He decided to help with the tea instead.

He heated water in a kettle and very quickly the water turned into steam.

Arthur noticed that as the steam reached the kitchen window it turned back into water (we say that the water <u>condensed</u>). The water began streaming down the glass.

6 What happens to the steam when it hits the window?

7 Why do you notice this more on a cold day?

Different boiling points

A test tube of alcohol was put into a beaker of very hot water.

The alcohol in the test tube started to boil even though the water was not boiling!

water at 90 °C

alcohol

8 Why is the alcohol boiling even though the water is not boiling?

To check what liquids are, scientists often measure their boiling points.

Substance	Boiling point (°C)
alcohol	78
water	100

9 Look at the diagrams.

   (a) Which liquid is water?

   (b) Which liquid is alcohol?

   (c) Which liquid might be paraffin?

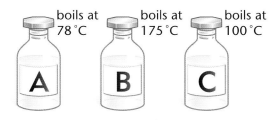

boils at 78 °C   boils at 175 °C   boils at 100 °C

A   B   C

WHAT YOU SHOULD KNOW (Copy and complete using the **key words**)

Melting and boiling

Many solids have a temperature at which they will melt. This is called the _____ _____ of the solid.

The temperature at which a liquid boils is called the _____ _____.
As a liquid boils, it changes into a _____.

Boiling point temperatures are always _____ than melting point temperatures.

1.6 Heat in, heat out

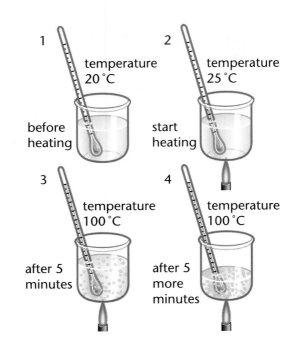

1 temperature 20 °C — before heating

2 temperature 25 °C — start heating

3 temperature 100 °C — after 5 minutes

4 temperature 100 °C — after 5 more minutes

■ Heating things doesn't always make them hotter

When you heat things they usually become hotter. But this does not always happen.

Look at the diagrams.

1 What happens to the water when you first start heating it?

2 What is the temperature of the water when it starts to boil?

3 What happens to the temperature of the boiling water when you keep on heating it?

The beaker is being heated as the water boils but the temperature is staying the same.
Energy from the hot flame makes the water change into a gas.

■ Melting ice

For an ice cube to melt it must take in energy. It takes this energy from the air or the dish it is on. To make the ice melt we have to make it hotter, so we have to **transfer** energy to the ice from its surroundings. This makes the surroundings colder.

4 For each of the ice cubes in the picture, say whether it would melt, and give a reason for your answer.

5 Which cube, A or B, would take the longest to melt? Explain your answer.

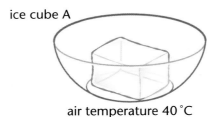

ice cube A

air temperature 40 °C

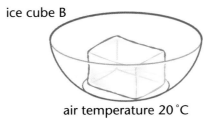

ice cube B

air temperature 20 °C

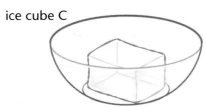

ice cube C

air temperature −2 °C

Getting rid of water

Anne left a measuring cylinder of water on a balance for a week.

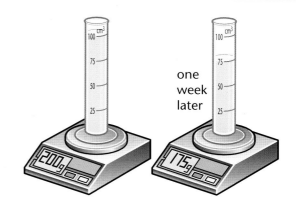

one week later

6 Give <u>two</u> things that have changed about the water in one week.

The water that has gone has changed into a gas. We call this change **evaporation**.

You can make evaporation happen more quickly by **heating** things.

You can make evaporation happen more quickly by **blowing** on the liquid surface.

7 Give <u>two</u> ways that a hair dryer helps water evaporate from your hair.

8 Which set of washing will dry quickest? Give <u>two</u> reasons for your answer.

sunny and breezy   dull and still

Cooling things down

Water evaporates from wet things. This makes these things a bit **colder**.

9 Look at the pictures. Which person will feel coolest? Give a reason for your answer.

10 How does sweating help you cool down?

air temperature 20 °C

dry person

person soaked in water at 20 °C

WHAT YOU SHOULD KNOW (Copy and complete using the **key words**)

Heat in, heat out

When we boil a liquid, we give _____ to the liquid.

When an ice cube is melted we _____ heat to the ice.

The change from liquid to gas is called _____.

We can make evaporation happen more quickly by _____ the liquid, and by _____ on the liquid surface.

Evaporation makes things get _____.

1.7 Other effects of heating and cooling

Heating things can change them from solid to liquid or from liquid to gas. Cooling things can do the opposite.

Heating and cooling can also change things in other ways.

■ How long is a piece of metal?

It depends on the temperature! If a bar of metal gets hot it will **expand**; this means it gets longer. If the metal cools down it will **contract**; this means it gets shorter.

1 Which picture shows telephone wires in summer?

2 Which picture shows telephone wires in winter?

■ Damaging heat

Many other substances expand when they get hot – not just metals.

If a substance can't expand when it gets hot, **push** forces are produced. If a substance can't contract as it cools, **pull** forces are produced. These forces can do lots of damage.

3 Copy this table. Complete it using the information in the pictures.

Example	Damage caused by contraction or expansion	How damage is prevented
telephone wires		
runway		

4 (a) What is the expanding concrete on the runway pushing against?

(b) Why does the bitumen stop the concrete cracking?

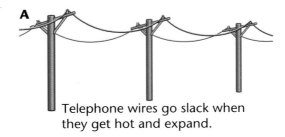

A

Telephone wires go slack when they get hot and expand.

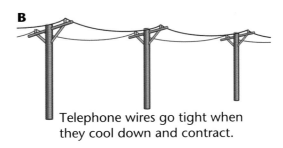

B

Telephone wires go tight when they cool down and contract.

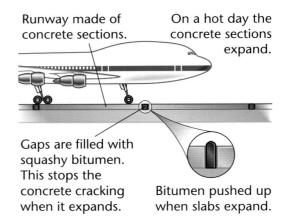

Runway made of concrete sections.

On a hot day the concrete sections expand.

Gaps are filled with squashy bitumen. This stops the concrete cracking when it expands.

Bitumen pushed up when slabs expand.

Telephone wires are put up so they are slack. If they contract in cold weather they get tighter but do not snap.

■ Expanding and contracting liquid

Like solids, liquids expand or contract when they get hot or cool down.

Mercury is a liquid metal found in many types of thermometer.

5 Write down the readings on both thermometers.

6 Describe what happens to the length of mercury in the thermometer when the temperature falls.

7 Does the mercury expand or contract when the temperature falls?

8 Wine bottles always have a gap at the top of the liquid inside the bottle. Explain why.

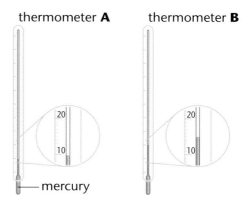

thermometer **A**   thermometer **B**

mercury

cork

air gap

wine

The force of an expanding liquid will push out the cork. Air is squashy so it makes room for the wine to expand.

■ Gases getting hot

Inside the wine bottle there is no room for the air to expand.
But air will expand when it is heated if there is nothing to stop it.

9 Explain what happens to the air inside the balloon as it gets hotter.

10 Does the balloon push or pull on the beaker when the air inside the balloon gets hot?

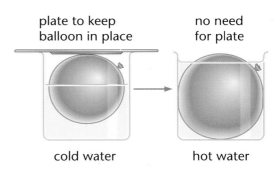

plate to keep   no need
balloon in place   for plate

cold water   hot water

WHAT YOU SHOULD KNOW (Copy and complete using the **key words**)

Other effects of heating and cooling

If a solid or liquid or gas is heated, it will _____.

If we cool the solid or liquid or gas down, then it will _____.

Expanding materials produce _____ forces. Contracting materials produce _____ forces. These forces can be very large and cause lots of damage.

1.8 Looking at change

The diagrams show some of the ways substances can change.

1 Write down <u>five</u> different ways that substances can change.

Even though substances may change in some ways, other things about the substance may stay the same.

■ Does the mass of things change?

You can find the **mass** of something by weighing it.

The diagrams show the mass of some ice before and after melting.

REMEMBER

The number of grams of a substance is called its mass.

2 (a) What was the mass of the ice cube before melting?

(b) What was the mass of the water after the ice had melted?

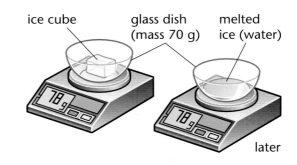

3 Copy and complete this sentence.

When ice changes to water, the _____ does not change.

The diagrams show the mass of some salt and some water before and after they are mixed.

4 Copy and complete the following.

Before: mass of salt   = _____ g
         mass of water   = _____ g
After: mass of salty water = _____ g

Take 10 g of salt.

Add it to 100 g of water, and stir.

You get 110 g of salt water.

5 Copy and complete this sentence.

When one substance dissolves in another, the total _____ does not change.

The same thing happens with the other changes on this page.

When something changes there is still the same amount of stuff so the mass stays the same.

■ Changing things back

Some changes are easy to change back. We say they are easy to **reverse**.

6 Write a sentence about the reverse of the changes in (a) and (b).

  (a) You can change a solid to a liquid by heating it.

  (b) You can change a gas to a liquid by cooling it.

7 Look at the diagrams.

  (a) How can you get the <u>salt</u> back from salt solution?

  (b) How can you get the <u>water</u> back from salt solution?

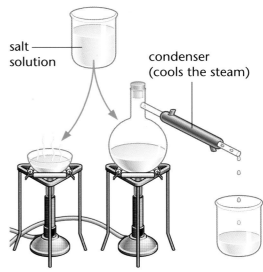

salt solution

condenser (cools the steam)

Boil off the water to get the salt.

To get the water, boil it off and condense it again; this is called distilling the water.

■ Still the same stuff

When water freezes, boils, expands or dissolves salt, it is still water. No new substances are produced.

Changes which do not produce new substances are called **physical** changes.

Some physical changes are easy to reverse. Some are not easy to reverse.

8 Look at the pictures of breaking glass and melting ice.

  (a) Why are these changes <u>physical</u> changes?

  (b) Which physical change is easier to reverse?

breaking glass

melting ice

WHAT YOU SHOULD KNOW (Copy and complete using the **key words**)

Looking at change

When things change, the _____ doesn't change.

Changes which don't produce new substances are called _____ changes.

Physical changes are usually easy to _____.

2.1 Mixtures

Lots of things are **mixtures**.

1 Write down the names of <u>two</u> mixtures.

A mixture of different sweets.

■ Air is a mixture

The air you breathe is a mixture of **gases**.

Air also has some solids in it like dust, insects, birds and planes!

Air is mainly a mixture of the gases **oxygen** and **nitrogen**. Oxygen is the one we need to stay alive.

A mixture of fruit and nuts.

2 Copy and complete this table.

Gas in the air	Percentage
nitrogen	
	21%
everything else	

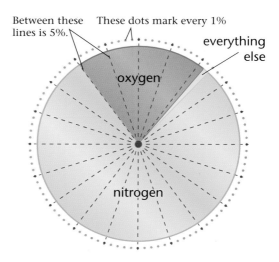

Pie chart of gases in the air.

■ Changing the mixture

You can change the **amount** of the things in a mixture. For example, in mixed fruit and nuts you can put more fruit and less nuts.

You change the mixture of gases in the air when you breathe. Your body picks the gas it needs out of the mixture of gases in the air.

3 Which gas does your body take from the air when you breathe?

4 Which gas do you add more of to the air when you breathe?

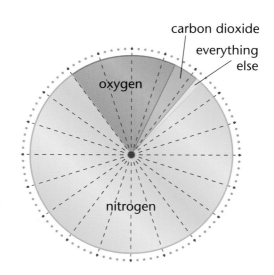

Pie chart of gases you breathe out.

What is in the sea

Sea-water is a mixture of lots of things. As well as fish and plants there is also salt.

A mixture of things can be **split** up. You can get the **salt** out of the sea by **evaporating** the water. The water goes into the air and leaves the salt behind.

5 How do people get salt from the sea in hot countries?

Heat from the sun evaporates the water. Salt is left behind.

How sea-water can be changed

You can change a mixture like sea-water by adding things to it.

Rivers carry substances to the sea. If a factory dumps poisonous waste into the river, the poison can damage sea life.

6 How can waste from an inland factory get into the sea?

7 Why is polluting the sea a bad idea?

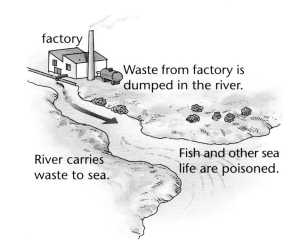

factory

Waste from factory is dumped in the river.

River carries waste to sea.

Fish and other sea life are poisoned.

WHAT YOU SHOULD KNOW (Copy and complete using the **key words**)

Mixtures

Air and sea-water are both _____.

Air is a mixture of _____. The two main gases in the air are _____ and _____.

The sea is a mixture of water, _____ and lots of other things.

Mixtures can be _____ up into their different parts. For example, you can get the salt out of sea-water by _____ the water.

You can change the _____ of different things in a mixture.

2.2 Taking out the bits

We can use a **sieve** to separate peas from water.

1 Why does the sieve trap the peas?

2 What would happen if the sieve's holes were larger than the peas?

peas in water

sieve

peas

water

You need a sieve with very small holes to strain bits of fruit out when you make fruit jelly. Two pieces of cotton sheet make a good sieve.

3 Why is the cotton sheet better than an ordinary sieve?

The juice goes through small holes in sheet, but the bits are trapped.

bits of fruit left behind

double thickness of cotton material fixed on with string

bowl

fruit juice without bits

Granny Smith's Fruit Jelly Recipe

Simmer fruit until tender.
Strain off the juice.
Add sugar and boil for 10 minutes.
Bottle in clean jars.

▩ Using paper

Kitchen paper has very tiny holes in it. They let liquids soak through. You can use kitchen paper to take bits of **solid** out of a liquid. You can also buy special paper to do this called <u>filter paper</u>.

Taking bits of solid out of a liquid like this is called **filtering**.

4 Copy the diagram. Then copy and complete this passage.

The liquid and bits of solid are poured into the _____ paper in the funnel.

The solid is trapped by the paper.
The solid is called the _____.

The liquid goes through the filter paper. It is called the filtrate.

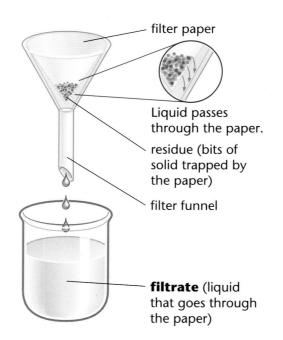

filter paper

Liquid passes through the paper.

residue (bits of solid trapped by the paper)

filter funnel

filtrate (liquid that goes through the paper)

Separating salt and pepper

You could use a magnifying glass and a pair of tweezers to **separate** salt and pepper. It would take a while!

Salt dissolves in water but pepper does not. This means you can separate them by filtering.

5   On a copy of the flow chart, write down these words in the correct boxes to show how to separate salt and pepper.

   ■ Evaporate the water to get the salt.

   ■ Filter.

   ■ Stir salt and pepper in some water.

   ■ Pepper stays on the filter paper.

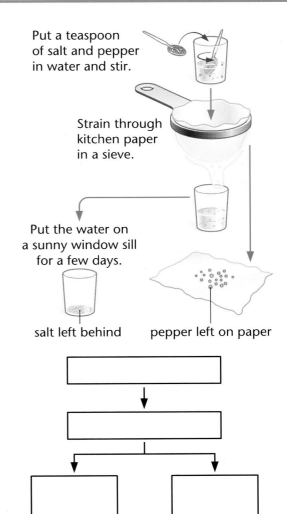

Put a teaspoon of salt and pepper in water and stir.

Strain through kitchen paper in a sieve.

Put the water on a sunny window sill for a few days.

salt left behind   pepper left on paper

What can you separate using filtration?

You can separate two things using filtering if one dissolves in a liquid but the other does not.

6   Which of these mixtures could you separate by stirring with water then filtering? (Use the information in the table. Give a reason for each answer.)

   (a) salt and sand

   (b) salt and sugar

   (c) sugar and pepper

   (d) pepper and sand

Substance	Does it dissolve in water?
salt	dissolves in water
sand	does not dissolve in water
sugar	dissolves in water
pepper	does not dissolve in water

WHAT YOU SHOULD KNOW (Copy and complete using the **key words**)

Taking out the bits

Filter paper acts like a very fine _____.

We can _____ a mixture of liquid and particles of solid using filter paper. We call this _____.

The _____ left behind in the filter paper is called the residue.

The liquid that goes through the filter paper is called the_____.

2.3 Getting the liquid back

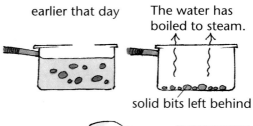

earlier that day   The water has boiled to steam.

solid bits left behind

A chef let his soup boil for too long. He was left with a pan of dried-up gunge and kitchen walls dripping with water.

1 What came out of the pan when the soup was boiling?

2 What stayed in the pan when the water boiled away?

3 Why did the water appear on the kitchen walls and windows?

Cold windows and walls make steam change back to water (it condenses).

Getting drinking water from the sea

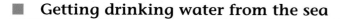

Sea water will poison you if you drink too much. This is because there is so much salt and other solid substances dissolved in it.

When we boil sea water, the water **boils** and turns into steam but the **solids** do not boil. We can **condense** the steam back into water. 'Condense' means change from gas to liquid.

4 What comes out of sea water as it boils?

5 What happens when the steam meets the cold wall of the beaker?

6 What substance collects on the wall of the beaker?

7 What would be left in the dish if you heated it until it dried up?

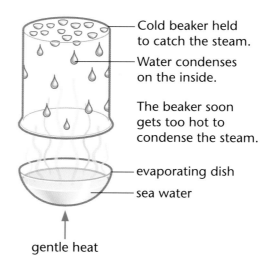

Cold beaker held to catch the steam.

Water condenses on the inside.

The beaker soon gets too hot to condense the steam.

evaporating dish

sea water

gentle heat

We can get drinking water from sea water by boiling it. We can condense the steam and collect the water. This water is pure and you can drink it. It is called **distilled** water. To make enough distilled water to drink we need something better than a beaker.

8 Can you use a beaker to condense steam for a long time? Explain your answer.

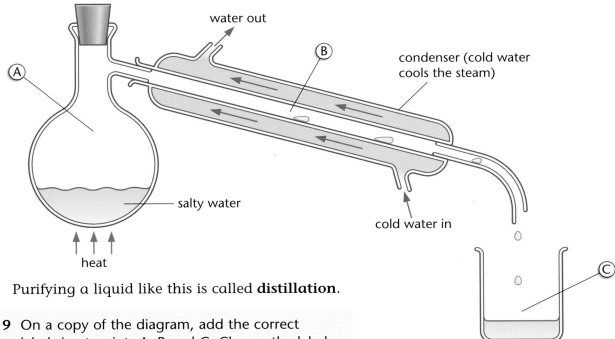

Distilling sea water.

Purifying a liquid like this is called **distillation**.

9 On a copy of the diagram, add the correct labels in at points A, B and C. Choose the labels from this list:

- Pure water is collected.
- The water changes to steam and the salt is left behind.
- The steam condenses to water.

When do you use distillation?

You use distillation to get a pure liquid when things are dissolved in it.

You use filtering to separate a solid from a liquid when they are not dissolved.

10 Copy the table, then complete it.

Mixture	What is wanted	Method of separation
sand and water	sand	
sugar dissolved in water	water	

WHAT YOU SHOULD KNOW (Copy and complete using the **key words**)

Getting the liquid back

When a solid dissolves in water we can get the water back by _____.

This works because the water _____ and turns into steam.

The steam is cooled to _____ it.

The _____ get left behind.

The water we get at the end is pure. It is called _____ water.

2.4 What's in a colour?

A pure dye contains only one colour. Black ink is made from two or more coloured dyes mixed together.

The pictures show one way of separating the dyes.

1 How does the water reach the ink spot?

2 What happens to the ink spot as the water soaks across the paper?

3 What different dyes are used to make black ink?

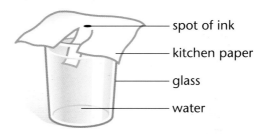

Using water to separate ink colours.

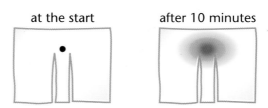

After 10 minutes the paper can be dried and the colours seen.

■ A better way of separating the dyes

Separating substances like this is called <u>chromatography</u>. The pattern of colours you get is called a **chromatogram**.

4 Which inks are made from only one dye?

5 What colours are in the green ink?

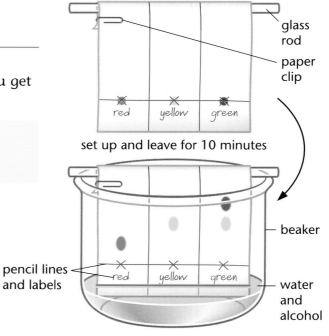

set up and leave for 10 minutes

Colours in different inks.

■ Who forged the cheque?

A chromatogram was made from the ink on a forged cheque.

Chromatograms were made from the pens used by two suspects.

6 (a) Who do you think forged the cheque?

  (b) Does the chromatogram prove beyond doubt who forged the cheque?

(Give reasons for your answers.)

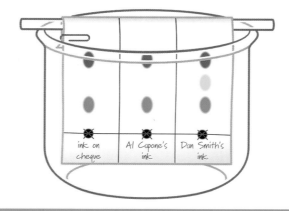

Spreading at different speeds

Chromatography is used to split up a mixture of substances that **dissolve** in the same liquid. The substances spread across the paper at different **speeds**.

7 Copy the diagram. Use coloured pens to copy the spots shown at the start and after 15 minutes. Then colour in the spots for after 7 minutes.

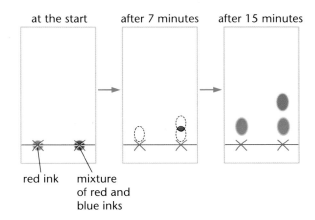

at the start   after 7 minutes   after 15 minutes

red ink   mixture of red and blue inks

More inks

Chromatography was used to split up some inks. A mixture of alcohol and water was used because all the inks would dissolve in it.

8 Brown ink is made from a mixture of yellow, blue and red inks. Copy the diagram and complete the section for the brown ink.

9 Why was a mixture of alcohol and water used to make the chromatogram?

10 Which inks shown on the diagram are made from only one colour?

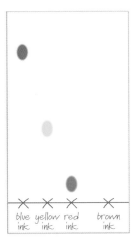

blue ink   yellow ink   red ink   brown ink

WHAT YOU SHOULD KNOW (Copy and complete using the **key words**)

What's in a colour?

Chromatography is used to split up a mixture of substances that _____ in the same liquid.

The substances spread out through the paper at different _____.

The pattern you get is called a _____.

2.5 Elements

There are about 750 000 words in the English language and they are all made out of just 26 letters joined together in different ways.

1 How many English words can you make from the letters E, I, L, and V? You don't have to use all the letters, and letters can be repeated.

Elements are substances that cannot be split into anything **simpler**. There are about 90 elements on the Earth.

All the other substances in the world are made from these elements joined together just like all the words are made from 26 letters.

2 What is the name for a substance that cannot be split into simpler substances?

3 About how many elements make up the substances on the Earth?

■ Is water an element?

Until the year 1800, people thought water was an element but they were wrong.

The diagram shows how we know that they were wrong.

4 What two elements make up water?

5 How can water be split up into its elements?

6 How can you tell that an electric current flows in the circuit?

7 Why was it impossible to do this experiment before 1794?

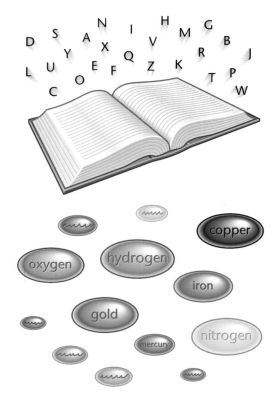

About 90 elements make millions of substances.

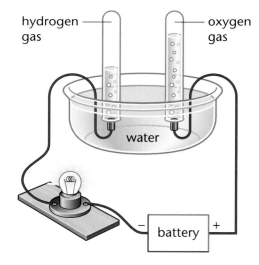

In 1800 an electric current was passed through water for the first time. The current splits the water into its elements.

DID YOU KNOW?

An electric current was first discovered in 1794.

Elements on the Earth

Some elements are more common than others.

8 Which <u>three</u> elements are the most common ones on the Earth?

Elements in common substances

Look at the chart of substances.

Carbon is an element. It is made of only one thing, carbon.

Water is not an element. It is made of two elements joined together, **hydrogen** and **oxygen**.

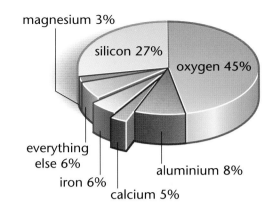

Pie chart showing elements in the Earth's crust.

magnesium 3%
silicon 27%
oxygen 45%
everything else 6%
iron 6%
aluminium 8%
calcium 5%

Substance	What is in it
water	hydrogen, oxygen
carbon	carbon
salt	sodium, chlorine
oxygen	oxygen
carbon dioxide	carbon, oxygen
limestone	calcium, carbon, oxygen
iron	iron
gold	gold

Substance	What is in it
sugar	carbon, hydrogen, oxygen
natural gas	carbon, hydrogen
sulphur	sulphur
magnesium oxide	magnesium, oxygen
nitrogen	nitrogen
copper	copper
iron sulphide	iron, sulphur
butane	carbon, hydrogen

9 Copy out the heading of the table below.
Complete it using the information above.

Some substances that are elements

WHAT YOU SHOULD KNOW (Copy and complete using the **key words**)

Elements

An element is a substance that cannot be split into anything _____.

Water is made from the two elements _____ and _____.

Altogether there are about 90 _____ that make up everything else.

2.6 Shorthand for elements

Scientists put all the elements into a special chart. On the chart each element has a **symbol**.

1 Copy the table. Then write the names of the elements by the symbols shown in the table.

Name of element	Symbol
	C
	S
	H
	O
	P
	Al

2 What do you notice about the symbol for each of these elements and its name?

Each symbol begins with a **capital** letter.

Sometimes we need to use a second letter. For example, N is the symbol for nitrogen. So we use the symbol Ne for neon. The second letter is always a small letter.

3 Copy and complete the table.

Name of element	Symbol
helium	
magnesium	
zinc	
chlorine	
copper	

The symbols for some elements are nothing like their names.

4 (a) What is the symbol for iron?

(b) Why does it have this symbol?

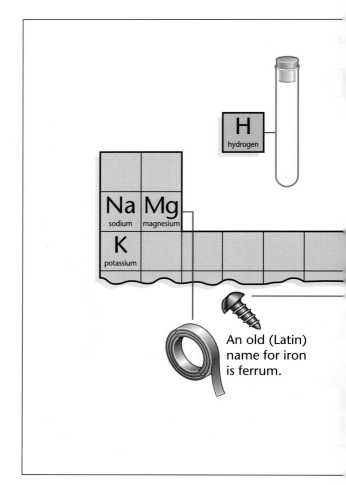

An old (Latin) name for iron is ferrum.

5 Copy and complete the table using the chart of elements to help you.

Name of element	Symbol
potassium	
	Au
sodium	

rt of a scientist's chart of the elements

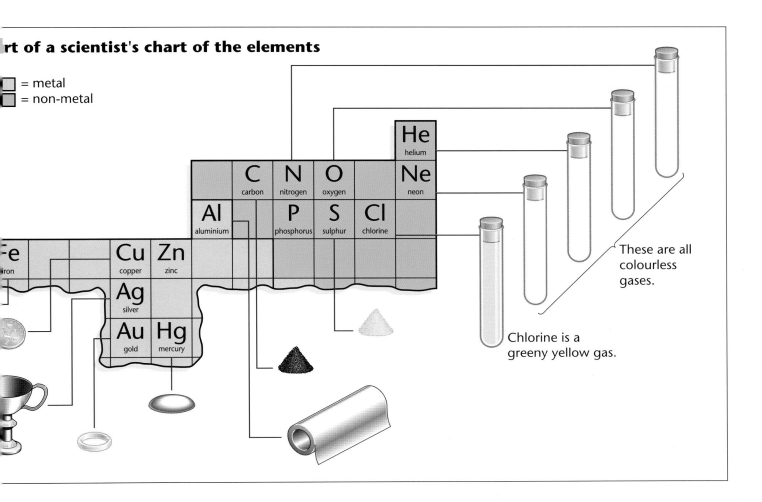

□ = metal
■ = non-metal

These are all colourless gases.

Chlorine is a greeny yellow gas.

6 Which element is a yellow solid but not a metal?

7 Write down the name of a gas which is coloured.

8 (a) Write down one thing that is the same about all the metals in the picture.

(b) Write down one thing that is different about some metals.

WHAT YOU SHOULD KNOW (Copy and complete using the **key words**)

Shorthand for elements

Every element has a _____. This is either one or two letters.

The first letter is always a _____ letter.

2.7 Putting elements together

Everything on the Earth is made from the elements. Sometimes the elements are found by themselves in the ground or in the air.

Use a copy of the scientists' chart of elements to help you answer these questions. Look back at pages 124–125 if you can't remember what the symbols stand for.

1 Which substances in the picture are elements?

This prospector is looking for gold.

A substance made from different elements joined together is called a **compound**.

2 Which substances in the picture are compounds?

Compounds have very different **properties** from the elements they are made from.

3 Copy and complete the table using the information in the box and the pictures.

Name of compound	Elements in the compound
water	
salt (sodium chloride)	

4 Describe one way in which water is different from both the elements it contains.

5 Describe one way in which salt is different from the two elements it contains.

REMEMBER

Scientists use a special chart of the elements.

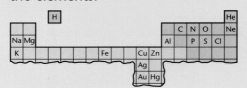

Air contains oxygen, nitrogen and carbon dioxide gases.

Clouds are made from tiny water droplets.

Ayers Rock in Australia is sandstone containing iron oxide (iron joined with oxygen).

There are tiny specks of gold mixed with the rock and dust.

DID YOU KNOW?

Water is hydrogen joined with oxygen. Water is a liquid and does not burn. Hydrogen and oxygen are gases. They make a mixture that can burn or even explode.

These are dangerous substances.

sodium metal

+

chlorine gas

crystals of sodium chloride

Making compounds

Iron and sulphur are both elements.

6   Describe what the fresh iron filings look like.

7   Describe what the sulphur looks like.

8   What must you do to make the iron and the sulphur join together to make a compound?

9   Write down <u>two</u> ways in which the new compound is different from what we started with.

If iron and sulphur are mixed together and heated, a new substance is made.

Compounds from burning

When iron and sulphur join together we say that a **chemical** reaction has happened. Burning is also a type of chemical reaction. When an element burns a compound is formed.

10   What does the magnesium look like:

    (a)   before burning,

    (b)   after burning?

11   Which other element takes part in the reaction when magnesium burns?

12   What is the name of the new compound formed when magnesium burns?

Although there are only about 90 elements, there are lots of different ways of putting them together. This means that there are millions of different compounds.

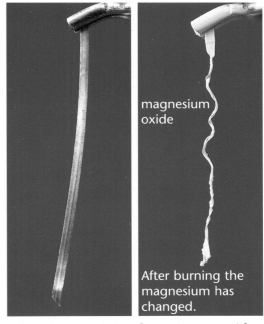

When the magnesium burns it reacts with oxygen from the air.

WHAT YOU SHOULD KNOW (Copy and complete using the **key words**)

Putting elements together

A substance which contains two or more elements joined together is called a _____.

Compounds have different _____ from the elements they contain.

Many compounds are formed by _____ reactions between elements.

2.8 Useful compounds

Water is probably the liquid that we know best. It is also the most useful compound known.

1 Make a list of the things that we use water for. The illustration gives some ideas.

Using water.

Using salt

Salt is also a very useful compound. Salt is a solid. It has been prized by people for a long time.

2 Look at the pictures. Write down a list of things that people use salt for.

Today we can make lots of other **compounds** from salt.

3 Look at the pictures. Write down <u>two</u> other compounds that we make from salt.

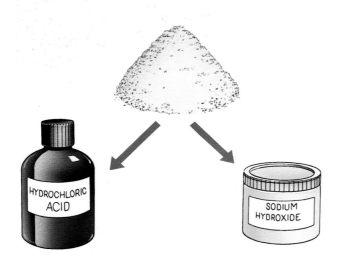

Using salt as a preservative.

Using salt as a flavouring.

Using salt to help thaw ice on roads.

A compound in the air

Carbon dioxide is a gas. Small amounts are present in the air. Carbon dioxide is a very important compound.

4 Write down <u>two</u> uses of carbon dioxide.

Two uses of carbon dioxide.

Whenever **carbon** burns in air, it usually makes carbon dioxide.

The charcoal fuel that we burn in barbecues is mainly carbon.

5 Copy and complete the word equation below that shows what happens when carbon burns.

carbon + oxygen → _____ di_____

Most fuels have carbon in them.

6 Write down the names of <u>five</u> other fuels which contain carbon.

When these fuels burn, they make the same gas.

7 Write down the name of this gas.

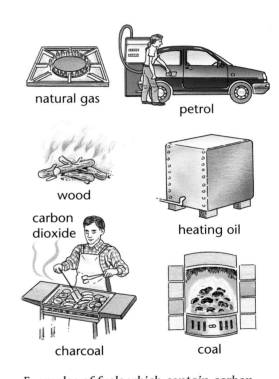

natural gas

petrol

wood

carbon dioxide

heating oil

charcoal

coal

Examples of fuels which contain carbon.

WHAT YOU SHOULD KNOW (Copy and complete using the **key words**)

Useful compounds

The best-known liquid in the world is _____.

A solid compound used to make lots of other substances is _____.

Air contains small amounts of _____ dioxide gas.

Water, salt and carbon dioxide are all very important _____.

3.1 Looking at metals

We use metals for many different things. The pictures show what we use some metals for.

1 Write down the names of <u>five</u> metals.

■ **What do we know about metals?**

There are many different metals. But most metals are like each other in lots of ways.

2 Choose one word or phrase from each pair that describes what <u>most</u> metals are like.

    (a) soft / hard

    (b) weak / strong

    (c) shiny / dull

    (d) tough / brittle

    (e) heavy or dense / light

    (f) conduct heat / do not conduct heat

    (g) conduct electricity / do not conduct electricity

    (h) liquid / solid

> We usually talk about 'heat', but the correct technical term is 'thermal energy'.

The words you have chosen (like 'hard' and 'strong') describe the <u>properties</u> of metals.

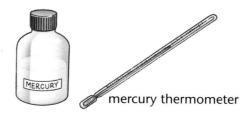

Mercury is the only metal that is not a solid at ordinary temperatures.

Steel is **hard** and strong.

Aluminium is shiny.

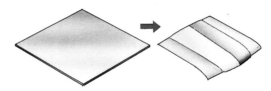

steel sheet   car bonnet

Steel is tough and can be stamped into different shapes without breaking.

brass   iron

Metal weights.

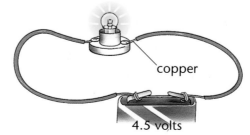

aluminium

heat travels through the metal from the flames

Metals **conduct** heat.

copper

4.5 volts

Metals conduct **electricity**.

■ Sorting out metals

People who work in scrap-yards sort out metals from other materials.

3 Copy the table. Then match each material with one of the parts of the scrap car.

Material	Part of car
plastic	
steel	
glass	
rubber	

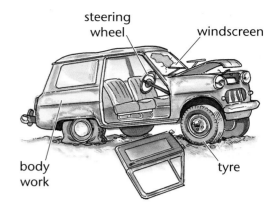

■ Working with scrap metals

People who work in scrap-yards must also sort out different metals from each other.

We use more steel than any other metal. Steel is made mainly of iron. Both iron and steel are **magnetic**. We can pick them up with a magnet. Most other metals are not magnetic.

4 Which objects in the drawing would a magnetic crane <u>not</u> pick up?

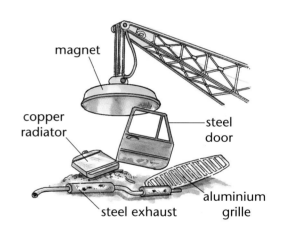

■ Metals and non-metals

There are millions of different substances in the world around us. They are made up of about 90 very simple substances that we call elements, joined together in different ways.

Most of these elements are metals. The rest of the elements are <u>non-metals</u>.

WHAT YOU SHOULD KNOW (Copy and complete using the **key words**)

Looking at metals

Metals are normally shiny and _____.

Metals conduct _____.

Metals _____ heat.

Iron and steel are _____.

3.2 Non-metals

Most of the elements are metals. But about a quarter of all the elements in nature are not metals. We call them **non-metals**.

Non-metals are a very mixed bunch!

The pictures show some of the non-metals at 20°C.

As you can see, non-metals are very different from each other. For example, some are solids, one is a liquid and some are **gases.**

Sulphur.

Iodine.

Bromine

Chlorine

Hydrogen   Nitrogen

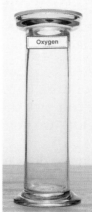
Oxygen

Phosphorus

You must keep this under water.

1 Copy the headings:

Solid   Liquid   Gas

(a) Now write down the names of the non-metallic elements under the correct headings.

(b) Write down the colour of each element under the name, for example: hydrogen (colourless)

Carbon. (diamond)

USEFUL RULE

Any element that is a **gas** at room temperature is also a non-metal.

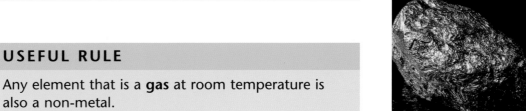
Carbon. (graphite)

How do we know if an element is a metal or a non-metal?

The biggest difference between metals and non-metals is that most non-metals do <u>not</u> **conduct** heat or electricity.

2 Look at the diagram. Copy and complete the sentence.

Sulphur does not conduct _____.

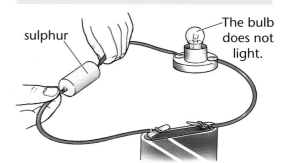

Does sulphur conduct electricity?

3 Copy and complete the sentence.

Carbon does not conduct _____.

The proper name for heat is thermal energy. Non-metals are poor conductors of thermal energy.

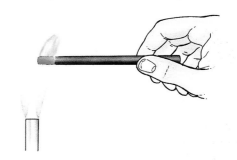

The carbon burns but the other end of the carbon rod does not get hot.

Another difference between metals and non-metals

Most metals can be bent many times before they break. Lead is a metal.

4 What happens when you hit (a) the lead strip and (b) the carbon rod?

Most non-metal solids break easily when you hit them. We say they are **brittle**.

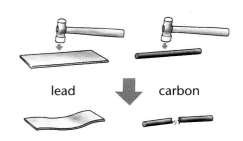

lead   carbon

WHAT YOU SHOULD KNOW (Copy and complete using the **key words**)

Non-metals

Elements that are not metals are called _____.

Non-metals can be solids, liquids, or _____.

If we know an element is a _____, then we also know that it is a non-metal.

Most non-metals do not _____ heat or electricity.

Solid non-metals are _____.

3.3 Where do we find non-metals?

There aren't as many non-metals as metals. But most of the things around us are made from **non-metals**.

The pie chart shows that your body contains 3% of metals. The rest of you is made up of non-metals.

1 What is the percentage of non-metals in the human body: 30% or 97% or 27% or 3%?

2 (a) What is the most common element in your body?

   (b) What percentage of your body is made of this element?

The most important element in living things is **carbon**. All life is based on the element carbon.

3 What percentage of your body is made up of carbon?

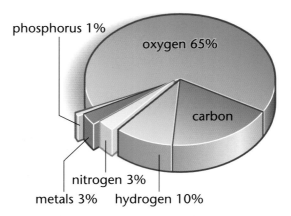

The elements in your body. (The percentages add up to 100.)

phosphorus 1%
oxygen 65%
carbon
nitrogen 3%
metals 3%
hydrogen 10%

DID YOU KNOW?

Phosphorus is so reactive that we store it under water. When phosphorus comes into contact with air, it bursts into flames.

■ Non-metals in food and drink

The things we eat and drink are made mostly of non-metals.

4 Write down the names of <u>three</u> non-metals that are found both in Coca Cola and in your body.

5 Why does it seem strange to find phosphorus in our bodies?

Coca Cola is mainly water but also contains phosphoric acid; this is made of hydrogen, phosphorus and oxygen.

Your body needs phosphorus to make its cells work.

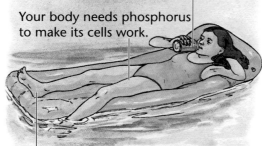

Most of your body is made up of water; this contains hydrogen and oxygen.

■ Non-metals in the air

The air around us is made from non-metals.

Look at the pie chart.

6   What are the two main gases we find in air?

7   What is the percentage of oxygen in the air?

Now look at the drawings.

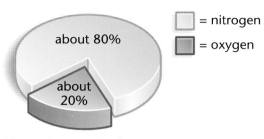

The main gases in the air.

Without oxygen, **burning** could not take place.

Without **oxygen**, we could not breathe.

If more than 25% of the air were oxygen, then fire would have destroyed all the trees.

8   Which element do we use when we breathe in?

9   Which element is needed for things to burn?

10 Nitrogen makes the air safe for living things. How does nitrogen do this?

■ Non-metals in the sea

The table shows the four most common elements in sea-water.

11 Copy and complete:

The three most common elements in sea-water are all _____.

Elements in sea water	Approximate %
oxygen	86
hydrogen	11
chlorine	2
sodium	1

(Look back to page 132 if you can't remember whether these elements are solids, liquids or gases at ordinary temperatures.)

WHAT YOU SHOULD KNOW (Copy and complete using the **key words**)

Where do we find non-metals?

Most of the things around us are made from _____.

Life is based on a non-metal called _____.

We need to breathe a non-metal called _____.

Oxygen is also needed for _____.

3.4 Elements of Thar

A star-ship left Earth to look for planets of distant stars. It found a planet called Thar.

Tharian scientists only know 15 of the elements. They don't even know about metals or non-metals.

■ **Metal or non-metal?**

Earth scientists tell the Tharians about the different properties of metals and non-metals.

1 Copy the table. Then complete it to show what the Earth scientists tell the Tharians.

Test	Metal	Non-metal
Does it conduct heat?		no
Does it conduct electricity?	yes	

2 Some elements are gases. What kind of element must a gas be – metal or non-metal?

3 The drawing shows six of the Tharian elements being tested. Copy out the table. Then complete it to show the results of the tests.

Thar element	Metal or non-metal?
cinz	
himule	
hongdery	
pulshur	
rolechin	
roni	

Elements and symbols on Thar

Earth scientists write out the list of 15 Tharian elements using Earth names.

They make one table for the gases and another table for the solid elements.

For the solid elements, they write down whether the element is a conductor or not.

The Earth scientists show the Tharians that these 15 elements are part of their own chart of the elements.

4 Copy the Earth scientists' chart of elements shown below. Write the symbols of the metals in blue and non-metals in red.

5 A Tharian element has the same letters in its name as the English name, but they are mixed up. Write down English names for:

cinz, himule, hongdery, pulshur, rolechin, roni.

Gases	Symbol
hydrogen	H
helium	He
nitrogen	N
oxygen	O
chlorine	Cl

Solid element	Symbol	Conductor?
carbon	C	no
sodium	Na	yes
magnesium	Mg	yes
aluminium	Al	yes
phosphorus	P	no
sulphur	S	no
calcium	Ca	yes
iron	Fe	yes
copper	Cu	yes
zinc	Zn	yes

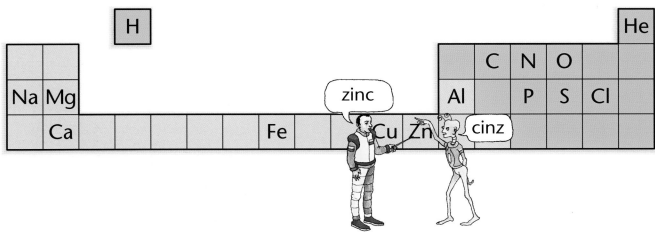

WHAT YOU SHOULD KNOW (Copy and complete using the key words)

Elements of Thar

An element is a metal or a _____.

Any element that is a _____ must be a non-metal.

We can test if an element is a metal or a non-metal. Metals conduct _____ and _____. Most non-metals do not conduct.

3.5 Metals reacting with oxygen

When we set off a sparkler, the sparks are tiny bits of burning iron. These are so hot that they burn as they fly through the air. Iron and oxygen (from the air) join together to make a new substance we call <u>iron oxide</u>. This is a chemical reaction.

1 (a) What do you see when iron and oxygen react together?

   (b) What new substance is produced?

■ Shooting stars, nature's sparklers

If you look at the sky when it's dark, you might see shooting stars. These are lumps of material from space. They mostly burn up as they go through the air.

But bigger lumps don't burn up completely so they hit the ground. We call them <u>meteorites</u>.

2 Are you more likely to see a shooting star during the daytime or during the night-time?

3 Look at the picture. What is a meteorite mainly made of?

■ The beginning of the Iron Age

The first iron that people ever used came from meteorites. By heating the meteorite until it was red hot, Early Iron Age people could shape the iron into tools and weapons.

When red-hot iron is hammered, it gives off lots of sparks. These sparks are iron burning in **oxygen** from the air.

4 What is the same about the chemical reactions in the sparkler, the shooting star and the blacksmith pictures?

iron + oxygen → iron oxide

Some shooting stars fall to the ground as meteorites.

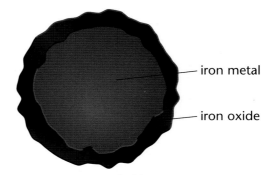

iron metal

iron oxide

A meteorite cut in half (a cross-section).

A blacksmith hammering red-hot iron.

Artificial shooting stars

If a ship at sea is in trouble at night, a flare can be used to show rescuers where the ship is.
The flare contains a metal called magnesium. Magnesium burns with a very bright flame:

magnesium + oxygen → magnesium oxide

5 What are the flares for?

6 Why is magnesium used in the flares rather than iron?

7 What chemical reaction occurs when magnesium burns?

A rescue flare burns with a bright white light.

Reactions of metals with oxygen

A teacher heats iron, magnesium and copper. The teacher then puts the metals into gas jars filled with oxygen. The diagram shows the reactions.

8 (a) Which metal burns brightest?

(b) Which metal burns dullest?

We say that metals that burn brightest are the most **reactive**.

9 Which is the most reactive of these three metals?

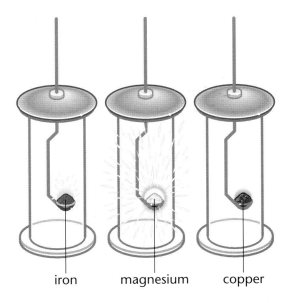

iron   magnesium   copper

WHAT YOU SHOULD KNOW (Copy and complete using the **key words**)

Metals reacting with oxygen

A few metals burn very easily in the air's _____.

Metals that burn brightest are the most _____.

3.6 Metals reacting with water

■ Does copper react with water?

In days gone by, people used **copper** kettles to boil water. Nowadays, we use copper pipes to carry hot water to the radiators that keep rooms warm.

1 Do you think that copper reacts with water or steam? Give a reason for your answer.

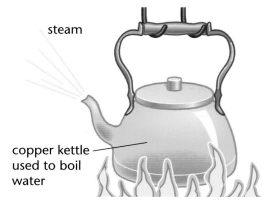

steam

copper kettle used to boil water

Copper kettles last for years.

■ Magnesium reacting with water

Remember how magnesium burns in air? That was a very fast reaction. Magnesium also reacts with cold **water** but only very slowly.

2 (a) How can you see that a reaction is taking place?

   (b) What gas is made in the reaction?

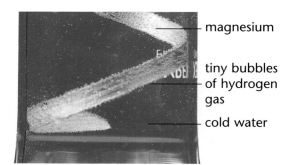

magnesium

tiny bubbles of hydrogen gas

cold water

Magnesium reacts very slowly with cold water.

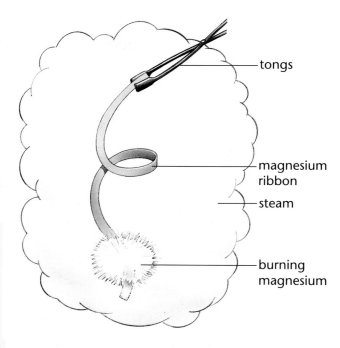

tongs

magnesium ribbon

steam

burning magnesium

The reaction goes very quickly if we put burning magnesium into **steam**.

3 Why do you think the reaction is faster in steam rather than in cold water?

4 Which metal, copper or magnesium, is more reactive?

5 What <u>two</u> new substances are made in the reaction between magnesium and steam?

Magnesium burns in steam.
Hydrogen and magnesium oxide are the two new substances made in this chemical reaction.

■ Sodium – a strange metal

Sodium is an unusual metal. Sodium is so soft that you can cut it with an ordinary table knife. It is so light that it floats on water.

Sodium is very reactive. It reacts very quickly with cold water. The reaction makes **hydrogen** gas.

Sodium will even react with the water vapour in the air. So we store sodium in oil.

sodium + water → sodium hydroxide + hydrogen

6   You must never pick sodium up with bare hands. Why do you think this is so?

7   Why is sodium stored in oil?

8   Which metal is more reactive, copper or sodium? Explain your answer.

9   Which metal is more reactive, magnesium or sodium? Explain your answer.

oil —

SODIUM

■ Metals for kettles

10   We can make a kettle out of copper. Could we make a kettle out of sodium or magnesium? Explain your answers.

11   Write out the three metals below, in order of their reactivity. Put the most reactive first, and the least reactive last.

    copper   magnesium   sodium

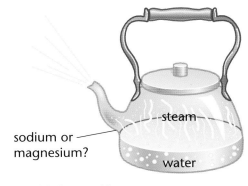

- - steam - -

sodium or magnesium?

water

Would this work?

WHAT YOU SHOULD KNOW (Copy and complete using the **key words**)

Metals reacting with water

Some metals, for example magnesium:
- react slowly with _____ ;
- react more quickly with _____ .

Few metals react quickly with water, for example _____ .

All these reactions make a gas called _____ .

Some metals do not react with water, for example _____ .

3.7 Which metals push hardest?

The main aim of the gladiators is to **push** the other gladiator off the platform.

A big gladiator can usually push much harder than a small gladiator.

1 If one gladiator is much bigger than the other, what result do you expect?

Metals behave like the gladiators. A reactive metal will try to 'push around' a less reactive metal.

In any fight between the two metals, we expect the more reactive metal to win.

2 Look at the copper and iron 'gladiators'. Which one will win?

Iron Maiden clobbers Copper Princess.

■ Can you coat a knife with copper?

Jill puts an old penknife blade into copper sulphate solution for two minutes. She then takes it out and looks at it.

3 (a) What did the blade look like before?

(b) What does the blade look like after?

Iron is more reactive than copper. So iron pushes copper out of copper sulphate.

We say that the iron **displaces** the copper. It takes the place of the copper in the copper sulphate.

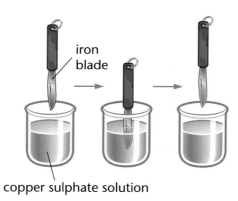

iron + copper sulphate → iron sulphate + copper

■ Where does the copper go?

The reaction makes a very thin layer of copper on the knife blade. If you scratch it, you can see the iron still underneath.

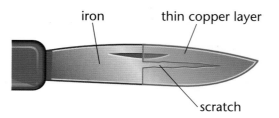

■ Can you coat a penny with iron?

Jill puts a bright, shiny, copper coin into iron sulphate solution for two minutes. She then takes it out and looks at it.

4 Has the coin changed?

Copper cannot push iron out of the iron sulphate because copper is less reactive than iron. So the coin does not change. There isn't a **displacement** reaction.

5 How does the copper behave in this reaction – like a small gladiator or big gladiator?

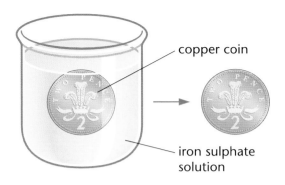

copper coin

iron sulphate solution

■ A three metal contest

Jill puts a strip of magnesium ribbon into a test-tube of iron sulphate and another strip into copper sulphate solution. After two minutes she takes the strips out.

6 What changes can you see? Copy and complete the table.

Name of solution	What the magnesium looks like	
	before the reaction	after the reaction
copper sulphate	silvery	
iron sulphate		black layer

7 Copy and complete the sentences.

Magnesium displaces copper from _____ sulphate and iron from _____ sulphate.

So magnesium is more _____ than both copper and iron.

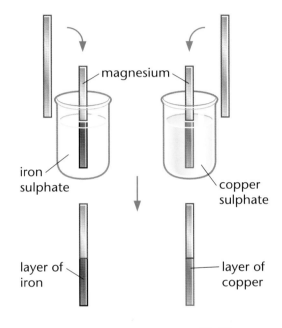

magnesium

iron sulphate

copper sulphate

layer of iron

layer of copper

WHAT YOU SHOULD KNOW (Copy and complete using the **key words**)

Which metals push hardest?

A reactive metal has a bigger _____ than a less reactive metal.

A reactive metal _____ a less reactive metal. We call this a _____ reaction.

3.8 Which metals react best?

Chemists look at the reactions of metals with oxygen and water. They also look at the displacement reactions of the metals. They then put the metals into a list in order of their **reactivity**. The <u>most</u> reactive go near the **top** and the <u>least</u> reactive go near the **bottom**. We call this list the **reactivity series**.

sodium	
magnesium	reactivity decreases
iron	
copper	

The reactivity series for the metals we have looked at so far.

■ Using the reactivity series

If we know where a metal is in the reactivity series, we can work out how it will react. We can do this before we even see the reactions. We call this **predicting**.

Chlorine is a very reactive gas. Most metals react with chlorine. But some will react better than others.

Chlorine is a <u>very</u> dangerous gas.

Only your teacher should use it. The following experiments also need to be done in a fume cupboard.

1   Which of the metals sodium, iron or copper do you expect to burn brightest in chlorine? Which do you expect to burn dullest?

2   The pictures show what actually happens. Write down the names of the three metals in order. Start with the metal that burns brightest in chlorine and finish with the one that burns least well.

3   Did your prediction agree with what really happens?

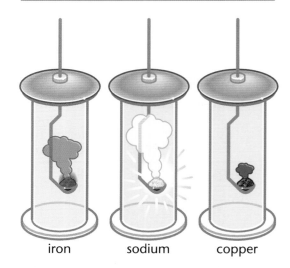

iron   sodium   copper

Metals burning in chlorine.

■ Adding more elements to the series

As you learn about more metals you can add them to the reactivity series.

4   (a) Potassium is more reactive than sodium. Copy the reactivity series from the top of the page. Then add potassium to it.

   (b) Silver is a less reactive metal than copper. Add silver to your reactivity series.

Making electricity out of a lemon

You can make electricity if you put two different metals into acid.

The diagram shows how Billy did this.

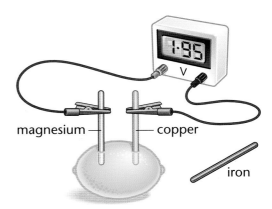

magnesium ——— copper

iron

You can make electricity like this because a lemon contains acid.

5 How do you know Billy made electricity?

6 As well as the magnesium and copper rods, Billy can use iron. Draw two other batteries that Billy can make using the lemon.

7 Billy's teacher did not let him use sodium. Why not?

REMEMBER

Sodium is a very reactive metal. It reacts so fast with water that it's dangerous.

Which battery is best?

You get a bigger voltage if the two different metals are a long way apart in the reactivity series.

Billy made three different batteries using copper, magnesium and iron. He labelled them A, B and C.

He measured the volts for each battery. He got:

0.5 volts,   1.5 volts,   2.0 volts.

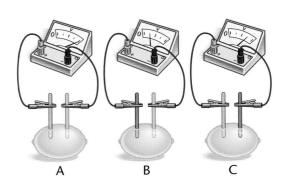

A   B   C

8 Match up these voltages with the batteries A, B and C.

9 Which pair of metals did Billy use for battery A? (Hint. Look at the diagram at the top of this page.)

WHAT YOU SHOULD KNOW   (Copy and complete using the **key words**)

Which metals react best?

We can list metals in order of _____. This list is called the _____ _____.

We put the most reactive at the _____ of the list, and the least reactive at the _____.

The reactivity series is useful for _____ how a metal will react.

4.1 Chemical changes

When you see something change, ask yourself:

'Has the change really made anything new?'

If the change makes a **new** substance, then it is a <u>chemical</u> change. If the change does <u>not</u> make a new substance, then it is a <u>physical</u> change.

◼ Playing with fire

Jane has two matches, A and B. She breaks match A into two. She strikes match B and it lights. After burning, match B is black.

1 (a) Which change makes new substances?

(b) Which is a chemical change?

◼ Dissolving

When we put sugar into a glass of water and stir, the sugar seems to disappear. We say the sugar <u>dissolves</u>. We know the sugar is there because the water tastes sweet.

If we leave this for a few days, the water dries up – it <u>evaporates</u>. We can see crystals of sugar in the bottom of the glass.

Dissolving sugar in water is a physical change.

2 Why is dissolving sugar in water not a chemical change?

◼ Do metals dissolve in acids?

If we add magnesium to dilute hydrochloric acid the magnesium does more than dissolve. It reacts with the acid to make new substances.

3 (a) What two new substances does this reaction make?

(b) Is it a physical or chemical change?

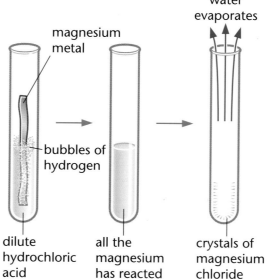

Chemical changes in living things

Chemical changes don't just happen in test-tubes. Every living thing needs **chemical changes** to stay alive.

For an egg to hatch into a baby chicken there must be lots of chemical changes.

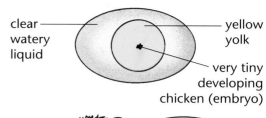

clear watery liquid — yellow yolk — very tiny developing chicken (embryo)

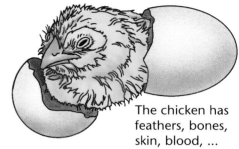

The chicken has feathers, bones, skin, blood, ...

4 When a chicken grows inside the egg,

   (a) what are the starting materials?

   (b) what new substances are made?

5 Why is the growth of a chicken inside an egg called a chemical change?

Chemical changes in us

We eat all sorts of food to stay healthy. But before our bodies can use food, it must be broken down into simpler substances. This is called <u>digestion</u>.

To stay alive, our bodies must make chemical changes all the time.

6 Copy and complete the following:

Digesting food is a _____ change.

7 Look at the pictures. Then copy and complete the sentences.

Combing your hair is a _____ change.
Growing your hair is a _____ change.

combing hair

I may look different, but have I made anything different?

growing hair

Our bodies make hair from substances we eat in our food.

WHAT YOU SHOULD KNOW (Copy and complete using the **key words**)

Chemical changes

Chemical changes always make _____ substances.

Life itself involves _____ changes.

4.2 Acids

We need to drink water to stay alive. But very few people drink pure water. We like lots of different flavours. Some people like lots of sugar in their drinks. Other people prefer a tangier taste.

One thing that many drinks have in common is that they contain <u>acids</u>. Many people seem to like the sour, sharp taste.

1 Write down a list of drinks that contain acids.

All these drinks contain acid.

■ Captain Cook's voyage

Captain Cook discovered Australia. He knew that eating fresh fruit would keep his sailors free from a dreadful disease called scurvy. So he made his men eat limes and lemons. During the long voyage of three and a half years, only one sailor died of scurvy. Afterwards, the British Navy made its sailors drink lime juice to keep them healthy.

This is why, even today, British sailors are often called 'Limeys'.

2 Copy and complete the sentences.

Lime juice tastes _____.
This is because it contains citric _____.
Lime juice prevents scurvy because it contains
_____.

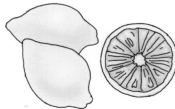

*Limes and lemons taste **sour** because they contain citric acid. They prevent scurvy because they contain vitamin C. This is also an acid, but very weak.*

■ Health warning

While many weak acids are harmless, there are other acids that are very powerful. Sulphuric acid is one of these.

Sulphuric acid is too dangerous to use in anything we eat or drink. It is very **corrosive**. The hazard warning sign shows you what this means.

3 What <u>two</u> things does the hazard warning sign tell you?

CORROSIVE

4 (a) Explain why you should <u>not</u> get sulphuric acid on your skin.

(b) Explain why you should <u>never</u> taste sulphuric acid.

5 Not all acids are as dangerous as sulphuric acid. Write down the names of two acids that are not dangerous. (Hint: remember the limes.)

■ Do acids dissolve everything?

In days gone by, a man tried to swindle a very wise king. He held up a bottle of a liquid and said:

'Your majesty, in this bottle I have a corrosive acid that will dissolve anything and everything.'

The king called for his guards and had the man thrown into prison.

6 How did the king know that the man was lying?

7 (a) What do we keep laboratory acids in?

(b) What does this tell us about these acids and glass?

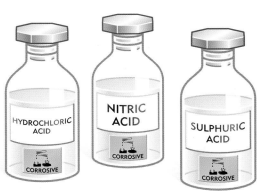

WHAT YOU SHOULD KNOW (Copy and complete using the **key words**)

Acids

Acids are substances that taste _____.

Some acids, like sulphuric acid, are dangerous because they are _____.

You should <u>never</u> taste laboratory acids.

4.3 How can we tell whether something is an acid?

When acids are dissolved in water, they look just like water. You could tell they are acids by tasting them. Anything that tastes sour is an acid. But many acids are too dangerous to taste.

1 Why can't you tell a liquid is an acid just by looking at it?

2 Why shouldn't we taste substances to see whether they are acids?

■ Using litmus to test for acids

We can use special **dyes** to check for acids. These dyes are called <u>indicators</u> because they change **colour** and indicate (tell us) whether the substance is an acid.

Litmus is a well-known indicator.

3 (a) What colour is litmus on its own?

(b) What colour is litmus when it is in acid?

4 Copy the table. Either shade each space in the litmus colour or write in the name of the colour.

A substance that turns litmus blue is called an <u>alkali</u>. Alkalis are the opposites of acids.

A substance that is neither an acid nor an alkali is <u>neutral</u>. Litmus does not change colour in neutral substances.

5 Look at the table again.

(a) Which one of the substances is neutral?

(b) Which three substances are alkalis?

6 Look at the bottles of alkalis. Copy and complete:

Alkalis have names that end in _____.
Like acids, alkalis are _____.

DID YOU KNOW?

Some 18th and early 19th century scientists believed that they had a duty to taste all the substances that they discovered. Not surprisingly, many of them died young.

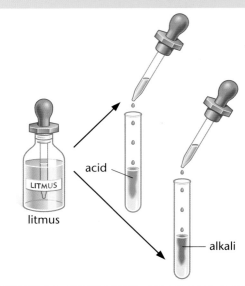

Substance	Turns litmus this colour
sodium hydroxide	blue
vitamin C	red
water	purple
calcium hydroxide	blue
carbon dioxide	red
hydrochloric acid	red
potassium hydroxide	blue

Sodium hydroxide and potassium hydroxide are alkalis. Like acids they are corrosive.

Universal indicator

Litmus has only three different colours. So it can only tell you if something is acidic, alkaline or neutral. It can't tell you that sulphuric acid is more acidic than lemon juice.

<u>Universal indicator</u> has all the colours of the rainbow. So it can tell you how strong an acid or an alkali is.

7 Copy out the table, but put the most acidic liquid first and the least acidic last.

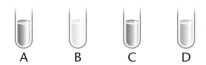

more acidic — neutral — more alkaline

Universal indicator turns different colours according to how acidic or alkaline a substance is.

A   B   C   D

Liquid	Colour with universal indicator
A	green
B	yellow
C	red
D	orange

The acidity scale

We use a special scale of acidity called the **pH** scale. (Say the letters 'pea–aitch'.)

- Acids have pH numbers **less** than 7.
- Alkalis have pH numbers **more** than 7.
- Neutral substances have a pH **equal** to 7.

8 (a) Which is more acidic, pH = 2 or pH = 6?

(b) Which is more alkaline, pH = 8 or pH = 11?

| 0 | 1 | 2 | 3 | 4 | 5 | 6 | 7 | 8 | 9 | 10 | 11 | 12 | 13 | 14 |

more acidic — neutral — more alkaline

The pH scale.

Using universal indicator to measure pH

Each colour in the universal indicator range has its own pH number.

9 Write the correct pH number by each liquid in your answer to question 7.

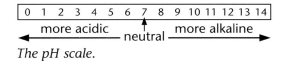

red   orange yellow green   blue   navy blue   purple

| 0–2 | 3–4 | 5–6 | 7 | 8–9 | 10–12 | 13–14 |

more acidic — neutral — more alkaline

WHAT YOU SHOULD KNOW (Copy and complete using the **key words**)

How can we tell whether something is an acid?

Indicators are special _____. They change _____ when mixed with acids or alkalis.

Universal indicator helps us to measure a substance's _____.

Alkalis have a pH of _____ than 7. Acids have a pH of _____ than 7.

Neutral substances have a pH _____ to 7.

4.4 Getting rid of an acid with an alkali

Chemists are a bit like magicians! They can't make rabbits disappear or turn them into carrots, but they <u>can</u> change things!

If you put one drop of hydrochloric acid on a glass slide then add one drop of sodium hydroxide, a bit of chemical magic takes place. The acid and the alkali react together to make salt – exactly the same salt that you put on food! The proper name for this salt is <u>sodium chloride</u>.

1 How do you know that adding sodium hydroxide to hydrochloric acid is a chemical change?

2 What <u>two</u> new substances does this reaction make?

REMEMBER

In chemical reactions new substances are made.

If you add just the right amount of alkali to an acid, you can make the acid disappear.

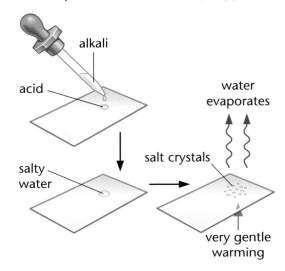

hydrochloric acid + sodium hydroxide → sodium chloride + water

How do you know how much alkali to add to the acid?

Things are not as simple as the first experiment suggested.

If you don't add enough alkali, you get some acid left.

If you add too much alkali, you get some alkali left.

When just the right amount of alkali is added to the acid, there is no acid or alkali left over.

The solution is <u>neutral</u>, so this kind of chemical reaction is called **neutralisation**.

3 Why is the chef's way of solving this problem not a good idea?

NEVER do this to check whether the acid has gone.

■ Neutralisation

We need to know exactly how much alkali we should add to the acid to make a perfectly neutral solution. We can't just guess, so we use an **indicator** to tell us.

Susan puts some acid in a test-tube. She adds a few drops of litmus indicator. Susan then uses a dropper to slowly add an alkali to the acid.

4 **(a)** At which point – A, B, or C – has the alkali just neutralised the acid?

(b) Susan wants some salt. Which is the best solution to evaporate?

If we add the acid to the alkali, we still get the same neutralisation reaction.

5 Copy the diagram. Colour solution Z correctly.

■ Can we use other acids and alkalis?

If we use a different acid or a different alkali, they will still neutralise each other.
One of the new substances produced is always **water**.
The other new substance is still called a **salt** but it is <u>different</u> from ordinary salt (sodium cloride).

We can use potassium hydroxide instead of sodium hydroxide to neutralise hydrochloric acid.

6 What salt do we now get?

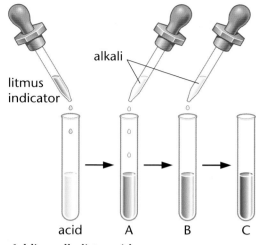

Adding alkali to acid.

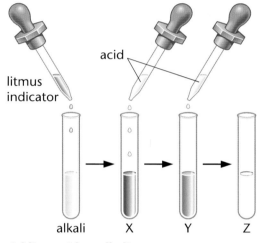

Adding acid to alkali.

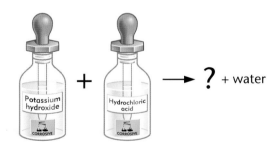

potassium hydroxide + hydrochloric acid → potassium chloride + water

---

WHAT YOU SHOULD KNOW (Copy and complete using the **key words**)

Getting rid of an acid with an alkali

When we mix an alkali with an acid, we get a reaction called _____.

Neutralisation reactions make two new substances, a _____ and _____.

To help us know when neutralisation is finished, we use an _____.

4.5 Using neutralisation reactions

Neutralisation reactions, where acid and alkali react together, don't just happen in test-tubes. They are very important in our daily lives.

Keeping your teeth healthy

Your mouth is full of bacteria. These feed on sugar from left-over food. Whenever bacteria eat sugar, they make acid. Acid then attacks your teeth.

When you brush your teeth, you remove bits of food and the bacteria.

Toothpaste also contains substances that neutralise the acid that rots your teeth. For example, some toothpastes contain bicarbonate of soda.

1 **(a)** Is toothpaste slightly alkaline, neutral or acidic?

(b) Why is this useful?

(c) Name a substance that is put into toothpaste to give it a pH of more than 7.

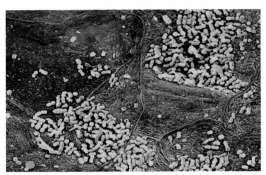

Bacteria on a human tongue.

The pH of this toothpaste is 8 because it contains bicarbonate of soda.

Curing upset stomachs

Too much acid in the stomach causes indigestion. Some people take medicines to neutralise the stomach acid.

2 Milk of Magnesia indigestion tablets contain magnesium hydroxide. This is a very weak alkali. Why couldn't the tablets contain sodium hydroxide?

3 How do medicines like Milk of Magnesia cure indigestion?

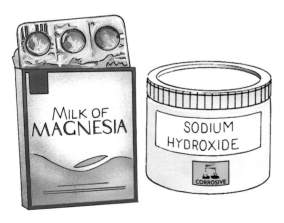

One of these is a medicine for indigestion.

Other indigestion cures contain magnesium **carbonate** or bicarbonate of soda. These neutralise acids but also make a gas called **carbon dioxide**.

4 Both magnesium carbonate and bicarbonate of soda make people burp. Why is this?

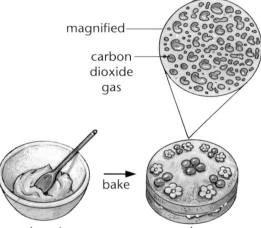

Baking a cake

Some cake recipes use baking powder. This contains bicarbonate of soda and crystals of a weak acid. When you make them wet, the acid and the bicarbonate of soda neutralise each other.

The reaction gives off carbon dioxide gas.

5 How does baking powder make the cake rise?

Trapped carbon dioxide gas makes the cake rise.

Neutralising acidic lakes

Scandinavian countries add crushed limestone to their lakes to neutralise the acidity that comes from acid rain.

Limestone is calcium carbonate. This neutralises acids and gives off carbon dioxide gas. Other carbonates and bicarbonates react with acid in the same way.

6 What would you see happen when the limestone is added to the acidic lake?

WHAT YOU SHOULD KNOW (Copy and complete using the **key words**)

Using neutralisation reactions

We can neutralise an acid with an _____.

We can also neutralise acids by using sodium bicarbonate or a _____. These react with the acid to give the gas _____ _____.

4.6 How do metals react with acids?

We know that when sugar dissolves in water, nothing new is made. Although the sugar seems to disappear, it is still in the water.

1 How could you prove that the sugar is still in the water?

2 Is dissolving sugar in water a chemical or physical change? Explain your answer.

REMEMBER

In a physical change, no new substances are made.

In a chemical change, new substances are made.

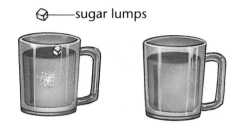

sugar lumps

■ **What happens when magnesium reacts with an acid?**

Look at the picture. The acid does not just dissolve the magnesium. It <u>reacts</u> with the magnesium. Two new substances are made.

3 What two new substances are made?

4 Copy and complete:

Because adding magnesium to dilute hydrochloric acid makes new substances, it is a _____ change.

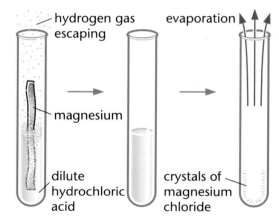

hydrogen gas escaping

evaporation

magnesium

dilute hydrochloric acid

crystals of magnesium chloride

We can write down what happens in the reaction like this:
magnesium + hydrochloric acid → magnesium chloride + hydrogen

5 Which one of these two sentences is the more accurate? Copy it down.

- The magnesium dissolves in the acid.

- The magnesium reacts with the acid.

■ **Investigating the gas made in the reaction**

If we test the gas with a lighted splint, we get a 'pop'. This is the chemical test for hydrogen.

6 Is this test for hydrogen a chemical or a physical change? Explain your answer.

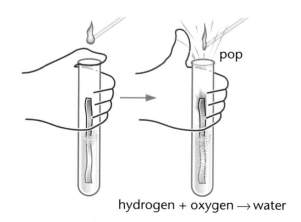

pop

hydrogen + oxygen → water

When magnesium reacts with the acid, the metal pushes **hydrogen** out of the acid.

We can collect the hydrogen gas in a balloon and let it go. With a little luck, the balloon might go as far as ten miles or so!

7 Write as much as you can about hydrogen gas, from the information on this page and page 156.

The balloon will rise up in the air. You can put your school address in a plastic bag and see where it goes.

Separating the salt made in the reaction

The other new material that is made when magnesium reacts with hydrochloric acid is a **salt**.

We make sure that all the acid is used up by using more magnesium than we need. The reaction has finished when there are no more bubbles of hydrogen produced.

We then filter off the left-over magnesium.

The diagrams show how you can get crystals of the salt that was made in the reaction.

8 Write down the following sentences in the correct order.

- Wait till there are no more bubbles of hydrogen.

- Cool and wait for crystals to grow.

- Add magnesium to the acid.

- Filter off the left-over magnesium.

- Boil off about half of the water.

9 Copy and complete.

When magnesium reacts with hydrochloric acid you get a salt called _____ _____.

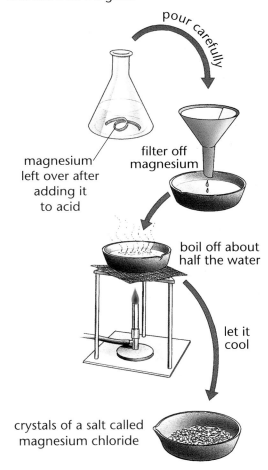

magnesium left over after adding it to acid

filter off magnesium

boil off about half the water

let it cool

crystals of a salt called magnesium chloride

WHAT YOU SHOULD KNOW (Copy and complete using the **key words**)

How do metals react with acids?

Metals react with dilute acids to make a _____.

Metals push _____ out of the acid.

4.7 Salt and salts

Salt is a very important substance. We put salt on our food. We also use salt to make lots of other useful chemicals.

1 Write down two ways of getting salt.

When we say or write the word **salt** in everyday life, what we usually mean is 'common salt'. Its chemical name is sodium chloride. This tells us that it is made of two simple substances that are called <u>elements</u>.

2 What two elements make common salt?

■ Looking at salt under the magnifying glass

Look at the picture of salt.

3 Copy and complete each sentence. Use the best describing word from each group.

   (a) Salt is made up of _____.
       drops / crystals / bits / specks

   (b) Each crystal is shaped like a _____.
       triangle / circle / cube / ball

   (c) Salt looks white but each crystal is really

       _____.
       red / blue / colourless / black

■ Looking at other salts

Sodium chloride is not the only salt. There are **hundreds** of different salts. Most of them dissolve in **water**.

Salts usually contain a metal element joined with at least one **non-metal** element.

The first name of the salt is that of the metal. The second name tells you the non-metal.

A salt mine in Cheshire.

Salt from the Australian seas. In hot dry places, people get salt by letting sea water evaporate.

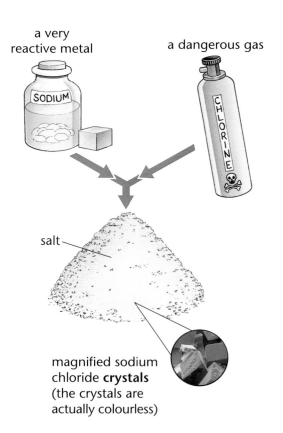

a very reactive metal

a dangerous gas

salt

magnified sodium chloride **crystals** (the crystals are actually colourless)

Potassium chloride

This looks and tastes like sodium chloride.

4 (a) Write down what crystals of potassium chloride look like.

(b) Write down the metal element and non-metal element that make this salt.

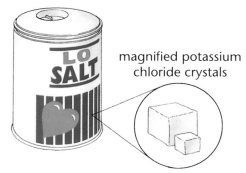

magnified potassium chloride crystals

Too much sodium in your diet can be bad for you. Lo Salt contains twice as much potassium chloride as sodium chloride.

Magnesium sulphate

This is made up of the metal element magnesium. The sulphate part of the salt contains the non-metal elements sulphur and oxygen.

5 What are the three elements in magnesium sulphate?

6 Do you think that magnesium sulphate is harmful? Explain your answer.

Magnesium sulphate is added to make it easier to float in this flotation bath.

Copper sulphate

Nearly all the salts of the metal copper are either green or blue.

7 Write down what crystals of copper sulphate look like.

8 What are the three elements that make up copper sulphate?

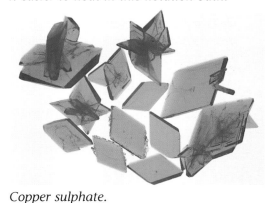

Copper sulphate.

WHAT YOU SHOULD KNOW (Copy and complete using the **key words**)

Salt and salts

We know sodium chloride as common _____.

There are _____ of different salts.

A salt usually contains a metal element joined to at least one _____.

Salts form _____.

Most salts dissolve in _____.

4.8 Other kinds of chemical reaction

■ Oxidation reactions

Oxygen joins on to many other elements. We say that oxygen oxidises other elements. We call these reactions **oxidation** reactions.

Some oxidation reactions are a big problem. Other oxidation reactions are very useful.

■ Rusting – a big problem

Oxygen from the air can react with iron.

1 Look at the diagram. Then copy and complete the following.

Both _____ and _____ must be present for rusting to take place.

Rusting is an _____ reaction.

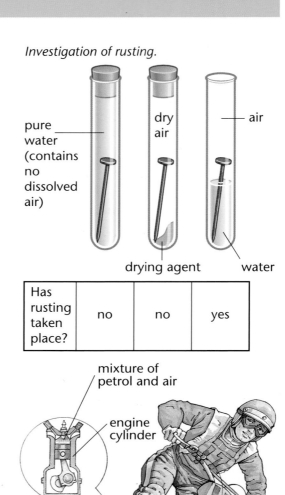

Investigation of rusting.

pure water (contains no dissolved air)

dry air

air

drying agent   water

Has rusting taken place?	no	no	yes

■ Combustion – a big help

Burning is a chemical reaction. The elements in the burning substances join with oxygen from the air. Heat and light energy are given out as flames.

Another word for burning is **combustion**.

All combustion reactions involve oxidation.

2 (a) What is burned in the motorbike?

  (b) Where does this reaction take place?

  (c) What else is needed for this to happen?

mixture of petrol and air

engine cylinder

Runs on petrol.

■ Respiration – the life giver

The food we eat helps us to keep warm and to move. The oxygen we breathe joins on to carbon and hydrogen in our food, and releases energy. This is an oxidation reaction called <u>respiration</u>. It is not burning or combustion because there are no flames inside your body.

Runs on food.

3 Copy and complete the sentences using these words: combustion, oxidation, respiration

The cyclist releases energy by _____.

The motorbike releases energy by _____.

Both are _____ reactions.

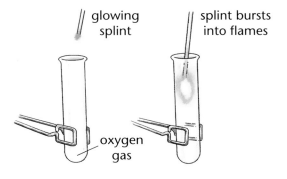

Test for oxygen.

Test for oxygen

Look at the picture of the test for oxygen gas.

4 Which <u>two</u> of the following best describe the reaction which happens in the test?

rusting, oxidation, respiration, combustion

Decomposition

Not all reactions involve elements <u>joining</u> together. Many reactions are like the one shown in the picture.

We can <u>break down</u> complicated substances into simpler ones. This breakdown is called **decomposition**. If we need heat to break a substance down, we call the reaction a <u>thermal</u> decomposition.

Thermal decomposition.

5 Look at the picture.

   (a) Which substance is being decomposed?

   (b) Write down the name of one of the substances it splits up into.

6 How does the teacher show that oxygen is given off when potassium nitrate is heated?

WHAT YOU SHOULD KNOW (Copy and complete using the **key words**)

Other kinds of chemical reaction

A chemical reaction that joins oxygen to a substance is called _____.

Examples of oxidation are rusting, respiration and _____.

If we heat a substance and it breaks down, we call this thermal _____.

4.9 Writing down chemical reactions

Hydrogen reacts with oxygen to make water.

Here is a quick way to write down what happens in this chemical reaction:

hydrogen + oxygen → water

the arrow means
'react to make'

This is called a word **equation**.

We always write word equations in the same way.

On the **left** we put what we <u>start</u> with.

On the **right** we put the **new** substance that we <u>finish</u> with.

> **1** Copy the diagram and put the following labels in the correct boxes:
>
> finishing substance, starting substance

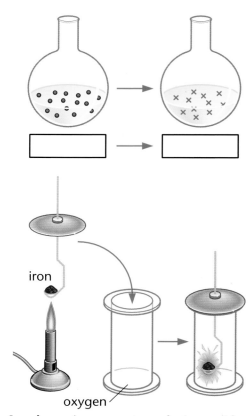

Iron burns in oxygen to make iron oxide.

■ **Remember burning?**

Jim burns some iron filings in oxygen.

He starts with iron and oxygen. He finishes up with iron oxide.

The word equation is

iron + oxygen → iron oxide

> **2 (a)** What two substances does this reaction start with?
>
> **(b)** What substance does this reaction finish with?

Julie burns some magnesium in air.
The magnesium reacts with the oxygen contained in the air.

> **3** Copy and complete the word equation below:
>
> magnesium + _____ → magnesium oxide

Burning magnesium in air makes magnesium oxide.

Naming two-element compounds

Metals can react with non-metals to make new substances. These contain the metal and non-metal joined together. They are called <u>compounds</u>.

We always start the name of the compound with the name of the metal. We write the name of the non-metal last.

Look at the examples. Notice that the name of the non-metal changes slightly.

4 Write down the name of the compound made by the reaction of:

   (a) magnesium + chlorine

   (b) copper + sulphur

5 Copy and complete the word equations.

   (a) copper + oxygen → copper _____

   (b) _____ + sulphur → iron sulphide

   (c) sodium + _____ → _____ chloride

   (d) copper + sulphur → _____ _____

   (e) _____ + chlorine → copper _____

6 Iron burns in chlorine.

   (a) What compound is formed?

   (b) Write a word equation for this reaction.

magnesium + oxygen → magnesium ox<u>ide</u>

sodium + chlorine → sodium chlor<u>ide</u>

iron + sulphur → iron sulp<u>hide</u>

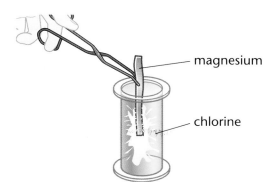

Magnesium burning in chlorine.

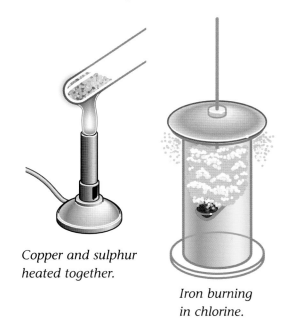

Copper and sulphur heated together.

Iron burning in chlorine.

WHAT YOU SHOULD KNOW (Copy and complete using the **key words**)

Writing down chemical reactions

Chemical reactions make _____ substances.

We show what happens in chemical reactions by writing a word _____.

We put what we start with on the _____.

We put what we finish with on the _____.

5.1 Different types of rock

There are hundreds of different types of rock. Some rocks are made from the same substance but they look different. This is because they were made in different ways.

Limestone is a fairly hard rock made from calcium carbonate.

Granite is a very hard rock.

Sandstone is a soft rock. You can scratch it with your nails.

Chalk is a soft rock made from calcium carbonate. You can rub bits off easily.

Marble is a rock made from calcium carbonate crystals. You can smooth and polish it.

1 Which <u>three</u> rocks are made from the same substance?

2 Which of the rocks would make the best building stone for a castle wall? Give a reason for your answer.

3 Which of the rocks shown can be made into thin tiles that you could use for the roof of a house?

Slate is a hard rock made of layers. It splits easily into sheets.

■ Some rocks react with acid

Chalk fizzes when acid is dropped on it. This happens because chalk is made from **calcium carbonate**.

4 Copy and complete the sentences.

When acid is dropped on chalk, a gas called _____ _____ is given off. This happens because chalk is made from calcium _____.

5 Which other rocks in the pictures at the top of the page will fizz when acid is added? Give a reason for your answer.

Carbon dioxide gas is given off.

■ Rocks can melt

When rocks get hot enough, they melt and change into a liquid called **magma**. This happens to rock inside the Earth.

6 What is the crust of the Earth made from?

7 What is the name for the hot, molten rock inside the Earth?

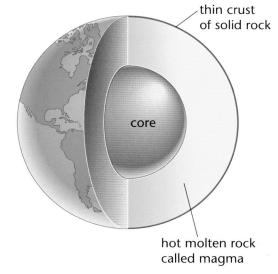

Cross-section through the Earth.

■ Molten rock can set hard

Sometimes magma comes up from inside the Earth. This happens when a volcano erupts. When magma cools, it sets hard.

Magma can also cool and set inside the Earth's crust.

8 Look at the diagram.

(a) What is the name for the rock hardened outside the Earth's crust?

(b) What is the name for the rock hardened inside the Earth's crust?

The new rocks that are made when magma sets are called **igneous** rocks.

9 Name two types of igneous rock.

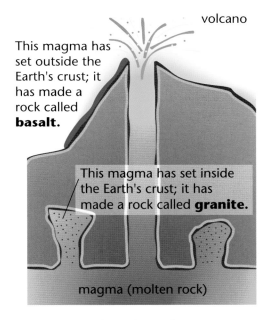

Cross-section through a volcano.

WHAT YOU SHOULD KNOW (Copy and complete using the **key words**)

Different types of rock

Carbon dioxide gas is produced when acid is put on _____ _____.

Hot liquid rock deep in the Earth is called _____.

Rocks made from magma are called _____ rocks.
Examples of igneous rocks are _____ and _____.

5.2 Getting new rocks from old

There are three ways of getting new rocks from old.

- New rocks are made when molten magma comes up through the Earth's crust and sets hard.

- New rocks are made under the sea from the bits that wear off old rocks.

- Rocks can also be changed into new ones by heat and pressure deep in the Earth's crust.

Rocks made under the sea

The diagram shows how this happens.

The new rocks are called **sedimentary** rocks.

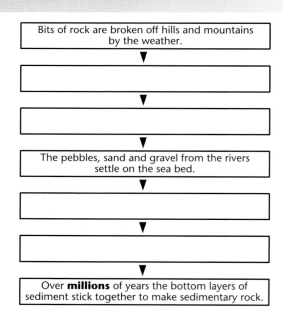

Weather breaks bits off the hills.

Streams and rivers carry bits of rock to the sea.

hills and mountains

The bits of rock (called sediment) settle at the bottom of the sea.

Older layers of sediment get squashed by newer layers; they gradually turn into rock such as sandstone or mudstone.

How sedimentary rocks are made.

1 Write down the name of a sedimentary rock.

2 On a copy of the flow chart, write down these words in the correct boxes to tell the story of sedimentary rocks.

- Layers of sediment get squashed as new sediment piles up on top.

- Bits of rock get into streams and rivers.

- The stuff that settles on the sea bed is called sediment.

- Rivers carry pebbles, sand and gravel to the sea.

Bits of rock are broken off hills and mountains by the weather.

▼

▼

The pebbles, sand and gravel from the rivers settle on the sea bed.

▼

▼

Over **millions** of years the bottom layers of sediment stick together to make sedimentary rock.

The story of sedimentary rocks.

Changing rocks with heat and pressure

Marble and limestone look different but they are both the same substance.

Marble has been made from limestone by **heat**. Its small grains have been changed into larger crystals. This has been done by heat deep in the Earth's crust.

Limestone.   *Marble.*

Slate is made from mudstone when it is squashed by the high **pressure** inside the Earth.

Mudstone.   *Slate.*

Rocks that are made by changing other kinds of rocks are called **metamorphic** rocks.

3 How is limestone changed into marble?

4 How is mudstone changed into slate?

5 What type of rocks are marble and slate?

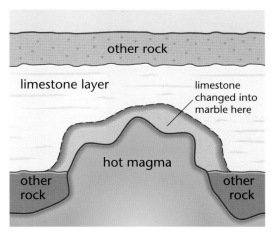

How limestone is changed to marble.

WHAT YOU SHOULD KNOW (Copy and complete using the **key words**)

Getting new rocks from old

New rocks made under the sea from the bits that wear off the old rocks are called _____ rocks. These rocks are formed over _____ of years.

Rocks can also be made from other rocks by _____ and _____. For example, heat changes limestone into _____, and pressure changes mudstone into _____.

Because marble and slate are both made by changing other rocks, we call them _____ rocks.

5.3 The rock cycle

Over **millions** of years the substances in the rocks shift round. This gradual shift is called the **rock cycle**.

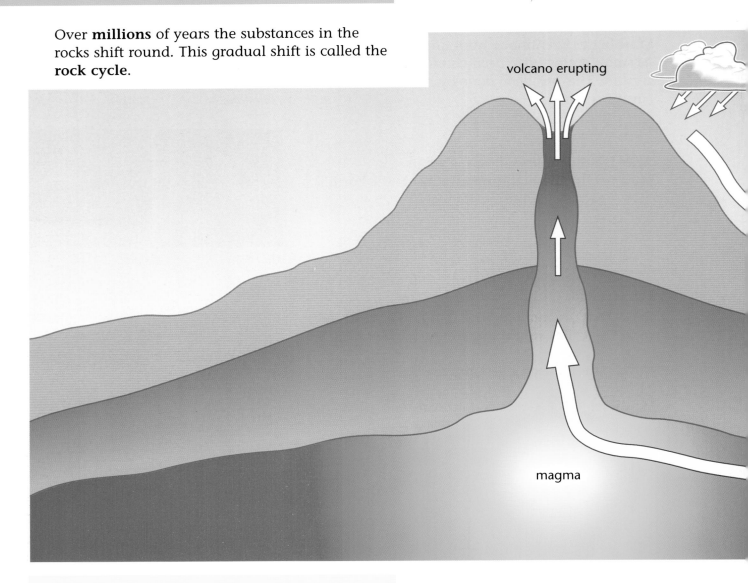

volcano erupting

magma

1 What type of rock is formed when magma cools and goes solid?

2 What breaks tiny pieces off rocks?

3 How do broken bits of rock get to the sea?

4 What is the stuff that settles on the bottom of the sea called?

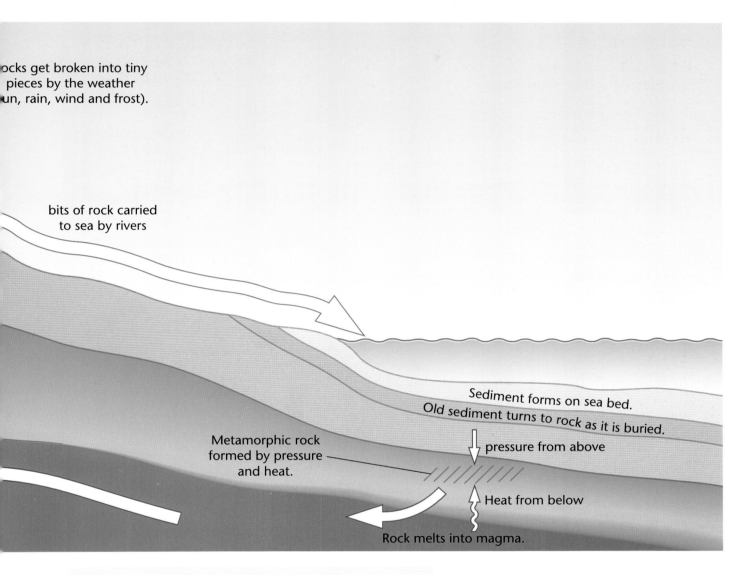

...ocks get broken into tiny pieces by the weather ...un, rain, wind and frost).

bits of rock carried to sea by rivers

Sediment forms on sea bed.
Old sediment turns to rock as it is buried.

Metamorphic rock formed by pressure and heat.

pressure from above

Heat from below

Rock melts into magma.

5　Where are sedimentary rocks formed?

6　What <u>two</u> things can change rock into metamorphic rock?

WHAT YOU SHOULD KNOW (Copy and complete using the **key words**)

The rock cycle

The substances that make up rocks shift around over _____ of years.

We call this shift the _____ _____.

5.4 How the weather breaks up rocks

Hot days, cold nights, rain, frost and wind all help to break up rocks.

When rocks are broken into pieces by the weather we call it **weathering**.

■ Heating and cooling can crack rocks

The surface of a rock gets a little bit bigger in the heat of the sun. We say that it <u>expands</u>.

The rock goes smaller again when it cools down at night. We say it <u>contracts</u>.

This constant heating and cooling can make **cracks** in the rock surface. It can even crack a whole rock.

1 What happens to the surface of a rock when it gets hot?

2 What can heating and cooling do to a rock?

3 What else can crack because of heating and cooling?

■ Water freezes and cracks rocks

Rain water gets into the cracks. Water **expands** when it freezes. This make the cracks bigger. Sometimes bits of rock **break** off.

4 What happens to water when it freezes?

5 Write the sentences in the correct order to say how water and freezing can break up rocks.

- ■ Bits of rock fall off.
- ■ Water freezes.
- ■ Water gets in the cracks in rocks.
- ■ The cracks in rocks become bigger.

REMEMBER

Rocks get broken up and carried to the sea.

The bits of rock then make new rocks.

This rock has been cracked by hot days and cold nights in the desert.

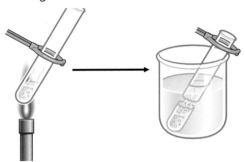

You should <u>never</u> put a hot test-tube into cold water. If you do, the glass may crack.

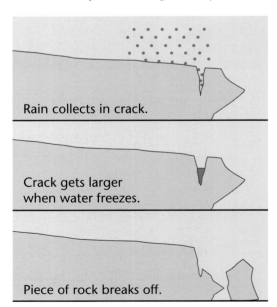

Rain collects in crack.

Crack gets larger when water freezes.

Piece of rock breaks off.

Two cases of weathering

The weathering of rocks makes varied scenery. A scree slope is made from lots of small pieces of broken rock.

6 What do you think made the screes at Wastwater?

7 The weather can also cause problems. Why do you think patched-up holes in the road become holes again in winter?

The screes at Wastwater in the English Lake District.

Wind can cause weathering

Bits of dust and sand blown by the **wind** can wear away rocks or buildings. This is called **erosion**.

Look at the picture.

8 (a) What has happened to parts of the rock?

(b) Why has this happened?

The holes in this rock have been worn away by sand blown by the wind.

WHAT YOU SHOULD KNOW (Copy and complete using the **key words**)

How the weather breaks up rocks

When rocks are worn away by the weather, we call it _____.

Changes in temperature from hot to cold can make _____ in the surface of a rock. Water gets in cracks and makes them bigger. This happens because water _____ when it freezes.

Sometimes freezing water makes bits of rock _____ off.

Rocks and building materials are also worn away by bits blown in the _____. This is called _____.

5.5 Acids in the air

It isn't just the weather that breaks up rocks. Acid gases in the air also attack rocks.

Look at the grid. It contains 100 x 30 small squares.

The grid shows the main gases in the air.

1 Write down the four main gases in the air.

2 Which gas makes up most of the air?

3 (a) How many small squares are in the grid?

(b) How many small squares are carbon dioxide?

(c) Is the amount of carbon dioxide in the air big or small?

The air always contains some **carbon dioxide**. In the last 150 years or so, the amount of carbon dioxide has increased. This is because of all the fuel that we burn.

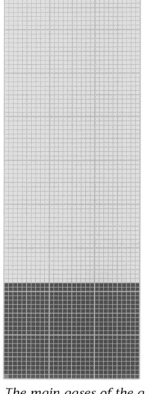

Key
nitrogen
oxygen
argon
carbon dioxide

The main gases of the air.

■ Making holes in rock

Carbon dioxide dissolves slightly in water and reacts with it to make a very weak **acid**. This weak acid reacts with some rocks like **limestone**, chalk and marble.

Over hundreds of thousands of years, carbon dioxide in rainwater chemically dissolved away large amounts of these rocks. This made caves and caverns.

4 Look at the photograph. What can happen when a lot of limestone gets dissolved away?

The limestone 'icicles' are called stalactites.

■ Weathering effects on buildings

Some buildings are made from limestone.

So rain containing carbon dioxide very slowly dissolves the outer layer of the stone. It gives the stone a worn look. This is called **chemical** weathering.

5 What causes limestone buildings to look older as the years go by?

■ Air pollution

When we burn fuels, we don't just put more carbon dioxide into the air. We also put gases such as sulphur **dioxide** and nitrogen **oxides** into the air. These are much more acidic than carbon dioxide. They cause much **faster** chemical weathering.

Most of the damage to the outsides of ancient buildings has taken place in the last 150 years. From the Industrial Revolution until recently, homes, factories, mills and other industries all burned solid fuel. This produced large amounts of smoke and gases.

6 Why do cathedrals such as York Minster employ teams of stone masons?

7 Which of the photos of York Minster shows newly repaired stonework?

8 Most of the damage to our ancient buildings has taken place during the last 150 years or so. Explain why.

Stonework on York Minster.

A

B

WHAT YOU SHOULD KNOW (Copy and complete using the **key words**)

Acids in the air

Air contains _____ _____.
This gas dissolves in rain water to make a very weak _____.
This attacks building stone such as _____. We call this process _____ weathering.

When we burn fuels we also make gases such as sulphur _____ and nitrogen _____. These are much more acidic and cause chemical weathering much _____.

5.6 Things we can do with limestone

Limestone is a very useful rock. The pictures show some of the things we can use it for.

1 Where do we get limestone from?

2 Write down <u>two</u> other uses for limestone.

Limestone quarry.

Limestone is used for buildings.

Crushed limestone can be spread on fields to make the soil less acidic.

■ Using limestone to make other things

We can use limestone to make other useful materials. To do this we have to use chemical **reactions**.

Limestone is a rock that is made mostly from calcium carbonate.

If you heat limestone strongly you produce a gas called carbon dioxide. The substance left behind is called **calcium oxide**.

Calcium oxide is also called **quicklime**.

3 Copy and complete the sentences.

When calcium carbonate is heated strongly, _____ _____ gas comes off.
Calcium oxide is left behind.
Calcium oxide is also called _____.
This process takes place in a _____.

Limestone is heated strongly in a lime-kiln to make quicklime.

What is quicklime used for?

We add water to quicklime to make **slaked** lime. We use slaked lime in many different ways, for example in glassmaking and mortar, and to spread on fields.

4 How is quicklime changed into slaked lime?

5 Write down <u>three</u> different uses for slaked lime.

Using mortar.

Making lime water

The other name for slaked lime is **calcium hydroxide**. Calcium hydroxide dissolves slightly in water. The solution is called lime water.

The diagram shows how to make lime water.

6 How can you make lime water?

slaked lime

filter paper

stir

water

lime water

Using lime water

Carbon dioxide gas makes lime water go milky. A reaction happens that makes calcium carbonate. Calcium carbonate does not dissolve in water so it appears as a white cloud of tiny particles.

7 What gas makes lime water go milky?

8 Why does the calcium carbonate appear as a white cloud?

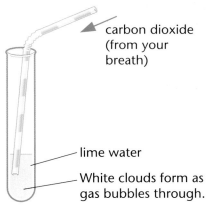

carbon dioxide (from your breath)

lime water

White clouds form as gas bubbles through.

WHAT YOU SHOULD KNOW (Copy and complete using the **key words**)

Things we can do with limestone

Chemical _____ are used to make useful materials.

If you heat limestone, you make it into a useful substance called _____ _____.
The other name for calcium oxide is _____.

If you add water to quicklime, you get another useful substance called _____ lime.
The other name for slaked lime is _____ _____.

Lime water is made by dissolving calcium hydroxide in water.
Lime water turns milky when _____ _____ is bubbled through it.

5.7 Getting metals from rocks

The rocks of the Earth's crust often contain metals. For example, we always find gold in lumps or as small bits of metal in the ground. Metals found like this are called **native** metals.

Native gold.

Native silver.

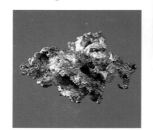
Native copper.

1   Look at the pictures. Write down the names of <u>two</u> other metals that we sometimes find as native metals.

■ Metal ores

Most metals cannot be found as native metals. They are always joined (combined) with other substances in rocks.

The rocks we get metals from are called **ores**.

Rock salt is mostly sodium combined with chlorine.

2   What is the name for any rock that we get a metal from?

3   What is the name for aluminium ore?

4   Which metal is in rock salt?

Bauxite is an ore that we get aluminium from. It is mainly aluminium combined with oxygen.

5   What is the name for the ore that contains lead joined with sulphur?

6   Copy and complete the table.

Metal	Ore
iron	
	galena
sodium	
	bauxite

Galena is an ore that we get lead from. It is mainly lead combined with sulphur.

Haematite is an ore that we get iron from. It is mainly iron combined with oxygen.

Extracting iron from iron ore

We get **iron** from iron ore by heating the ore with coke in a **blast** furnace. The diagram shows what happens.

7 What is blown into the blast furnace?

8 What happens to the iron oxide in the blast furnace?

9 How do you get the iron out of the blast furnace?

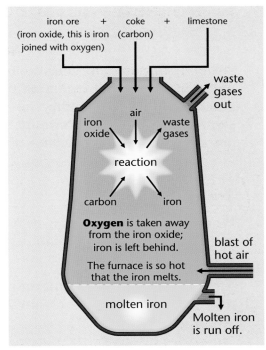

Inside a blast furnace.

Extracting aluminium from aluminium ore

To get **aluminium** you have to melt aluminium oxide and pass electricity through it. This is called **electrolysis**.

10 What is the aluminium oxide split up into?

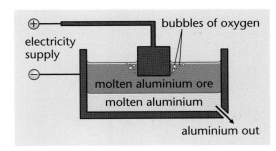

WHAT YOU SHOULD KNOW (Copy and complete using the **key words**)

Getting metals from rocks

You can find some metals like gold, silver and copper as lumps in the ground. These are called _____ metals.

Most metals come from rocks called _____.

Iron ore contains oxygen joined with _____.

We get the iron from the ore by taking away the _____. This is done by heating it in a _____ furnace.

We have to use electricity to extract _____ from aluminium oxide. This process is called _____.

177

5.8 A problem with metals

When metals are new, they are usually bright and shiny. But most metals start to go dull very quickly. This is because they can join with substances from the air. We say that metals **corrode**. Corrosion is a chemical **reaction**.

■ Rusting

When iron corrodes, we say that it <u>rusts</u>. Rusting is a chemical reaction. It can damage anything made from iron.

Ann wants to find out what makes iron nails go rusty. The diagrams show what she did.

1 Look at the diagrams. Then copy and complete the table.

Tube	What's in the tube with the iron nail?	Did it rust? (Yes or No)
A	Only _____	No
B	Only _____	_____
C	_____ and _____	_____

2 Copy and complete the sentence.

Iron will only rust when _____ and _____ are present together.

■ Protecting iron and steel from rusting

Steel is made mainly from iron. So most steel goes rusty too. Steel is a very useful metal for making things but it has to be protected from rusting.

3 Write down <u>three</u> common uses for steel.

4 Write down <u>three</u> ways in which rusting is prevented.

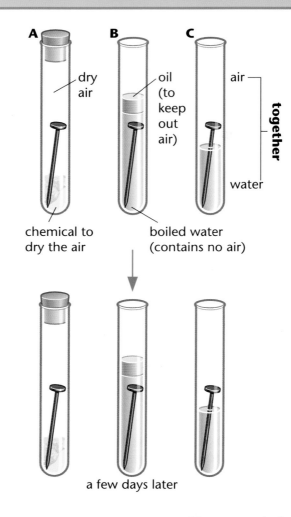

A — dry air; chemical to dry the air

B — oil (to keep out air); boiled water (contains no air)

C — air; water; together

a few days later

Oily bicycle chain.

Tins are made from steel coated with tin.

Galvanised steel screw (steel coated with zinc).

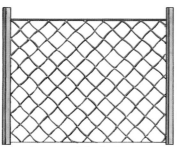

Plastic-coated link-chain fence.

When the bonnet of a car gets hit with a stone, the paint can get chipped. Once the steel starts to rust, the rest of the steel rusts faster.

5 Explain why a rust spot forms where the paint gets chipped.

6 What could you do to prevent the rust spot from spreading?

To repair this rust spot, you need to sand-paper the rust off, and then repaint the shiny metal.

▪ Bronze statues

Sculptors often make metal statues from bronze. **Bronze** does not rust but it does corrode. This reaction makes the statues go green.

7 Which side of the statue has been cleaned? Give a reason for your answer.

Just as with stone, polluted air attacks **metals** faster than clean air.

8 Where would the statues corrode fastest – in a big city, small town or country village?

This statue is being cleaned. They do this by removing the corroded metal on the surface.

WHAT YOU SHOULD KNOW (Copy and complete using the **key words**)

A problem with metals

Rusting is a chemical _____ .

Iron only rusts when in both air and water _____ .

Metals such as _____ do not rust. But they do _____ .

Polluted air causes much faster corrosion of _____ .

5.9 Why do we keep on polluting the air?

We know that polluted air damages stone and makes metals corrode faster. We know that when we burn fuels, we make pollution.

Fuels must be very important to us if we keep on doing something that is harmful.

■ What are fuels and why do we burn them?

A **fuel** is something that we can easily and safely burn. Burning fuels give out **energy**.

1 Look at the drawing. Write down for each letter (A, B, C and D) which fuel is being used.
The fuels are:

charcoal, wax, paraffin and gas.

Burning fuels give us light and make things hotter.

■ Exhaust fumes from cars

Cars burn petrol or diesel fuel. Some of the energy is turned into useful movement energy.

But in the car engine, **nitrogen oxides** are made, as well as lots of other harmful gases. The exhaust fumes from cars can make people ill.

2 Why do you think the police officer is wearing a gas mask?

■ Poor air quality

Weather forecasters tell us when the air quality is going to be bad.

People with chest problems are told to stay indoors on days when the air quality is poor.

More people now have difficulty breathing.

3 When the air quality is going to be bad, people are asked not to use their cars if at all possible. Why is this?

4 Why do you think some cities have pollution meters in their city centres?

5 Most drivers don't want to give up their cars even though they might make people ill. Why do you think this is?

Air pollution meter.

■ Making electricity

Electricity makes our lives very comfortable.

6 Write down a list of things in your house that use electricity.

A lot of coal, oil and gas is burned in power stations to make electricity.

Unfortunately, these fuels contain small amounts of sulphur. This burns to make sulphur **dioxide**.

Power stations have very tall chimneys. These put the pollution high up in the air. The sulphur dioxide gas dissolves in raindrops to make dilute sulphuric acid or **acid rain**.

The acid rain can come down hundreds of miles away. So it affects the environment of other countries.

7 What is the effect of acid rain on the Scandinavian lakes and forests?

8 Why do you think we keep on making acid rain?

We can turn the energy of burning fuels into electricity. All these things use electricity.

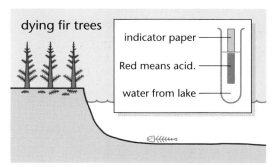

dying fir trees

indicator paper

Red means acid.

water from lake

The effect of acid rain on Scandinavian lakes and forests.

WHAT YOU SHOULD KNOW (Copy and complete using the **key words**)

Why do we keep on polluting the air?

Something that we can burn easily and safely is called a _____.
When fuels burn, they release _____.

Car engines make harmful gases called _____ _____.

Power stations produce some sulphur _____. This makes _____ _____.

1.1 How to make things move

We often want to start things moving.
The diagrams show some examples.

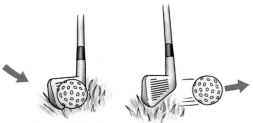

The golf club hits the ball.   *The ball moves.*

1 Copy and complete the table.

	What you do to start it moving
golf ball	
drawer	
buggy	

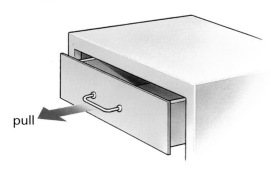

pull

*The drawer moves in the same **direction** as you pull it.*

Pushing things, pulling things and hitting things
are all ways of starting things moving. They
move because you make a **force** act on them.

2 Look at the diagrams again. Then copy and
complete the sentences.

A force acting on an object makes it _____.
The object moves in the same _____ as
the force.

push

The buggy moves along.

■ Making things move faster

It suddenly starts raining. So the man wants to
make the buggy move faster. The diagram shows
how he can do this.

3 Copy and complete the sentences.

To make the buggy move faster, the man must
push it with a bigger _____.
This force must be in the same _____ as the
buggy is moving.

bigger
pushing
force

The buggy moves faster.

■ Making things move slower

The man with the buggy now has to go downhill. The buggy starts to move too fast, so he needs to slow it down. The diagram shows how he can do this.

pull

buggy slows from this speed

to this

*A force in the **opposite** direction slows the buggy down.*

4 Copy and complete the sentences.

To make something slow down you need a _____. The force must be in the _____ direction to the way the thing is moving.

■ Making things change direction

A football is moving <u>across</u> the goal mouth. The attacker wants the ball to go <u>into</u> the goal. The diagram shows how he can do this.

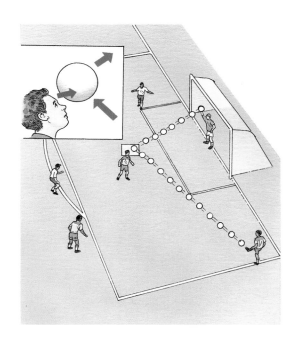

5 Copy and complete the sentences.

To change the direction that the ball is moving, the attacker must make a _____ act on it.

The attacker wants the ball to turn to the right. So he must head it with a force from the _____.

WHAT YOU SHOULD KNOW (Copy and complete using the **key words**)

How to make things move

To start something moving, to speed it up or to change its direction, you must make a _____ act on it. This force must be in the same _____ as you want the thing to move.

If you want to slow something down, the force must be in the _____ direction to the way it is moving.

1.2 Why do things slow down?

Moving things often slow down by themselves. This happens even when we <u>don't</u> want it to.

1 (a) What happens to a bicycle if you stop pedalling?

(b) What must you do to keep the bicycle going at the same speed (or, in other words, to stop it from slowing down)?

A bicycle will slow down by itself unless you keep pedalling.

Things slow down because there is a force acting on them. This force acts in the **opposite** direction to the way they are moving. We call this force a **friction** force.

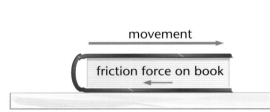

smooth table top

If you give a book a push, it will slide across a table. A table top is smooth. There is only a small friction force. The book slides a long way before it stops.

■ Sliding friction

When two things **slide** over each other, there is a friction force between them.

This friction force can be large or small. The diagrams show why.

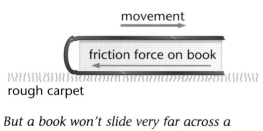

rough carpet

But a book won't slide very far across a carpet. A carpet isn't very smooth. There is a large friction force. The book doesn't slide very far before it stops.

2 Copy and complete the sentences.

The friction force on a moving object always acts in the opposite _____ to the way the object is moving.
So it makes the object _____ down.

There is less friction if the object is sliding over a _____ surface.

■ Friction with the air

In tennis, the ball is moving through the <u>air</u> most of the time. But this doesn't mean there isn't any friction.

There is a friction force between the ball and the air. This friction force is called <u>air resistance</u> or **drag**.

Some tennis players can serve a ball at 120 miles per hour. The ball slows down to about 90 miles per hour by the time it gets to the other player.

3 Look at the diagram. Then copy and complete the sentences.

A tennis ball _____ down as it travels through the air.
This is because of air _____ or _____.

4 A shuttlecock slows down a lot faster than a tennis ball. Explain why.

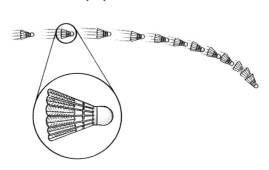

There is a lot of drag on the feathers of a badminton shuttlecock, so it slows down quickly.

■ Why a bicycle slows down

If you stop pedalling, a bicycle slows down. This is because of friction. The diagram shows where this friction occurs.

5 (a) Write down the <u>two</u> friction forces that slow down a bicycle.

(b) Which of these two forces slows down the bicycle more?

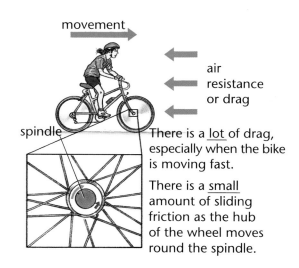

movement

air resistance or drag

spindle

There is a <u>lot</u> of drag, especially when the bike is moving fast.

There is a <u>small</u> amount of sliding friction as the hub of the wheel moves round the spindle.

WHAT YOU SHOULD KNOW (Copy and complete using the **key words**)

Why do things slow down?

Moving things slow down because of _____ forces.
Friction forces act in the _____ direction to the way an object is moving.

There is friction between things which _____ over each other.

There is also friction when things move through the air. This is called air resistance or _____.

1.3 How to reduce friction

When a bicycle is moving, friction forces act on it all the time. So we have to keep pedalling to keep the bicycle moving.

We want to make these friction forces as small as we can. Then we don't need to waste so much energy pedalling.

1 Write down <u>two</u> friction forces that slow down a bicycle.

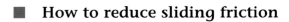

*You can reduce friction if you lubricate moving parts with **oil**.*

■ How to reduce sliding friction

There is a little bit of sliding friction on a bicycle. It is mainly where the hubs of the wheels spin around the spindles.

The diagrams show how we can make this friction as small as possible.

2 Write down <u>three</u> ways of reducing the friction between the hub and the spindle of a bicycle wheel.

REMEMBER

There is always a friction force:
■ when two surfaces slide across each other;
■ when things move through the air.

This friction force is always in the <u>opposite</u> direction to the movement.

ball bearing

*Sliding surfaces must be **smooth**. If they are rough, or rusty, there will be a lot of friction.*
*Ball **bearings** reduce friction because they roll rather than slide.*

How to reduce air resistance

When people design a car, they need to think about its air resistance or drag. They can make the air resistance smaller by changing the car's shape. The diagrams show how.

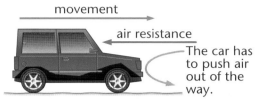

The shape of this car gives it a lot of resistance.

3 Copy and complete the sentences.

To reduce the drag on a car, we must make it a
_____ shape.
The air can then _____ past it more easily.

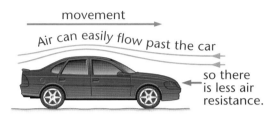

*We say this car has a **streamlined** shape.*

How to save petrol

A car with a more streamlined shape uses less petrol to do the same journey at the same speed.

The diagram shows how you can do the same journey in the <u>same</u> car but using less petrol.

At 50 m.p.h. the car travels 50 miles on a gallon of petrol.

4 Copy and complete the table.

Speed (miles per hour)	Petrol used (miles per gallon)
50	
70	

5 Copy and complete the sentences.

At 70 miles per hour there is a lot more _____ _____ than there is at 50 miles per hour.

So you do [more/the same/fewer] miles on each gallon of petrol.

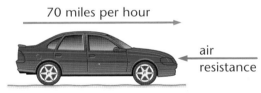

At 70 m.p.h the car travels 30 miles on a gallon of petrol.

WHAT YOU SHOULD KNOW (Copy and complete using the **key words**)

How to reduce friction

You can reduce sliding friction between hubs and spindles:
- by using _____ surfaces
- by using ball _____
- by lubricating moving parts with _____.

You can reduce air resistance by giving things a _____ shape.

1.4 Making good use of friction

Friction is often a nuisance. So we usually want to reduce it.

But friction can also be very helpful. Then we want to increase it.

■ Slowing down

To slow down a car or a bicycle, we use the **brakes**.

The diagram shows how the brakes on a bicycle work.

1 Write down the following sentences in the right order. The first one is in the correct place.

- ■ You squeeze the brake lever to pull the cable.
- ■ There is a force of friction between the rubber blocks and the wheel.
- ■ The wheel slows down.
- ■ The rubber blocks press against the wheel.

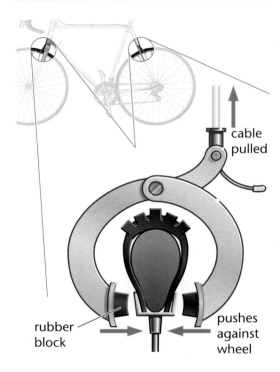

cable pulled

rubber block

pushes against wheel

How bicycle brakes work.

■ Using drag to slow things down

Brakes use **sliding** friction to slow things down.

You can also use **air resistance** to slow things down. The diagram shows how air resistance slows down a parachutist.

2 (a) Why do people use a parachute when they jump out of a plane?

(b) How does the parachute work?

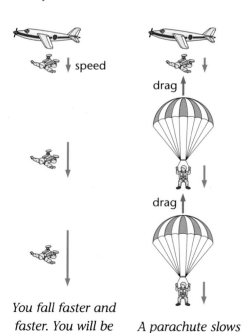

speed

drag

drag

You fall faster and faster. You will be killed or injured when you hit the ground.

A parachute slows you down so you can land safely.

■ Walking on ice

The friction force is sometimes big enough to stop two surfaces from sliding across each other.

You use a friction force like this when you walk. That is why it is difficult to walk on ice.

3 Look at the diagrams. What happens if you try to walk on slippery ice?

Mountaineers fasten crampons to their boots so they can walk on ice.

4 How do the crampons work?

Metal spikes on crampons dig into the ice. This makes a very big friction force.

■ Getting a grip

Tyres must grip the road. If they don't grip hard enough, the car or bicycle will **skid**.

5 Look at the diagram. Then copy and complete the sentences.

To make tyres grip, there must be a lot of _____ between the tyres and the road.

To make the friction forces big, we make tyres from _____ and make road surfaces _____.

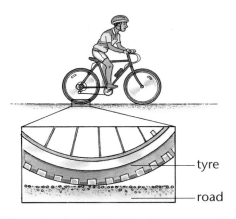

*There is a lot of **friction** between a rubber tyre and a rough road surface.*

WHAT YOU SHOULD KNOW (Copy and complete using the **key words**)

Making good use of friction

Between tyres and the road there must be a lot of _____.
If there isn't, the tyre might _____.

You slow down cars and bicycles by using the _____.
These use _____ friction to slow the wheels down.

A parachute uses _____ _____ to slow the parachutist down.

1.5 Balanced forces

You need a force to <u>start</u> something moving or to <u>change</u> its speed or direction.

But forces are also acting on things that are staying still and on things that are moving at a steady speed.

■ Holding up a suitcase

A suitcase which isn't moving still has forces acting on it. The diagram shows these forces.

1 Copy and complete the sentences.

When you hold a suitcase above the ground:
- the _____ of the suitcase pulls down
- your arm pulls _____.

These two forces _____, so the suitcase stays still.

If something is staying still, the forces that act on it must be **balanced**.

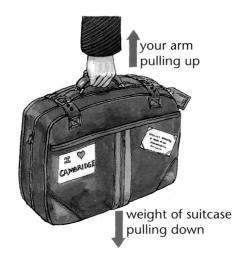

The two forces balance, so the suitcase stays still.

■ More things staying still

The diagrams show some more things which aren't moving.

2 Copy and complete the table.

	Which forces balance?	
	upwards force	downwards force
wood floating	water pushing	
helium balloon		
child standing		

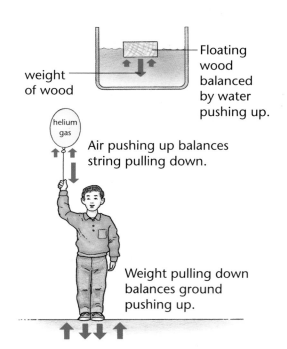

■ Falling at a steady speed

The diagram shows the forces acting on a parachutist.

3 (a) What <u>two</u> forces are acting on the parachutist?

(b) Why does the parachutist fall at a steady speed?

When something falls at a steady speed, there are still forces acting on it. It falls at a steady speed because the forces acting on it are <u>balanced</u>.

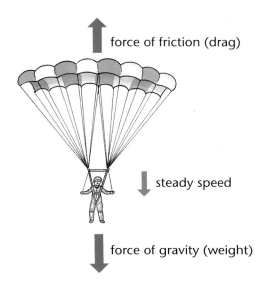

The forces balance, so the parachutist falls at a steady speed.

■ Cycling at a steady speed

A bicycle is moving at a steady speed.
So its speed isn't changing.

There are still forces acting on the bicycle.
But these forces are <u>balanced</u>.

4 Look at the diagram. Then copy and complete the sentences.

There are two forces that affect the speed of the bicycle:
■ the force of _____
■ the _____ force, caused by pedalling.

The bicycle goes at a steady speed because the two forces are _____ .

Balanced forces don't change the way things move. To change the way something moves, you need an **unbalanced** force.

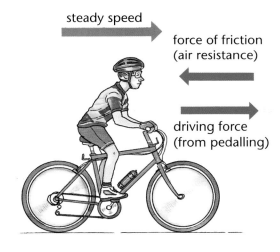

The two forces balance, so the bicycle goes at a steady speed.

WHAT YOU SHOULD KNOW (Copy and complete using the **key words**)

Balanced forces

A force doesn't always change the way something moves.
This is because the force may be _____ by another force.

To change the way something moves, you need an _____ force.

1.6 How hard is it pressing?

Walking on snow isn't easy.

It's a lot easier if you wear snow shoes.

1 Look at the pictures. Why do snow shoes make it easier to walk on snow?

■ How do snow shoes work?

You're still the same weight when you wear snow shoes. In fact, the snow shoes will make you a little bit heavier.

But you don't sink into the snow.

The diagrams at the bottom of the page show why.

2 Copy and complete the sentences.

Snow shoes work by spreading out your _____ over a much bigger _____.

When you spread your weight out over a bigger **area** of snow, you press down less on each bit of snow. We say that there is less **pressure** on the snow.

■ How much do snow shoes reduce the pressure?

The diagrams show the areas of an ordinary shoe and a snow shoe.

3 Copy and complete the sentences.

The area of a snow shoe is five times _____ than the area of an ordinary shoe.

So the pressure of a snow shoe on the snow is five times _____.

Your feet sink into soft snow.

If you wear snow shoes, your feet don't sink in.

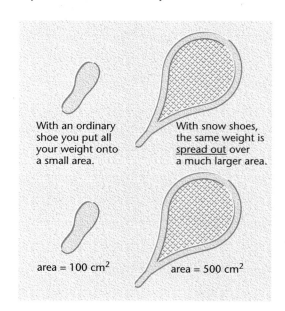

With an ordinary shoe you put all your weight onto a small area.

With snow shoes, the same weight is spread out over a much larger area.

area = 100 cm^2

area = 500 cm^2

■ Riding on soft sand

It's hard to ride a racing bike on soft sand.

It's a lot easier on a mountain bike.

The diagrams show why.

4 (a) Why is it hard to ride a racing bike across sand?

(b) Why doesn't the mountain bike sink into the sand so much?

5 Copy and complete the sentences.

With fatter tyres the weight is spread over a _____ area. So there is a _____ pressure on the sand.

A racing bike sinks into the sand. It has thin tyres so there is a big pressure on the sand.

A mountain bike has fat tyres so there is a small pressure on the sand.

■ Cutting cheese with a knife

It's easy to cut cheese with a sharp knife.

But it's much harder if you use the wrong side of the blade!

The diagrams show why.

6 Copy and complete the sentences.

The sharp edge of a knife blade is much thinner than the _____ edge.
So the same force produces a much bigger _____ on the cheese.

7 The sharp edge of the knife is 100 times narrower than the blunt edge. How many times bigger is the pressure on the cheese, using the same force?

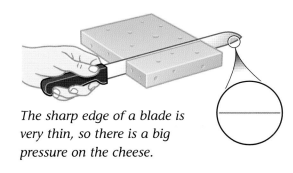

The sharp edge of a blade is very thin, so there is a big pressure on the cheese.

It's a lot harder to cut cheese with the blunt edge of a blade. This edge of the blade is 100 times thicker.

WHAT YOU SHOULD KNOW (Copy and complete using the **key words**)

How hard is it pressing?

If you spread out a force over a big area, it will only produce a small _____.

To get a big pressure, you must make a force act on a small _____.

1.7 Using forces to make things turn

Some things are fixed to the ground, so we can't make them move <u>along</u>. But we can sometimes make them move <u>round</u>.

■ Making a roundabout turn

The diagrams show a roundabout in a children's playground.

1 Copy and complete the sentences.

You can make the roundabout turn by _____ it.

Pushing it one way makes it turn round _____ wise.
Pushing it the other way makes it turn round _____ wise.

The roundabout turns around a point called the _____ .

■ Moving a see-saw

The diagram shows what happens when a boy sits on the right-hand side of a see-saw.

2 Copy and complete the sentence.

The see-saw turns _____ wise.
It turns around its _____ point.

3 Copy the diagram of a girl on a see-saw. Then complete it to show what happens.

You can use a force to:
- start something moving;
- make it move faster;
- slow it down;
- make it move in a different direction.

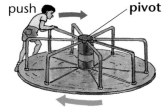

If you push like this the roundabout goes round the same way as the hands of a clock. We say it turns <u>clockwise</u>.

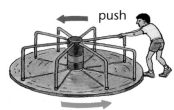

If you push the opposite way the roundabout turns **anti-clockwise**.

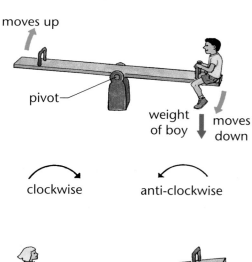

■ Balancing a see-saw

The diagram shows how the turning forces on a see-saw can **balance**.

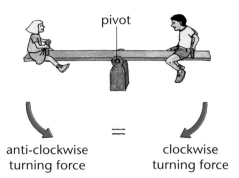

pivot

4 Copy and complete the sentences.

The clockwise turning force is the same as the _____ turning force.
So the forces _____.

anti-clockwise turning force = clockwise turning force

■ Turning forces in everyday life

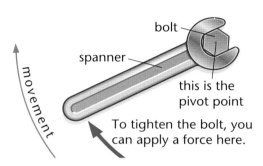

bolt
spanner
this is the pivot point
movement
To tighten the bolt, you can apply a force here.

You often use a turning force to do things. For example, you can use a spanner to tighten a bolt.

5 Which way do you turn a bolt to tighten it?

You also use a turning force to close a door.

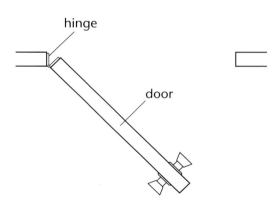

hinge
door

6 Make a copy of the diagram of the door. Show on the diagram:

(a) the pivot point;

(b) where you apply a force to close the door.

WHAT YOU SHOULD KNOW (Copy and complete using the **key words**)

Using forces to make things turn

Forces can make things turn around a _____ point.

If a force makes something turn clockwise, the opposite force will make it turn _____.

If a clockwise turning force is the same as an anti-clockwise turning force, the forces _____.

1.8 How fast is it moving?

We sometimes want to know how fast something is moving.

Look at the top picture of a car and a lorry. They both go past a lamp-post at the same time.
The lower picture shows how far the car and the lorry travel in the next second.

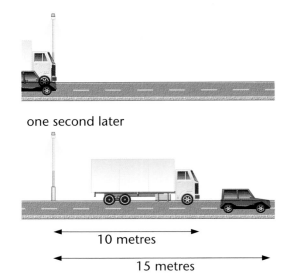

one second later

10 metres

15 metres

1 (a) Which is moving faster, the car or the lorry?

(b) Give a reason for your answer.

The car is moving faster than the lorry. We say that the car has a higher **speed** than the lorry.

■ Thinking about speed

The speed of something is how far it travels in a certain time.

For example, the lorry in the pictures travels 10 metres in one second.
So its speed is 10 metres per second.
[Note: 'per second' means 'in one second'.]

2 Look again at the pictures of the car and the lorry. What is the speed of the car?

3 Look at the pictures of the walker and the cyclists. What is the speed:

(a) of the walker?

(b) of the cyclists?

The walker travels 5 kilometres in one hour.

These cyclists travel 50 kilometres in one hour.

How to work out speeds

To work out the speed of something you need to know:

- how far it travels (a **distance**);
- the **time** it takes to travel this distance.

You can then work out its speed like this:

speed = distance travelled ÷ time taken

Example

A car goes 120 miles in 2 hours.

speed = distance travelled ÷ time taken
$$= 120 ÷ 2$$
$$= 60$$

So the car's speed is 60 miles per hour.

4 Work out the speeds of the things shown in the pictures on this page. (Use a calculator if you want to.)

Average speeds

Most things don't travel at the same speed all the time. For example:

- the train stops at some stations;
- the athlete has to build up to full speed.

So the speeds you worked out were their **average** speeds.

Concorde travels 3000 miles in 2 hours.

This athlete runs 100 metres in 10 seconds.

This Eurostar train travels 240 kilometres in $1\frac{1}{2}$ hours.

WHAT YOU SHOULD KNOW (Copy and complete using the **key words**)

How fast is it moving?

The distance something travels in a certain time is called its _____.

You can work out speed like this: speed = _____ travelled ÷ _____ taken

Many things don't move at the same speed all the time. So the speed we work out is their _____ speed.

1.9 Working out the pressure

The pressure that a force produces depends on the **area** that the force acts on.

So you can get <u>different</u> pressures with the <u>same</u> force.

This idea is used with a drawing pin.

How a drawing pin uses pressure

When you use a drawing pin you get:

- a <u>small</u> pressure on your thumb;

- a <u>big</u> pressure on the notice-board.

The diagram shows how this happens.

1 (a) Why do you want a small pressure on your thumb?

  (b) How do you get this small pressure?

2 (a) Why is the pressure of the sharp end of a drawing pin on the notice board very big?

  (b) Why do you want this pressure to be very big?

How much bigger is the pressure on the notice-board?

The head of the drawing pin has an area a thousand times bigger than the point of the drawing pin.

The same force acts on both.

3 How many times bigger is the pressure of the drawing pin on the notice-board than on your thumb?

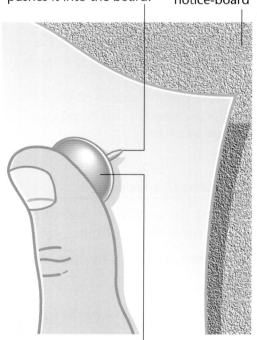

The point of the drawing pin has a small area, so a large pressure pushes it into the board.   notice-board

The head of the drawing pin has a large area, so the pressure is small and doesn't cut your thumb.

force on board

This is the <u>same</u> force, but on a much smaller area.

force of thumb

■ Measuring forces

We measure forces in units called **newtons** (N for short).

The diagrams give you an idea of how big a newton of force is.

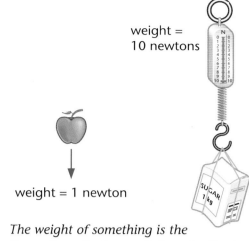

weight = 10 newtons

weight = 1 newton

The weight of something is the force of gravity that pulls it to the Earth.

4 Copy and complete the sentences.

The weight of an apple is about _____ newton.

The force of gravity on a kilogram is about _____ N.

■ Working out the pressures

Pressure is the **force** on a certain area. So you can work out a pressure like this:

pressure = force ÷ area

The example shows you how to use this idea for the drawing pin.

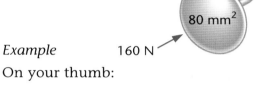

Example   160 N   80 mm^2

On your thumb:

$$pressure = force ÷ area$$
$$= 160 ÷ 80$$
$$= 2 \text{ newtons per mm}^2$$

■ Working out the pressure on snow

The diagrams show a girl's ordinary shoe and her snow shoe.

As the girl walks, she puts all her weight on to one foot and then on to the other foot.

5 Work out the pressure of the girl's foot on the snow as she walks:

(a) with ordinary shoes;

(b) with snow shoes.

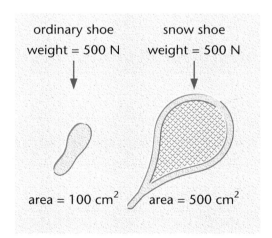

ordinary shoe
weight = 500 N

snow shoe
weight = 500 N

area = 100 cm^2

area = 500 cm^2

WHAT YOU SHOULD KNOW (Copy and complete using the **key words**)

Working out the pressure

The pressure of a force depends on the _____ it acts on.

Forces are measured in _____ (N for short).

You can work out pressure like this: pressure = _____ ÷ area

2.1 How you see things

You need **light** to see things.

When it's dark, you can't see very well.
If it's completely dark, you can't see anything
at all.

1 Look at the diagrams.

   (a) Why can you see the light bulb?

   (b) Why can you see the chair and the carpet?

   (c) Why can't you see the chair or the carpet
   when it's dark?

*The light bulb sends out light. Other things
in the room reflect this light. You see when
light goes into your eyes.*

■ A problem with corners

Even when it is light, you can't see round
corners. The diagram shows why.

2 Copy and complete the sentences.

   The driver of the blue car can't see the _____
   car. This is because light from the red car travels in
   _____ lines.
   Light doesn't travel round _____.

3 **(a)** Can the driver of the red car see any part of
   the blue car?

   (b) Explain your answer on a copy of the diagram.
   (Leave out the red line so that it doesn't get
   in the way.)

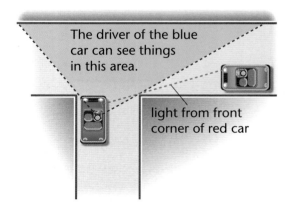

The driver of the blue
car can see things
in this area.

light from front
corner of red car

Light travels in straight lines.

■ Shadows

Light can't go through most solid things. So if you put something like a pencil in the way of a beam of light, you get a **shadow**.

The diagram shows why.

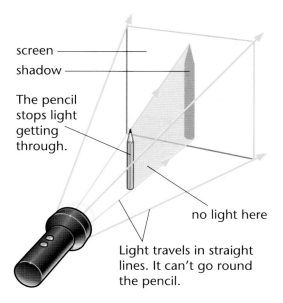

screen —
shadow —

The pencil stops light getting through.

no light here

Light travels in straight lines. It can't go round the pencil.

4 Copy and complete the sentences.

Light can't go through a pencil.

Light travels in straight _____.
So it can't go _____ the pencil either.

This is why the pencil makes a _____.

5 What shape is the shadow of the pencil?

■ Why is it light on a cloudy day?

During the day we can see because of light from the Sun.

Even on a cloudy day there is still plenty of light. The diagram shows why.

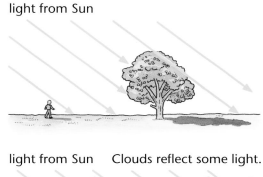

light from Sun

6 (a) Why is it light on a cloudy day?

   (b) Why is it not as light on a cloudy day as on a sunny day?

   (c) You can't see the Sun or the sky on a cloudy day. What else don't you see on a cloudy day? (Look carefully at the picture.)

light from Sun   Clouds reflect some light.

But some light gets through.

WHAT YOU SHOULD KNOW (Copy and complete using the **key words**)

How you see things

You can only see when there is some _____.
The things you see either give out light or _____ light into your eyes.

Light travels in _____ _____. So it can't go round _____.

When light can't pass through something, it makes a _____.

2.2 Reflecting light

Some things give out **light**. This makes them easy to see.

We can see other things because they **reflect** the light that falls on them.

1 Write down the names of <u>five</u> things that give out light.

2 How can you see:

(a) the Moon;

(b) the pages of a book you read at night?

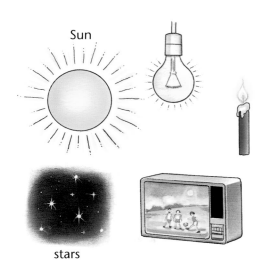

Some things give out their own light.

We can see other things because they reflect light.

■ How most things reflect light

A spotlight shines on a picture.

The diagram shows why you can see the picture from all parts of the room.

3 Copy and complete the sentences.

The picture reflects light in _____ directions. This is because the surface of the picture has lots and lots of tiny _____ .

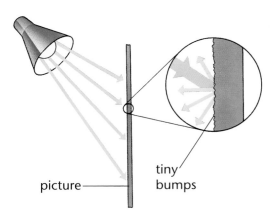

*The picture has a bumpy surface. So it reflects light in <u>all</u> **directions**.*

■ Reflection from very shiny surfaces

Shiny surfaces reflect light in a special sort of way.

4 Look at the diagrams.

(a) What can you use a very shiny surface for?

(b) Write down the names of <u>two</u> shiny surfaces you can see your reflection in.

mirror (glass with silvered back)

polished metal spoon

You can see your own reflection in these.

■ How a mirror reflects light

Some pupils decided to find out how a mirror reflects light. The diagram shows what they did.

The pupils then moved the ray-box so the beam of light hit the mirror at a different **angle**.

The table shows their results.

5 Copy and complete the sentence.

A mirror reflects a ray of light at the _____ angle as it strikes the mirror.

This is an easy way to show a mirror.

ray strikes mirror at 49°   ray reflects from mirror at 49°

A ray-box makes a narrow beam of light. We call this a <u>ray</u>.

Angle that light strikes mirror	Angle that light reflects from mirror
20°	20°
37°	37°
49°	49°
66°	66°
81°	81°

WHAT YOU SHOULD KNOW (Copy and complete using the **key words**)

Reflecting light

We can see some things because they give out _____.

We can see other things because they _____ light into our eyes.

Most things reflect light in all _____.

Shiny surfaces, such as mirrors, reflect light at the same _____ as the light strikes them.

2.3 Using mirrors

Other people can see you because light is reflected from your face.

To see your own face you need to use a mirror.

The diagram shows how this works.

1 Copy and complete the sentence.

   On the diagram angle P and angle Q are

   _____.

2 Draw a diagram to show how the girl sees her own lips to put on lipstick.

   We can use mirrors to do many other useful jobs.

angle P

angle Q

mirror

■ Seeing round corners

You can use a mirror to help drivers to see round a dangerous corner.

The diagram shows how the driver of the blue car can see the red car through the mirror.

When she looks past the corner, the driver of the blue car can <u>just</u> see the front of the yellow car.

The driver of the blue car can also see the yellow car through the mirror.

3 On a copy of the diagram, draw lines to show the <u>two</u> ways the driver of the blue car can see the yellow car. (Leave out the red lines so they don't get in the way.)

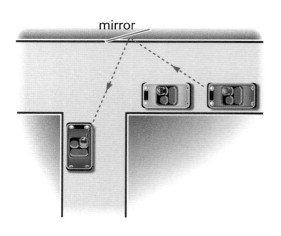

mirror

■ Seeing over the top of things

To see over the top of something you need to use a <u>periscope</u>.

The diagrams show some of the ways you can use a periscope.

4 Write down <u>three</u> things that a periscope can be used for.

battleship

submarine

seeing over a crowd

woodpecker

birdwatcher

■ How a periscope works

You can make a periscope using two mirrors.

The diagram shows how you can do this.

5 Copy and complete the table.

Angle	Number of degrees
A	45°
B	_____°
C	90°
X	_____°
Y	_____°
Z	_____°

6 Copy and complete the sentences.

At each mirror, the light changes direction by an angle of _____°.

To do this:

■ it strikes the mirror at _____°

■ it is reflected at _____°.

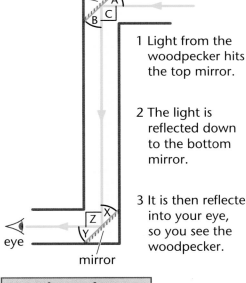

mirror

1 Light from the woodpecker hits the top mirror.

2 The light is reflected down to the bottom mirror.

3 It is then reflected into your eye, so you see the woodpecker.

eye

mirror

A right angle is 90°.

WHAT YOU SHOULD KNOW (Copy and complete using the **key words**)

Using mirrors

mirror

When light is reflected from a mirror, angles X and Y are _____.

X   Y

You should be able to use this idea to explain other uses of mirrors in the same sort of way as you have on these pages.

2.4 Colours of the rainbow

On pictures we often show the Sun as yellow.

But the light from the Sun is really **white**.

White light isn't just one colour. It's lots of different colours all mixed up together.

You can see all these colours in a **rainbow**.

1 What splits up sunlight into all the colours in a rainbow?

2 Write down a list of the colours of the rainbow in the right order. Start from the outside with <u>red</u>.
   Use these colours in your list:
   blue green orange red violet yellow

Drops of rain can split up sunlight into all the colours of the rainbow.

■ Making your own 'rainbow'

The diagram shows how you can use a **prism** to split up white light into all the colours of the rainbow.

We call these rainbow colours a **spectrum**.

3 Copy and complete the sentences.

   We can split up a narrow beam of white light using a prism made of _____ _____.

   We call all the different colours of light a _____.

4 Draw a box about 5 cm wide and 2 cm high.

   Colour a spectrum inside the box. (Coloured pencils are best because you can shade the colours into each other.)

   Then label the colours in your spectrum.

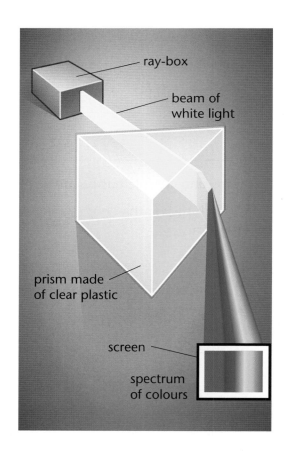

ray-box

beam of white light

prism made of clear plastic

screen

spectrum of colours

■ Using coloured filters

Another way to get coloured light from white light is to use coloured **filters**.

Filters let some colours of light pass through. But they stop other colours. We say that the filters **absorb** these other colours.

The diagrams show how filters work.

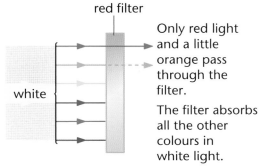

Only red light and a little orange pass through the filter.

The filter absorbs all the other colours in white light.

How a red filter works.

5 When you send white light through a red filter it comes out red. Explain why.

6 Copy the diagram of the yellow filter.

Then add words to the diagram to explain how it works.

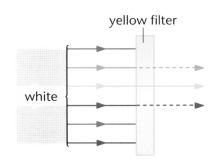

How a yellow filter works.

■ Using more than one filter

The diagram shows what happens when you send white light through a blue filter and then through a yellow filter.

7 What light passes through both filters?

8 (a) What happens if you send white light through a blue filter and then through a red filter?

(b) Draw a diagram to explain your answer.

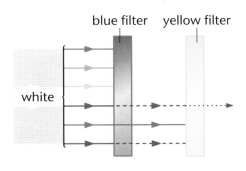

Two filters together.

WHAT YOU SHOULD KNOW (Copy and complete using the **key words**)

Colours of the rainbow

Light from the Sun is _____.

When white light is split up by drops of rain, we get a _____.

We can split up white light into colours using a _____ made of clear plastic. We call the colours a _____.

We can also make coloured light from white light by using _____. Filters let some colours pass through but _____ other colours.

2.5 Why do things look coloured?

We can see things because they reflect light.

But sunlight and the light from most lamps is <u>white</u>.

So we need to explain why many of the things we see are <u>coloured</u>.

■ Why a postbox looks red

A postbox looks red in white daylight.

The diagram shows why.

1 Copy and complete the sentences.

A postbox looks _____.
This is because red paint reflects mainly
_____ light.
It _____ most other colours.

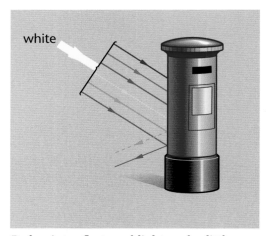

white

Red paint reflects red light and a little orange. It absorbs other colours.

■ Why grass looks green

Things look coloured because they **reflect** some colours of light and **absorb** other colours.

The diagram shows why grass looks green.

2 (a) What colour of light does grass <u>mainly</u> reflect?

(b) What other colours does grass <u>partly</u> reflect?

(c) What happens to the colours of light that are <u>not</u> reflected?

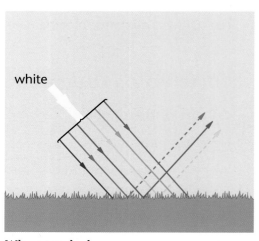

white

Why grass looks green.

■ Why isn't everything coloured?

Some things aren't coloured. They are white or black or some shade of grey.

The diagrams show why.

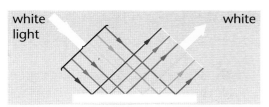

*A white surface reflects **all** colours a lot.*

3 (a) Copy and complete the table.

Surface	What it reflects
white	
black	
grey	

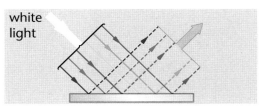

A grey surface reflects all colours a bit.

(b) Copy and complete the sentences.

White things and grey things don't look coloured. This is because the light they reflect contains all the _____ of the spectrum.

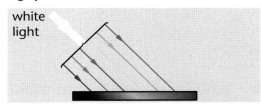

*A **black** surface hardly reflects any colour.*

■ Looking at things in coloured light

Things look their normal colour when we see them in <u>white</u> light.

They look different in coloured light.

in white light

4 Look at the diagrams. Then copy and complete the table.

	How it looks in red light	How it looks in green light
postbox		
grass		

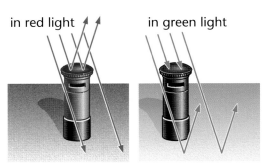

in red light   in green light

WHAT YOU SHOULD KNOW (Copy and complete using the **key words**)

Why do things look coloured?

Things look coloured in white light because they _____ some colours of light but _____ other colours.

White things and grey things don't look coloured because they reflect the same amount of _____ the colours of the spectrum.

Things which reflect hardly any light at all look _____.

2.6 Comparing light and sound

We all need to know what's going on in the world around us. We find out mainly by looking and listening.

This means that we use **light** and **sound** to find out about our surroundings.

1 Look at the picture. Then copy and complete the sentences.

We use our _____ to see the _____ reflected from things around us.

We use our _____ to hear _____.

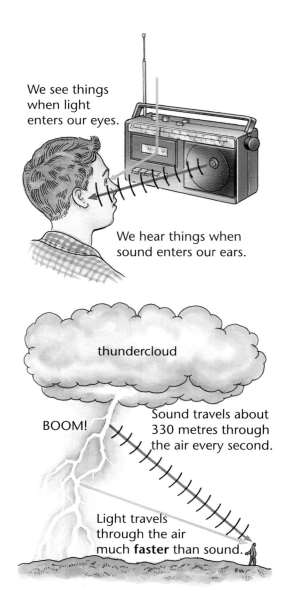

We see things when light enters our eyes.

We hear things when sound enters our ears.

thundercloud

BOOM!

Sound travels about 330 metres through the air every second.

Light travels through the air much **faster** than sound.

■ Seeing and hearing in a thunderstorm

During a thunderstorm you see flashes of lightning. These make the sound we call thunder.

Light takes hardly any time at all to travel through the air. You see the lightning a short time before you hear the thunder. The diagram shows why.

2 Why do you see lightning before you hear thunder?

3 You see a flash of lightning. Three seconds later you hear thunder.

  How far away was the lightning?

If you hear thunder 4 seconds after seeing lightning, the lightning is
4 × 330 = 1320 metres away.

■ Fainter and fainter

As a thunderstorm moves further away, the sound of the thunder isn't so loud. The flashes of lightning aren't so bright either.

We say that the light and sound get **fainter**.

4 Why does light get fainter as it gets further away?

Light spreads out more as it gets further away. So it is fainter.

■ Another difference between light and sound

An accident on a satellite causes a HUGE explosion.

5 People on Earth <u>see</u> the explosion. But they do not <u>hear</u> it. Why not?

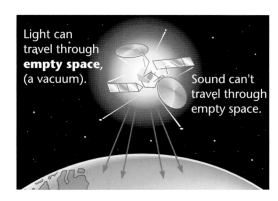

Light can travel through **empty space**, (a vacuum).

Sound can't travel through empty space.

■ Differences between sounds

You know that light can be many different **colours**.

In the same way, sounds can have a different **pitch**.

We say that some sounds have a <u>higher</u> or <u>lower</u> pitch than others.

6 Look at the pictures. Then answer the questions below.

(a) Which plays notes of a higher pitch, a cello or a violin?

(b) During his teens, a boy's voice 'breaks'. What does this mean?

(c) Where do you find the lowest notes on a keyboard?

violin   cello

Small musical instruments play notes with a higher pitch than large ones.

A man's voice has a lower pitch than a young boy's voice.

The pitch of notes gets higher as you move this way along the keyboard.

Each key on a keyboard plays a note with a different pitch.

WHAT YOU SHOULD KNOW (Copy and complete using the **key words**)

Comparing light and sound

We see when _____ enters our eyes. We hear when _____ enters our ears.

Light travels _____ than sound through the air.

The further light and sound travel, the _____ they get.

Light, but not sound, can travel through _____ _____.

Light can be different _____. Sounds can have a different _____.

2.7 Making and hearing sounds

Things that vibrate make sounds.

There are lots and lots of different sounds. They are all made by things which **vibrate**.

We often use musical instruments to make sounds.

1 Look at the diagrams of musical instruments. Then copy and complete the table.

Instrument	What vibrates to make a sound
saxophone	the air inside it

saxophone

The air inside this vibrates when you blow.

guitar

The strings vibrate when you pluck them.

drum

The drum skins vibrate when you hit them.

■ Sound from radios and TVs

Many of the sounds we listen to every day come from radios, TVs and CD players.

2 Look at the diagram. What part of a radio produces sounds?

The loudspeaker in a radio produces sounds.

■ How sounds reach your ears

The diagram shows how the sound from a loudspeaker reaches your ears.

3 Copy and complete the following.

loudspeaker makes ____ → vibrations travel through the ____ → vibrations enter your ____

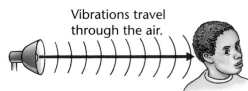

Vibrations travel through the air.

The loudspeaker makes vibrations.

The vibrations enter your ear.

■ What else can sound travel through?

Most of the sounds you hear travel through **air** before they reach your ears.

Sound can also travel very well through **solids** and **liquids**.

4 Write down:

(a) one example of a sound travelling through a solid;

(b) one example of a sound travelling through a liquid.

Whales can send sounds to each other for hundreds of kilometres.

earthquake

Earth

Sound vibrations from an earthquake travel through the Earth. Scientists use special instruments to 'listen' to earthquakes thousands of kilometres away.

■ What happens when a sound enters your ear?

The diagram shows what happens when sound vibrations travel through the air into your ear.

5 Write down these sentences in the right order to explain how you hear. The first and the last are in the correct place.

- ■ Your pinna collects sound vibrations in the air.

- ■ Vibrations pass on to small bones inside your ear.

- ■ The vibrations in the air strike your eardrum.

- ■ Your eardrum vibrates.

- ■ The vibrations in the air travel down your ear canal.

- ■ Your inner ear sends a signal to your brain.

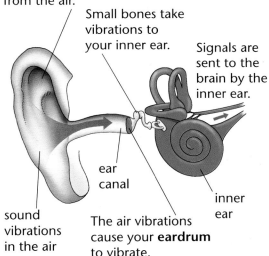

Your external ear (pinna) collects sound vibrations from the air.

Small bones take vibrations to your inner ear.

Signals are sent to the brain by the inner ear.

ear canal

inner ear

sound vibrations in the air

The air vibrations cause your **eardrum** to vibrate.

WHAT YOU SHOULD KNOW (Copy and complete using the **key words**)

Making and hearing sounds

Sounds are made when things _____.
These vibrations then travel through the _____ to your ears.

Sounds can also travel through _____ and _____.

When sounds enter your ear, they strike your _____ and make it vibrate.

2.8 Different sounds

There are lots of different sounds.

Some sounds are **louder** than others.

The pictures show how you can make the <u>same</u> sound louder.

1 Write down <u>three</u> ways of making a sound louder.

■ Why are some sounds louder than others?

All sounds are caused by **vibrations**. These vibrations are often too small to see. But you <u>can</u> see the strings on a guitar vibrate.

2 Look at the diagram. Then copy and complete the sentences.

When you pluck a guitar string harder, the sound is _____.
This is because the vibrations are _____.

Another way of saying that vibrations are large is to say that they have a big **amplitude**.

■ Danger! Loud sounds

Very loud sounds can be dangerous.

3 Why are very loud sounds dangerous?

4 How can workers prevent their ears from being damaged by loud sounds?

People who work in loud noise should wear ear protectors.

Making a louder sound.

Hit the drum harder.

Turn up the volume control.

String plucked gently:

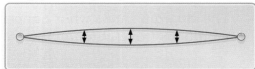

small vibrations, quiet sound.

String plucked harder:

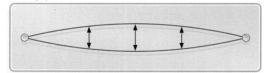

larger vibrations, louder sound.

Very loud sounds can damage your ears.

■ Another difference between sounds

Some sounds are louder than others. Sounds can also have a different **pitch**.

5 Copy and complete the sentences.

Small musical instruments make sounds with a higher _____ than larger ones.

■ Why do sounds have different pitches?

The pitch of a sound depends on **how many** vibrations there are each second.

We call this the **frequency** of the sound.

Sounds that have a high frequency also have a high pitch.

We measure frequency in **hertz** (Hz for short).

6 How does the pitch of a sound depend on its frequency?

7 Look at the diagram.

(a) What is the lowest frequency that most people can hear?

(b) What happens to the highest frequency people can hear as they get older?

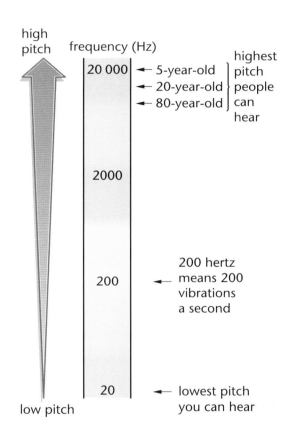

high pitch

frequency (Hz)

20 000 ← 5-year-old ⎫ highest pitch
← 20-year-old ⎬ people can hear
← 80-year-old ⎭

2000

200 hertz means 200 vibrations a second

200

20 ← lowest pitch you can hear

low pitch

WHAT YOU SHOULD KNOW (Copy and complete using the **key words**)

Different sounds

Sounds can be different in two ways:
- one sound can be _____ than another;
- the sounds can have a different _____.

Loud sounds are caused by large _____. We say that these vibrations have a big _____.

The pitch of a sound depends on _____ _____ vibrations there are each second. This is called the _____ of the sound.

A frequency of 200 _____ (Hz for short) means 200 vibrations each second.

2.9 How to bend light

REMEMBER

Light travels in straight lines.
It can't go round corners.

Light <u>usually</u> travels in straight lines.

But you can make light bend using water.

The diagram shows you how.

1 At first, Kris can't see the coin in the metal can. Why not?

2 When Sam fills the can with water, Kris can then see the coin. Explain why.

Light bends when it passes from water into air. We say that it is **refracted**.

■ Describing refraction

We sometimes want to say which <u>way</u> light is refracted.

The diagram shows how you can do this.

Look carefully at the key words on the diagram.

3 Copy and complete the sentences.

Where the water ends is called a _____.

A normal is a line at _____ angles (90°) to the boundary.

When light crosses the boundary from water into air, it is refracted away from the _____.

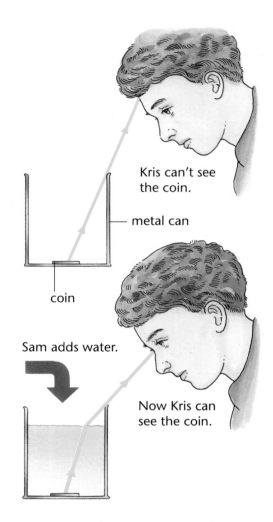

Kris can't see the coin.

metal can

coin

Sam adds water.

Now Kris can see the coin.

The **normal** is a line at **right angles** to the boundary.

This ray of light is refracted **away from** the normal.

The **boundary** is where the water ends.

air

water

■ Refraction works both ways

Light is also refracted when it travels from air into water.

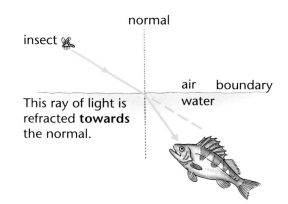

normal

insect

This ray of light is refracted **towards** the normal.

air   boundary
water

4 Look at the diagram. Describe what happens to a ray of light from the insect as it passes into the water.

■ More examples of refraction

The diagrams show what happens to light when it crosses the boundaries between different substances and at different angles.

Light travelling along a normal is <u>not</u> refracted.

5 Copy each diagram.

Underneath each diagram describe what happens like this:

A   When light passes from <u>glass</u> into <u>air</u> at <u>60°</u> to the boundary it is <u>refracted away from the normal</u>.

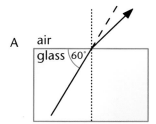

A   air
glass 60°

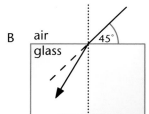

B   air 45°
glass

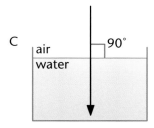

C   air 90°
water

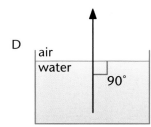

D   air
water
90°

WHAT YOU SHOULD KNOW (Copy and complete using the **key words**)

How to bend light

Light bends when it passes across the _____ between two different substances. We say that the light is _____.

A line at 90° to a boundary is called a _____.

When light passes from glass or water into air, it is refracted _____ _____ the normal.

When light passes from air into glass or water, it is refracted _____ the normal.

When light crosses a boundary at _____ _____, it is not refracted.

3.1 Making electricity by rubbing

The Ancient Greeks discovered electricity thousands of years ago. The diagram shows how they discovered it.

1 **(a)** How did the Ancient Greeks make electricity?

   (b) How did they <u>know</u> they had made it?

   (c) How did electricity get its name?

When we rub amber, we say that it becomes **charged** with electricity.

The electrical charge stays on the amber. So we call it **static** electricity. ('Static' means 'not moving'.)

Amber looks like orange glass. The Ancient Greeks used it to make jewellery.

■ Charging a comb

We don't use amber much today. But we do make lots of things from <u>plastic</u>.

You have charged a piece of plastic with electricity lots of times. You do this when you comb your hair.

*If you rub a piece of amber with a cloth, it will **attract** bits of paper and dust.*

2 Look at the diagram. Then copy and complete the sentences.

When you use a comb, it rubs against your hair. The comb becomes charged with _____. So it will _____ small bits of paper or dust.

DID YOU KNOW?

Our word 'electricity' comes from the Greek word for amber.

When you use a comb, it rubs against your hair.

The comb will then attract bits of paper and dust.

■ Making a balloon stick to the ceiling

A balloon will stick to the ceiling if you charge it with electricity. The diagram shows how you can do this.

3 (a) How can you charge a balloon with electricity?

(b) Why does the balloon now stick to the ceiling?

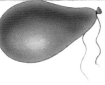

You can charge a balloon by rubbing it against your sweater.

Release the balloon near the ceiling. There is a force of attraction between the charged balloon and the ceiling. This holds the balloon up.

■ Making your own lightning

When you take off a sweater, it rubs against your blouse or your shirt. Sometimes you can hear crackles. If it is dark you can see tiny sparks.

4 (a) What causes the sparks when you take off a sweater?

(b) Why does taking off a sweater make electricity?

You can only get an electrical charge if the things you rub together are made of <u>different</u> materials.

5 A boy wears a cotton sweater on top of a cotton shirt. When he takes the sweater off, he <u>doesn't</u> produce an electrical charge. Why not?

Another way to make static electricity.

WHAT YOU SHOULD KNOW (Copy and complete using the **key words**)

Making electricity by rubbing

If you rub an object with a different material, it becomes _____ with electricity. The electrical charge stays where it is, so we call it _____ electricity.

A charged object will _____ other things such as bits of dust or paper.

3.2 Two sorts of charges

Two rulers are made from the same kind of white plastic.

You can charge the rulers by rubbing both of them with a cloth. The diagrams show how you can then test the electrical charges on the rulers.

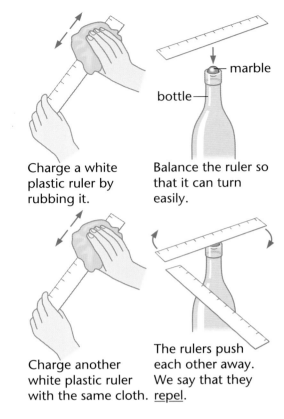

Charge a white plastic ruler by rubbing it.

Balance the ruler so that it can turn easily.

marble

bottle

Charge another white plastic ruler with the same cloth.

The rulers push each other away. We say that they <u>repel</u>.

1 What do the electrically charged rulers do to each other?

2 Copy and complete the sentences.

Both white rulers are made of the same kind of _____.

They are both rubbed with the same _____.
So the electrical charge on both rulers must also be the _____.

Two objects that have the <u>same</u> electrical charge repel each other.

■ Testing a different plastic

A clear ruler is made from a different kind of plastic.

Some pupils charge a clear plastic ruler by rubbing it with a cloth. They then test it with a charged white plastic ruler. The diagram shows what happens.

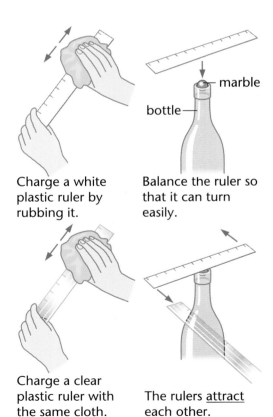

Charge a white plastic ruler by rubbing it.

Balance the ruler so that it can turn easily.

marble

bottle

Charge a clear plastic ruler with the same cloth.

The rulers <u>attract</u> each other.

3 Copy and complete the sentences.

The clear plastic ruler _____ the white plastic ruler.
But if two charges are the <u>same</u>, they repel each other.
So the electrical charge on the clear plastic must be _____ from the electrical charge on the white plastic.

■ **What do we call the different charges?**

The charge on a clear plastic ruler is different from the charge on a white plastic ruler. This is because the rulers are made of different kinds of plastic.

A clear plastic ruler is made from acrylic plastic. When you charge something made from acrylic plastic, you give it a **positive** (+) charge.

A white plastic ruler is made from polythene. When you charge something made from polythene, you give it a **negative** (–) charge.

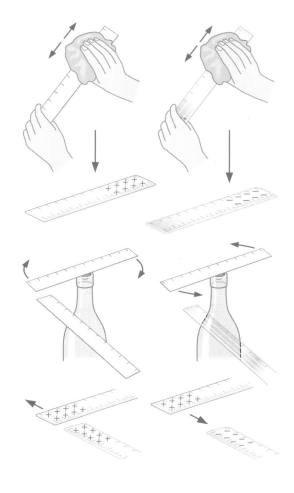

4 Copy and complete the table.

Charge on first object	Charge on second object	Do they attract or repel?
+	+	
+	–	
–	–	

<u>Different</u> charges **attract** each other.

Charges that are the <u>same</u> **repel** each other.

■ **Another look at combing your hair**

Sometimes, when you comb your hair, it won't lie flat. The diagram shows why.

5 Copy and complete the sentences.

When you comb your hair you give all the hairs a _____ charge.
So the hairs _____ each other.

Your hairs all have negative charges, so they repel each other.

The comb has a positive charge.

WHAT YOU SHOULD KNOW (Copy and complete using the **key words**)

Two sorts of charges

Electrical charges can be _____ (+) or _____ (–).

A positive charge and a negative charge _____ each other.

Two charges that are the same _____ each other.

3.3 Electric currents

You can make <u>static</u> electricity by rubbing things together. But to be really useful, electrical charges must be <u>moving</u>.

When charges move they make an electric current. Electric currents can do lots of useful jobs.

■ A safe electric current

We can get an electric current from the mains. You just plug in and switch on.

But mains electricity is very dangerous. For experiments, you need a <u>safe</u> electric current.

1 Look at the diagrams. Then copy and complete the sentences.

To get a safe electric current we can use a

_____.

If we join cells together we get a _____.

■ Connecting up a cell

To get an electric current from a cell, you need to connect it into a circuit. The diagram shows how to do this.

2 Copy and complete the sentence.

An electric current flows:

- from the cell,
- through a _____ wire,
- through the _____,
- through another _____ wire,
- back to the other end of the _____.

3 You can't <u>see</u> electricity. So how do you know that an electric current is flowing in this circuit?

*You can use a **cell** to get an electric current that is safe for experiments.*

Two (or more) cells joined together make a **battery**.

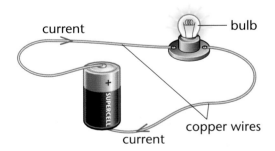

■ Adding a switch to the circuit

If you want to turn a current on or off, you use a **switch**.

4 Look at the diagrams. Then copy and complete the sentence.

To switch off a current, you must _____ the circuit.

A current can only flow if there is a **complete** circuit.

If the circuit is broken there is no current and the bulb doesn't light.

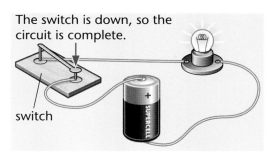

The switch is down, so the circuit is complete.

switch

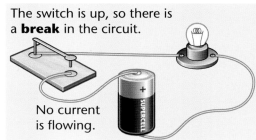

The switch is up, so there is a **break** in the circuit.

No current is flowing.

■ Conductors and insulators

If you make a circuit using string, it doesn't work.

5 How do you know that an electric current does <u>not</u> flow through the string?

6 Copy and complete the sentences.

An electric current <u>will</u> flow through copper. So we call copper a _____.

An electric current <u>won't</u> flow through string. So we call string an _____.

An electric current can only flow if there is a complete circuit made of **conductors**.

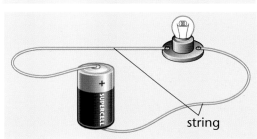

string

An electric current <u>won't</u> go through string. We say that string is an <u>insulator</u>.

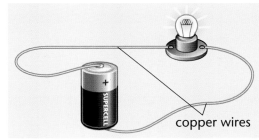

copper wires

An electric current <u>will</u> go through copper. We say that copper is a <u>conductor</u>.

WHAT YOU SHOULD KNOW (Copy and complete using the **key words**)

Electric currents

You can get a safe electric current from a _____.

Two or more cells joined together is called a _____.

A current will only flow if there is a _____ circuit of _____.

To stop a current flowing you must make a _____ in the circuit. You usually do this using a _____.

3.4 Other things that attract and repel

It isn't only electrically charged objects that can attract things.

Some rocks that you find in the ground will attract things made from **iron** or steel. We say that these rocks are **magnetised**.

The diagrams show some of the things that magnetised rocks can do.

Some rocks are magnetised. They attract things made of iron or steel.

1 What things will magnetised rocks attract?

2 Hundreds of years ago, explorers used magnetised rocks to find out the direction they were travelling. Explain how they did this.

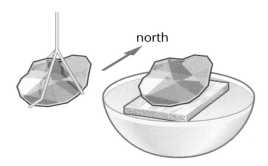

A magnetised rock always points the same way if you hang it up or float it on water.

■ Magnets made by people

We don't need to use magnetic rocks any more. Scientists can <u>make</u> magnets in all shapes and sizes. We use these modern magnets for many different jobs.

3 Look at the diagrams. Write down <u>two</u> different uses for modern magnets.

4 (a) What do we call the end of a magnet which points north?

(b) What do you think we call the <u>other</u> end of a magnet?

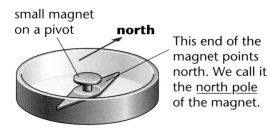

small magnet on a pivot

north

This end of the magnet points north. We call it the <u>north pole</u> of the magnet.

A magnetic compass tells you where north and south are.

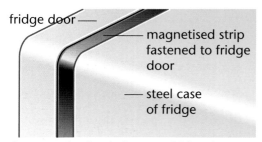

fridge door

magnetised strip fastened to fridge door

steel case of fridge

A magnetised strip keeps a fridge door closed.

▪ What do magnets do to each other?

The diagrams show what happens when you bring the **poles** of two magnets near to each other.

N = north pole   S = south pole

5 Copy and complete the table.

Pole of first magnet	Pole of second magnet	Do they attract or repel?
S	N	
S	S	
N	N	

Two poles that are <u>different</u> attract each other.

Two poles that are the <u>same</u> repel each other.

These magnets **attract** each other.

These magnets push each other away. They **repel**.

▪ Finding the north and south poles of a magnet

To find the north and south poles of a magnet, you can hang the magnet up or float it.

The diagrams show you another way to find out.

These magnets also repel.

A compass needle is a magnet

north

This end of the compass needle is a north pole.

6 Copy and complete the sentences.

End A of the magnet is a _____ pole because it repels the _____ pole of the compass needle.

End B of the magnet is a _____ pole because it repels the _____ pole of the compass needle.

End A repels the N pole of the compass needle and attracts the S pole.

End B attracts the N pole of the compass needle and repels the S pole.

WHAT YOU SHOULD KNOW (Copy and complete using the **key words**)

Other things that attract and repel

Some rocks attract things made of _____ or steel. We say that the rocks are

_____.

If a magnetised rock or a magnet is free to move, one end will point _____ and the other end will point south. The ends of a magnet are called the _____.

The north pole of one magnet will _____ the south pole of another magnet. Two poles that are the same _____ each other.

3.5 Magnetic fields

Magnets attract pieces of iron or steel that are near to them. They can also attract or repel other magnets.

The area around a magnet where it pushes or pulls is called a magnetic **field**.

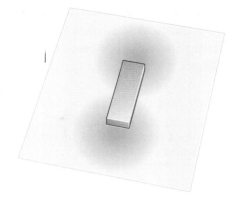

1 Look at the diagram. Then copy and complete the sentence.

As you go further away from a magnet, the magnetic field gets _____.

The pushing and pulling effect of a magnet gets smaller as you get further away. We say that the magnetic field gets <u>weaker</u>.

■ Exploring a magnetic field

You can see the shape of the magnetic field around a **bar** magnet using tiny bits of iron. We call these iron **filings**.

The diagrams show you how to do this.

2 Write down the following sentences in the right order. (The first sentence is in the correct place.) Use the diagrams to help.

- Put a card on top of a bar magnet.

- Tap the card with your finger.

- Sprinkle iron filings on evenly.

- The iron filings now show you the magnetic field pattern of the magnet.

The lines that show you the shape of the magnetic field are called lines of magnetic **force**.

3 Which parts of the bar magnet do all the lines of magnetic force come out from (or go in to)?

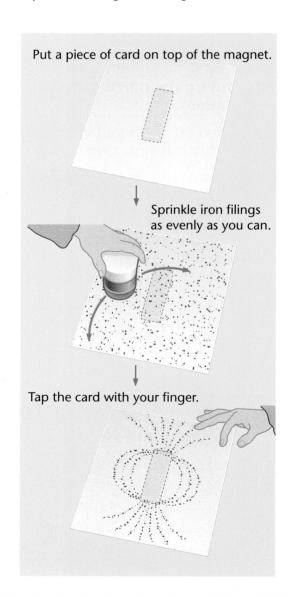

Put a piece of card on top of the magnet.

Sprinkle iron filings as evenly as you can.

Tap the card with your finger.

Another way of exploring a magnetic field

You can also find the shape of a magnetic field using a small magnetic **compass**. The diagrams show you how to do this.

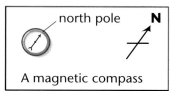

north pole

A magnetic compass

N **1** Put a compass anywhere in a magnetic field. Put a dot at each end of the compass needle.

N **2** Move the compass so that its south pole is where the north pole was before. Add a dot.

N **3** Keep on moving the compass in the same way. Add a dot each time.

4 Keep on until you get back to the magnet or come to the edge of the paper. Do the same thing again lots of times, starting off with the compass in a different place each time.

Join the dots to get lines of magnetic force. The arrows show which way the **north** pole of a compass points.

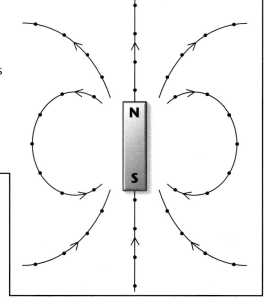

4 (a) What are the lines of the magnetic field pattern called?

(b) What do the arrows on the lines show?

WHAT YOU SHOULD KNOW (Copy and complete using the **key words**)

Magnetic fields

The area around a magnet is called a magnetic _____.

You can explore a magnetic field using iron _____ or a small magnetic _____.

The lines on a magnetic field are called lines of magnetic _____.

The arrows show the direction that the _____ pole of a compass needle will point.

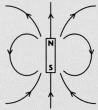

The magnetic field around a _____ magnet.

3.6 Using an electric current to make a magnet

You can get a safe electric current using a cell or a battery of cells. But cells soon run out of energy.

A low voltage power supply is often better. It will give you a safe electric current for as long as you want.

1 Look at the diagram. Then copy and complete the following.

To get a current from a low voltage power supply you must:

■ switch it _____;

■ connect the terminals to a _____ circuit.

A bulb uses an electric current to produce light. You can also use an electric current to make a magnet.

This red light tells you the power supply is switched on.

The two terminals of the power supply are connected to a complete circuit.

■ Making a magnet

You can make a magnet by sending an electric current through a **coil** of wire.

The magnet works better if you put an iron bar down the middle of the coil. This is called an iron **core**.

iron core

switched on

coil of wire

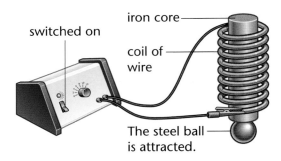

The steel ball is attracted.

2 How can you tell that the electric current makes the coil and core into a magnet?

3 (a) What happens to the steel ball when you switch the current off?

(b) Why does this happen?

This magnet needs an electric current to make it work, so we call it an **electromagnet**.

switched off

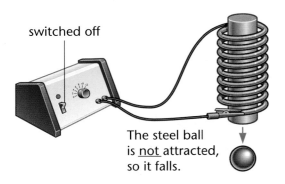

The steel ball is <u>not</u> attracted, so it falls.

■ Picking up paper clips

Suppose you drop a packet full of paper clips on to a fluffy rug. An easy way to pick up the paper clips is to use a magnet.

4 Look at the diagrams.

  (a) You can pick up the paper clips with a permanent magnet. What's the problem with this?

  (b) How would an electromagnet solve this problem?

A bar magnet stays magnetised all the time. We call it a <u>permanent</u> magnet.

You have to pick the paper clips off.

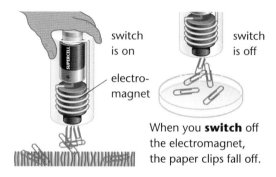

switch is on

switch is off

electro-magnet

When you **switch** off the electromagnet, the paper clips fall off.

■ The magnetic field around an electromagnet

You can find the shape of a magnetic field around an electromagnet with a small magnetic compass. Lines of magnetic force show you the shape of a magnetic field.

5 Copy and complete the sentences.

End X of the electromagnet is a magnetic _____ pole.
End Y of the electromagnet is a magnetic _____ pole.

The lines of magnetic _____ around the magnet show you the shape of its magnetic _____.

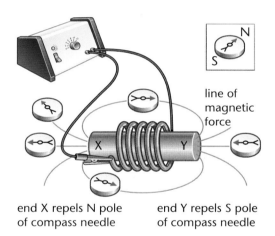

line of magnetic force

end X repels N pole of compass needle   end Y repels S pole of compass needle

*The magnetic field of an electromagnet is the same shape as the field of a **bar** magnet.*

WHAT YOU SHOULD KNOW (Copy and complete using the **key words**)

Using an electric current to make a magnet

You can make a magnet by passing an electric current through a _____ of wire. This is called an _____.

The magnet works better with an iron _____ inside the coil.

The magnetic field of the electromagnet is the same shape as for a _____ magnet.

An electromagnet is very useful because you can _____ it off.

3.7 Building up circuits

You can make a simple circuit by connecting a bulb to a cell.

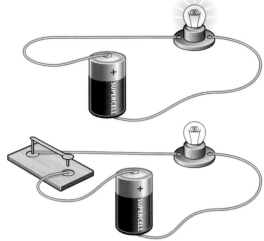

■ Adding a switch to the circuit

The circuit is more useful if you add a switch. The diagram shows how you can do this.

1 How does a switch turn a current off?

2 Copy and complete the sentences.

When the switch is on, an electric current flows through the switch <u>and then</u> through the _____.

We say that the switch and the bulb are connected in _____.

You can <u>break</u> the circuit with a switch. No current then flows.

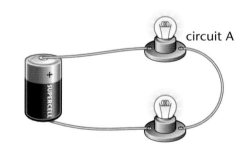

*When the circuit is complete, a current flows through the switch <u>and then</u> through the bulb. So we say that the switch and the bulb are connected in **series**.*

■ Adding another bulb to the circuit

You can add another bulb to the circuit in two different ways. The diagrams show you how.

3 Copy and complete the table.

	How the bulbs are connected	How bright the bulbs are
circuit A	in _____	
circuit B	in _____	

circuit A

A current flows through one bulb <u>and then</u> through the other.

circuit B

*Each bulb is connected <u>separately</u> to the cell. We say they are connected in **parallel**.*

■ An easy way to draw circuits

It's useful to have a quick and easy way to draw electrical circuits. You can do this using special **symbols** for bulbs, cells and switches. The diagram shows you how.

4 Copy and complete the table.

	Symbol
cell	
bulb	
switch (on)	
switch (off)	

When we draw circuits using symbols, we call them **circuit diagrams**.

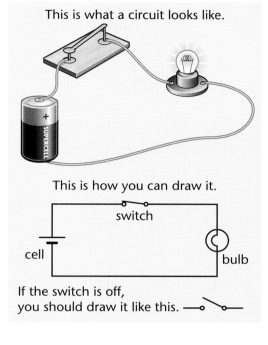

This is what a circuit looks like.

This is how you can draw it.

switch

cell   bulb

If the switch is off, you should draw it like this. ●─○ ╲○

■ Looking at circuit diagrams

The diagrams show three different circuits, X, Y and Z.

5 Copy each circuit diagram. Then copy and complete this sentence underneath <u>each</u> diagram (<u>three</u> times altogether).

The bulbs in this circuit are connected in _____ with each other.

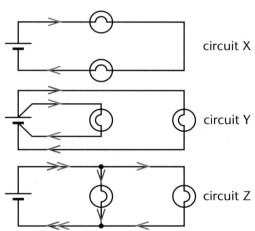

circuit X

circuit Y

circuit Z

WHAT YOU SHOULD KNOW (Copy and complete using the **key words**)

Building up circuits

If a current flows through one bulb <u>and then</u> through another, we say that the bulbs are connected in _____.

If two bulbs are connected <u>separately</u> to a cell or a power supply, we say that they are connected in _____.

We can draw circuits using special _____ for cells, bulbs, and switches.
Circuits drawn with these symbols are called _____ _____.

You should know the symbols for bulbs, cells and switches.

3.8 Using series and parallel circuits

Remember, it's useful to have switches in electrical circuits. You can then turn the current on or off.

Where you put a switch in a circuit depends on the kind of circuit it is in.

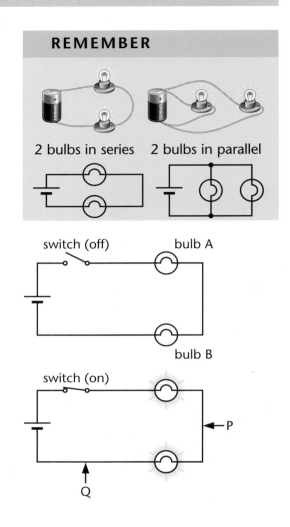

REMEMBER

2 bulbs in series   2 bulbs in parallel

■ Putting a switch in a series circuit

The diagram shows where you can put a switch into a series circuit.

1 Which bulb(s) does the switch turn on and off?

2 Copy and complete the sentence.

The switch is put in _____ with the two bulbs in the circuit.

You could also put the switch at position P or position Q in the circuit. It will still be in **series** with both bulbs.

3 Draw a circuit diagram with the switch (on) at position P.

If two bulbs are connected in series, the same switch turns **both** of them on or off.

■ What if one bulb breaks in a series circuit?

The diagram shows a circuit with two bulbs connected in series. Neither of the bulbs lights up.

4 (a) Why doesn't bulb A light up?

(b) Why doesn't bulb B light up?

The bulb with a broken filament is just like a **switch** which is off.

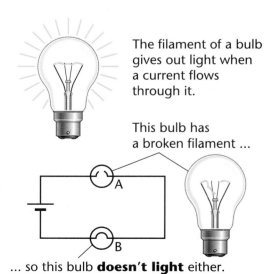

The filament of a bulb gives out light when a current flows through it.

This bulb has a broken filament ...

... so this bulb **doesn't light** either.

■ Putting a switch in a parallel circuit

circuit X

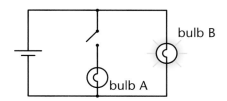

In a parallel circuit, you need to decide whether you want the switch to switch off both bulbs or just one bulb. Then you can choose the right place to put the switch.

5 Look at circuit X. Which bulb does the switch turn on and off?

6 Draw a circuit diagram which has a switch for turning bulb B on and off, but <u>not</u> bulb A.

circuit Y

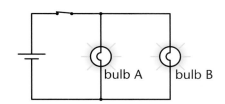

Circuit Y shows where a pupil puts a switch.

7 The pupil breaks the circuit with this switch. What happens to each bulb?

■ What if one bulb breaks in a parallel circuit?

The diagram shows what happens if the filament of one of the bulbs breaks.

The filament of this bulb is broken...

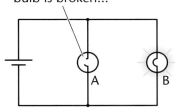

...but this bulb **stays on**.

8 (a) Why doesn't bulb A light up?

(b) Why does bulb B stay lit?

WHAT YOU SHOULD KNOW (Copy and complete using the **key words**)

Using series and parallel circuits

You must put a switch in _____ with the bulb that you want to switch on or off.

If two bulbs are in series, the switch will turn off the current to _____ of them.

A bulb with a broken filament is just like a _____ which is off.

In a series circuit, if one bulb breaks, the other bulb _____ _____.

In a parallel circuit, if one bulb breaks, the other bulb _____ _____.

3.9 Using electromagnets

You can **switch** electromagnets on and off. This makes them useful for many jobs. For example, you can use an electromagnet to make a relay or a buzzer.

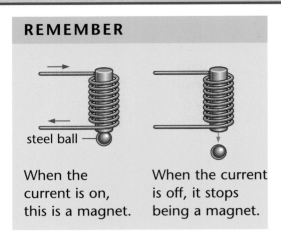
■ A relay

A relay is a special kind of switch. It uses a small current to switch on a much larger current.

The diagram shows a simple relay. The current to the relay is switched off.

1 Copy and complete the sentences.

The springy _____ strip is not touching the contact.
So there is a _____ in the circuit that goes to the powerful lamp.
This means that the lamp is switched _____.

The next diagram shows what happens when you switch on the current to the relay.

2 Write down the following sentences in the right order. (The first sentence is in the correct place.) Use the diagram to help.

- You press the switch.
- The electromagnet becomes magnetised.
- The springy steel strip touches the contact.
- A large current flows through the lamp.
- A small current flows through the coil.
- The electromagnet pulls the steel strip down.

When you stop pressing the switch, the springy steel strip moves away from the contact. This switches the powerful lamp off.

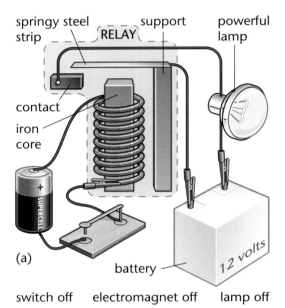

springy steel strip RELAY support powerful lamp

contact

iron core

(a) battery 12 volts

switch off   electromagnet off   lamp off

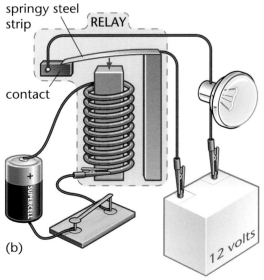

springy steel strip RELAY

contact

(b) 12 volts

switch on   electromagnet on   lamp on

A buzzer

The diagram shows how you can make a buzzer.

When you press the switch, the springy steel strip vibrates. This makes a buzzing sound.

3 What is used for the core of the electromagnet in the buzzer?

The diagrams show how the buzzer works.

4 Copy and complete the flow chart.

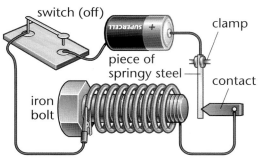

How to make a buzzer.

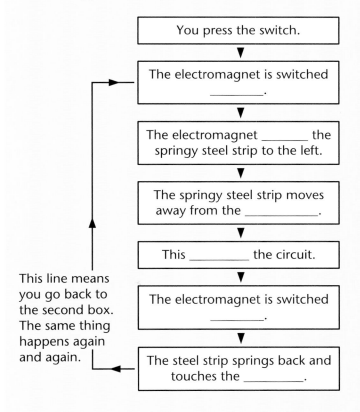

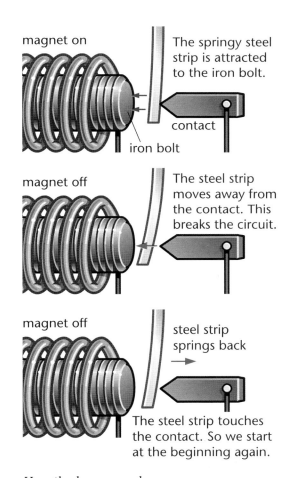

How the buzzer works.

WHAT YOU SHOULD KNOW (Copy and complete using the **key words**)

Using electromagnets

Electromagnets are very useful because you can easily _____ them on and off.

You may be given a diagram of something which uses an electromagnet.
You must be able to explain how it works, like you did with the relay and buzzer.
Electromagnets can do lots of different jobs, but they all work in the same way.

4.1 Switch on for energy

We need energy for many different things.

1 Look at the pictures. Then write down <u>four</u> things that we need energy for.

■ Getting the energy we need

We often get the energy we need from **electricity**.

Suppose you need some hot water to make a cup of coffee. All you have to do is put water into a kettle, plug it in and switch it on.

2 Look at the pictures again. Then copy and complete the table.

What we need energy for	What we can switch on to get it
to make something hot	■ kettle ■ _____
to make something move	■ _____ ■ _____
to produce sound	■ _____ ■ _____
to produce light	■ _____ ■ _____

■ Talking about energy

To make a light bulb work, we must supply it with electricity. We say that we <u>transfer</u> energy to the light bulb by electricity.

The bulb gives out light to its surroundings. We say that the bulb **transfers** energy to its surroundings by light.

drill   food mixer

We need energy to make things **move**.

light bulb   TV set

We need energy to produce light.

kettle   microwave oven

We need energy to make things hot.

cassette player   PA system

We need energy to produce sound.

We can get all these kinds of energy from electricity.

■ Describing energy transfers

You transfer energy to an electric kettle by electricity.

The electric kettle then transfers energy to the water inside it. This makes the water <u>hotter</u>. So we say that the electric kettle transfers energy to the water as **thermal** energy.

Here is a simple way to write down the energy transfers to and from the kettle:

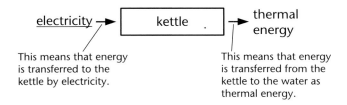

<u>electricity</u> → | kettle | → thermal energy

This means that energy is transferred to the kettle by electricity.

This means that energy is transferred from the kettle to the water as thermal energy.

3 Look at the pictures. Then copy and complete the following.

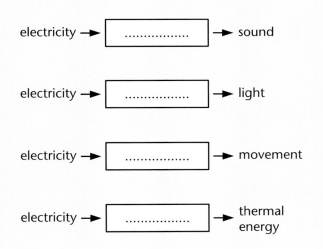

electricity → [.................] → sound

electricity → [.................] → light

electricity → [.................] → movement

electricity → [.................] → thermal energy

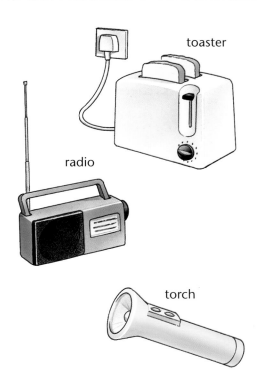

toaster

radio

torch

fan

We transfer energy to all these things by electricity. They then transfer energy to their surroundings.

WHAT YOU SHOULD KNOW (Copy and complete using the **key words**)

Switch on for energy

We need energy for light, for sound, to make things hot and to make things _____.

We transfer energy to a light bulb by _____. The bulb then _____ energy to its surroundings by light.

When something becomes hotter, it has more _____ energy.

4.2 Energy from fuels

We often get the energy we need from electricity.

We can also get energy by <u>burning</u> things. The things we burn to get energy are called **fuels**.

1 Look at the pictures. Then write down the names of <u>five</u> fuels.

People used to burn coal to heat their homes.

Today, most people prefer gas.

Car engines burn petrol or diesel fuel.

During a power cut you can burn a wax candle.

Many people burn gas for cooking.

In some parts of the world, most people burn wood for cooking.

■ What happens when fuels burn?

We burn fuels to <u>transfer</u> energy from them.

2 Look at the pictures. Then write down <u>three</u> reasons why we want to transfer energy from fuels.

Burning fuels always makes the things around them <u>hotter</u>. So we say that burning fuels transfers **thermal** energy to the surroundings.

3 Copy and complete the following.

We burn fuels to make things hotter.

We burn fuels to produce light.

We burn fuels to make things move.

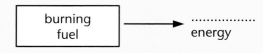

| burning fuel | → | .... energy |

Why fuels can transfer energy

When we burn a fuel, it transfers energy to its surroundings. So the fuel must <u>store</u> energy to start off with.

4 Look at the diagrams. Then copy and complete the sentences.

Fuels store energy in the chemical _____ that they are made of.
So we say that they store _____ energy.

*Fuels, like everything else, are made of chemical substances. The chemical substances in fuels store energy. So we say that fuels store **chemical** energy.*

stored chemical energy → | burning fuel | → thermal energy

What else do fuels need to burn?

Fuels by themselves won't burn. The diagrams show what else they need so that they can burn.

5 (a) What else do fuels need so they can burn?

(b) Where do they usually get this from?

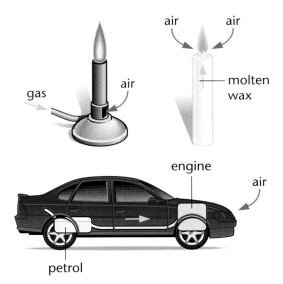

*Fuels won't burn without **oxygen** from the air.*

WHAT YOU SHOULD KNOW (Copy and complete using the **key words**)

Energy from fuels

We sometimes get the energy we need by burning _____.
The energy stored in fuels is called _____ energy.

When we burn fuels, energy is transferred to the surroundings as _____ energy.

For fuels to burn, _____ is also needed.

4.3 Using fuels to make electricity

Power stations burn mainly these fuels.

Electricity is very handy when we want to transfer energy.

But we don't find electricity just lying around ready for us to use. We have to <u>make</u> electricity. We say that electricity has to be **generated**. This happens at a power station.

To generate electricity, we need to have some energy to start off with. We say that we need an energy <u>source</u>.

Most electricity is generated using the energy from **fuels**.

1 Write down the names of the <u>three</u> main fuels that are burned in power stations.

Coal stores **chemical** energy.

The coal is burned.

■ What happens at a power station

The diagram shows how electricity is generated using the energy from coal.

2 Copy and complete the sentences.

The energy stored in coal is called _____ energy. Burning coal makes things hotter. So we say that _____ energy is transferred to the surroundings.

3 Copy and complete the energy flow diagram for a power station.

This transfers the stored energy as **thermal** energy.

chemical energy in fuel → | furnace and boiler | → thermal energy (in steam) → | .... | → movement (or kinetic) energy → | .... | → electricity

REMEMBER

We can take electricity to where we want it through wires.
Then we can transfer the energy to the surroundings the way we want to:
■ by light; ■ by sound;
■ as thermal energy; ■ as movement.

■ Nuclear power stations

Nuclear power stations use a fuel called <u>uranium</u>.

The box tells you about the differences between nuclear power stations and power stations that burn coal, gas or oil.

4 Write down <u>one</u> difference between nuclear fuel and fuels like coal, gas and oil.

5 (a) Why are nuclear reactors dangerous?

(b) How are workers in a nuclear power station protected from this danger?

Using nuclear fuel

You don't burn uranium. You put it into a nuclear reactor. It then splits up into other substances and transfers a lot of thermal energy to its surroundings. This energy is transferred to water to make steam.

Nuclear reactors give out very dangerous radiation. So thick walls are built round them to protect workers in a nuclear power station.

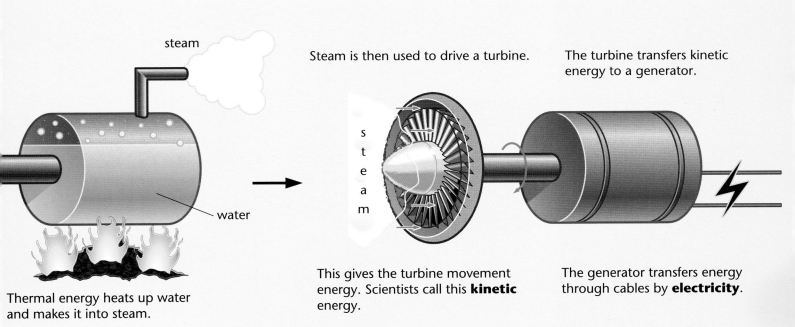

steam

Thermal energy heats up water and makes it into steam.

water

Steam is then used to drive a turbine.

steam

This gives the turbine movement energy. Scientists call this **kinetic** energy.

The turbine transfers kinetic energy to a generator.

The generator transfers energy through cables by **electricity**.

WHAT YOU SHOULD KNOW (Copy and complete using the **key words**)

Using fuels to make electricity

Electricity is _____ in power stations. The main energy sources used are all _____.

In a power station:

.... energy in fuel → | boiler and furnace | → .... energy (in steam) → | turbine | → movement (or ....) energy → | generator | → ....

241

4.4 Some other ways of generating electricity

To generate electricity we must first have energy of some other kind. We say that we need an energy **source**.

We often use <u>fuels</u> as our energy source.

One problem with fuels is that they produce harmful substances when they burn. We say they cause <u>pollution</u>.

The pictures on this page and the next show some <u>cleaner</u> energy sources we can use to generate electricity. But these energy sources still cause problems.

Power stations which burn fuels pollute the air with harmful gases.

■ Wind

We use the **wind** to generate some of our electricity.

You need <u>lots</u> of wind generators, usually on the tops of hills. Even then, the wind doesn't blow all the time.

1 (a) Write down <u>one</u> advantage of using wind generators rather than ordinary power stations.

(b) Write down <u>two</u> disadvantages of using wind generators.

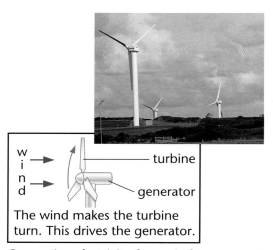

The wind makes the turbine turn. This drives the generator.

Generating electricity from wind.

■ Hydro-electricity

Hydro-electric power stations generate electricity using **water trapped behind dams**.

The water stores energy because it is high up. We can transfer this stored energy to a turbine by letting the water flow downhill.

2 What do we call the energy stored by things which are high up?

3 Copy and complete the energy transfer diagram for a hydro-electric power station.

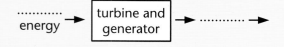

The water level behind the dam is high, so the water stores energy. We call this <u>potential</u> energy.

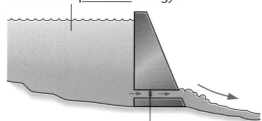

Water drives this turbine as it flows past, and the turbine drives a generator. The generator transfers energy through cables by electricity.

Producing hydro-electricity.

■ Waves

Energy from the **waves** could generate a lot of electricity.

4 The wave machines we have at the moment don't make very much electricity. Why not?

Water moves up and down inside the tube. This drives air through the turbine.

Small machines fastened to cliffs work all right. Nobody has built really big machines out at sea yet.

■ Tides

At the coast, the level of the sea gets higher twice every day. We say that there is a <u>high tide</u> twice a day.

The diagrams show how we can use the **tides** to generate electricity.

5 Copy and complete the sentences.

Water is trapped behind a _____ at high tide.

When the tide goes out, the water behind the barrage is _____ than the sea outside.
So the water stores _____ energy.

You can transfer this stored energy to a _____ as kinetic energy.
This then drives a generator.

6 Bird-lovers do <u>not</u> like tidal barrages. Why not?

When the tide goes out there is plenty of food in the mud for wading birds.

When the barrage is built the mud flats in the estuary are flooded all the time.

You can build a barrage across an estuary. This traps water when the tide comes in. When the tide goes out, the water is higher behind the barrage. So you can generate electricity just like you can with a dam. Lots of wading birds find food in the mud in estuaries. Their feeding ground will be flooded by building a barrage.

■ Energy from hot rocks

Deep down in the ground the rocks are hot. You can use the hot rocks to change water into steam. Then you can use the steam to generate electricity.

7 Why is the energy stored in hot rocks called <u>geothermal</u> energy?

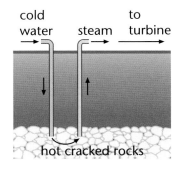

cold water   steam   to turbine

hot cracked rocks

The energy in hot rocks is called **geothermal** energy. 'Geo' means 'Earth'.

WHAT YOU SHOULD KNOW (Copy and complete using the **key words**)

Some other ways of generating electricity

To generate electricity we need an energy _____.

Some of the energy sources we can use, besides fuels, are: [name <u>five</u> other sources].

4.5 Thank you, Sun!

Lots of energy reaches us from the **Sun** every day. The diagrams show how we can transfer this energy.

1 Copy and complete the following.

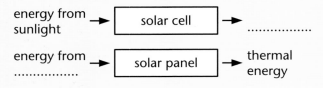

energy from sunlight → | solar cell | → ....

energy from .... → | solar panel | → thermal energy

The Sun is very important to us. Most of our other energy sources wouldn't be there without the Sun.

■ Wood

Trees need energy from the Sun to grow. This energy is stored in the wood the trees are made of.

Without the Sun there would be no wood.

2 Copy and complete the sentence.

Wood stores _____ energy.

All plants store energy as they grow. We say that they store energy in their <u>biomass</u>.

■ Fuels from the ground

Coal, gas and oil were all formed millions of years ago under the ground.

The diagrams show how coal was formed.

3 (a) What was coal made from?

(b) What other fuels were made in the same sort of way?

(c) Coal, gas and oil are called <u>fossil fuels</u>. Why is this?

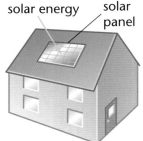

Energy is transferred to solar cells and solar panels by sunlight.

solar energy

Energy is transferred from solar <u>cells</u> by electricity. The cells are very expensive to make for the amount of electricity they produce.

array of solar cells

solar energy   solar panel

Energy is transferred from solar <u>panels</u> as thermal energy. This heats water to use in the house.

Energy is transferred to trees by sunlight. Trees store this energy as they grow. So trees are stores of chemical energy. You can burn the wood as a fuel.

How coal was formed.

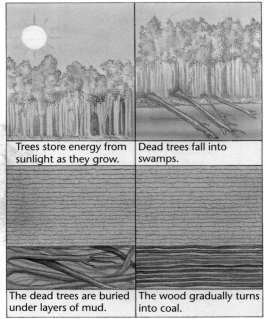

| Trees store energy from sunlight as they grow. | Dead trees fall into swamps. |
| The dead trees are buried under layers of mud. | The wood gradually turns into coal. |

Oil and gas are formed in the same way from plants and animals that lived in the sea. Because these fuels are made from the remains of dead plants and animals, they are called <u>fossil</u> fuels.

Wind, waves and rain

The Sun heats up some places on Earth more than others. This is what causes winds.

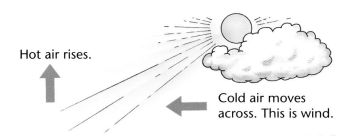

Hot air rises.

Cold air moves across. This is wind.

Energy from the Sun heats up the ground. This heats up the air above it.

Without the Sun there would also be no waves and no rain. The diagram on the right shows why.

4 Explain how energy from the Sun:

(a) produces wind;

(b) produces waves;

(c) keeps on filling up the water behind dams.

No Sun needed

The diagrams show a few energy sources that don't need the Sun.

5 (a) Which two energy sources depend on radioactive materials?

(b) Which energy source depends mainly on the Moon?

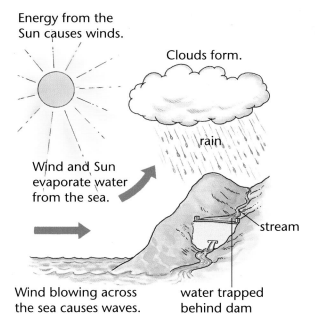

Energy from the Sun causes winds.

Clouds form.

rain

Wind and Sun evaporate water from the sea.

stream

Wind blowing across the sea causes waves.

water trapped behind dam

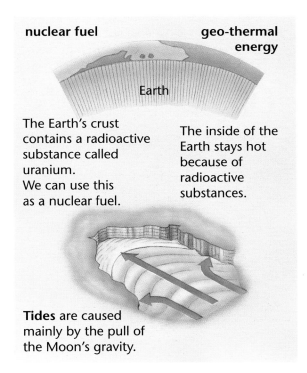

nuclear fuel

geo-thermal energy

Earth

The Earth's crust contains a radioactive substance called uranium. We can use this as a nuclear fuel.

The inside of the Earth stays hot because of radioactive substances.

Tides are caused mainly by the pull of the Moon's gravity.

WHAT YOU SHOULD KNOW (Copy and complete using the key words)

Thank you, Sun!

Most of our energy sources depend on energy from the _____.

Energy sources which don't depend on the Sun are: [name three]

4.6 Will our energy sources last for ever?

Some of our energy sources will last for billions of years. They won't run out because the energy is being **replaced** all the time.

We say that these energy sources are **renewable**.

1 Solar energy is a renewable energy source. Explain why.

The Sun will keep on shining for about 5 billion more years.

So solar energy is a <u>renewable</u> energy source.

■ Energy sources which will run out

Other energy sources <u>will</u> eventually get used up. Then there won't be any more energy from those energy sources.

So we say that these energy sources are **non-renewable**.

2 Oil is a non-renewable energy source. Explain why.

Oil takes millions of years to form. We get most of our oil and gas by drilling through the rocks under the North Sea.

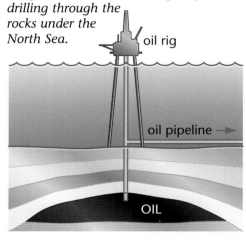

We have already used up a lot of the oil on Earth. Most of the rest will be used up during the next fifty years.

3 Most of the oil is burned as fuel. Write down <u>five</u> things that we use fuels from oil for.

4 What else is oil used for besides fuel?

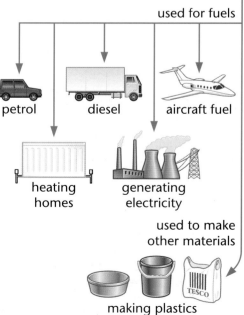

■ Renewable or non-renewable?

Solar energy is a renewable energy source.

Oil is a non-renewable energy source.

The pictures show most of our other energy sources.

5 For each picture:

(a) write down the name of the energy source;

(b) say whether it is renewable or non-renewable;

(c) give a reason for your answer.

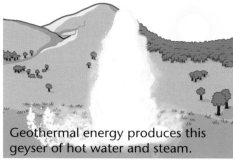
Geothermal energy produces this geyser of hot water and steam.

There is enough radioactive material left to keep the Earth hot inside for at least a billion years.

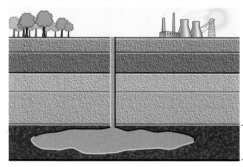

Coal was formed from trees which died millions of years ago.

coal seam

Winds are caused because the Sun heats up the Earth more in some places than in others.

Tides are caused mainly by the Moon as the Earth spins round each day.

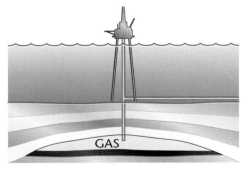
GAS

Gas was formed from the dead bodies of things which lived in the sea millions of years ago.

Waves are caused when the wind blows across the sea.

Waves can transfer energy to rocking 'ducks'.

WHAT YOU SHOULD KNOW (Copy and complete using the **key words**)

Will our energy sources last for ever?

Some energy sources will last for ever because the energy is constantly being _____. We say that these energy sources are _____.

Some energy sources will eventually run out. We say they are _____ energy sources.

You should know whether or not each energy source on these pages is renewable.

4.7 Energy for your body

We need sources of energy to keep power stations working to generate electricity for us.

Our bodies also need a constant supply of energy to keep them alive and well.

1 How does your body get the energy it needs?

2 (a) What <u>two</u> types of food supply most of your energy?

(b) Write down <u>three</u> examples of each of these types of food.

3 Copy and complete the sentence.

The food we eat stores _____ energy.

■ What does your body need energy for?

Your body is made of lots of tiny cells. All these cells need energy to work properly.

The photos show two other reasons why your body needs energy.

REMEMBER

Things which are hot have a lot of **thermal** energy.

Things which are moving have **kinetic** energy.

4 Look at the photographs.
Then copy and complete the following energy transfer diagrams.

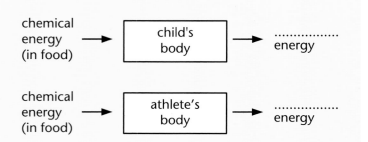

These foods give you most energy.

Carbohydrates   Fats

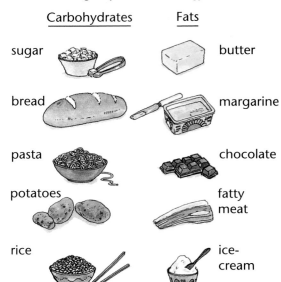

sugar   butter

bread   margarine

pasta   chocolate

potatoes   fatty meat

rice   ice-cream

Foods like these store **chemical** energy.

The girl needs energy to keep warm.

The athlete needs energy to move.

■ Energy for lifting things

Things which are high up store energy. So to lift things up you have to transfer energy to them.

You transfer more energy walking uphill than walking the same distance on the flat.

5 What do we call the energy something has because it is high up?

■ Who transfers most energy?

Three girls are all the same weight. The drawings show what each girl does one afternoon.

6 **(a)** Which girl transfers most energy? Which girl transfers least energy?

(b) Give reasons for your answers.

7 Copy and complete the following.

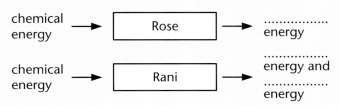

chemical energy → | Rose | → .... energy

chemical energy → | Rani | → .... energy and .... energy

■ A falling book

Daisy falls asleep. Her book falls to the floor.

8 Copy and complete the following.

_____ energy $\xrightarrow[\text{book falls}]{\text{as the}}$ _____ energy

Daisy lies on the sofa reading a book.

Rose walks along a flat beach.

Rani walks up a steep hill.

WHAT YOU SHOULD KNOW (Copy and complete using the **key words**)

Energy for your body

Your body gets the energy it needs from _____.

Food stores _____ energy. Your body transfers the energy from food mainly as _____ energy and _____ energy.

When you lift something up, you give it more _____ energy.

4.8 Ways of storing energy

Fuels and food store energy.

Many other things store energy too. The energy can be stored in several different ways.

■ Storing energy in chemicals

All the things in the diagram store **chemical** energy.

1 Copy and complete the table.

Chemical energy

What stores it	Is it a food or a fuel?	What you do to transfer the stored energy
potatoes	food	eat them
firewood		
petrol		
bread		

■ Storing energy by lifting things up

We can store energy in things by lifting them up. This stored energy is called <u>potential</u> energy.

Because we lift things up against the force of gravity, the energy they store is **gravitational** potential energy.

2 Look at the diagrams. Then write down <u>two</u> things that work by transferring gravitational potential energy.

3 Copy and complete the sentence.

You can transfer gravitational potential energy by letting the things that store it move _____.

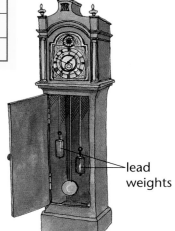

lead weights

When you wind up the clock, you lift up the weights. Energy stored by the weights is transferred to the clock as the weights slowly fall <u>down</u>.

Water is at a higher level behind the dam. In a hydro-electric power station, the energy stored by the water is transferred to generate electricity. This happens when the water flows <u>down</u>.

■ Another kind of potential energy

We can store energy in some things by changing their shape. We can do this by stretching them, bending them or squeezing them.

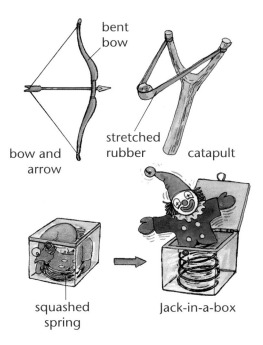

bent bow

bow and arrow · stretched rubber · catapult

squashed spring · Jack-in-a-box

4 Look at the diagrams. Then copy and complete the table.

What changes its shape	How do we change its shape?
bow	
catapult rubber	
spring	

The stored energy is called **elastic** potential energy.

5 Copy and complete the sentence.

A bent bow, stretched rubber and a squashed spring all store _____ potential energy.

■ A problem with electrical energy

Electricity is great for **transferring** energy. But you can't **store** electricity.

You have to store energy in some other way. Then you can transfer the stored energy to give you electricity when you need it.

This is what happens with batteries.

6 Copy and complete the sentences.

A battery stores _____ energy. It transfers energy by _____ when you connect it into a circuit.

Charging up batteries.

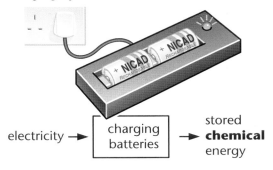

electricity → charging batteries → stored **chemical** energy

Using the batteries in a circuit.

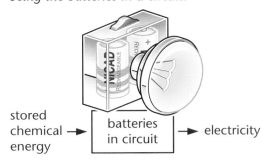

stored chemical energy → batteries in circuit → electricity

WHAT YOU SHOULD KNOW (Copy and complete using the **key words**)

Ways of storing energy

You can store energy as _____ energy, _____ potential energy or _____ potential energy.

Electricity is great for _____ energy, but you can't _____ electricity.

Batteries store energy as _____ energy.

4.9 You don't only get what you want

When it gets dark, we just switch on a light bulb.
The light bulb transfers energy to its
surroundings as light.
But not <u>all</u> the electrical energy that we transfer
to the bulb is transferred from the bulb as light.

1   Look at the diagram. Then copy and complete the
sentences.

Energy is transferred from a light bulb only partly
by _____.
Energy is transferred from a light bulb mostly as
_____ energy.

This light bulb transfers energy to its
surroundings :
- *partly by light;* ———
- *mostly as thermal energy.* ∿∿

■ All the energy goes somewhere

Whenever you transfer energy:

- only <u>part</u> of the energy is transferred in the
way you want;

- but **all** the energy is transferred in <u>some</u> way.

The diagram shows what happens to all the
energy transferred to a light bulb.

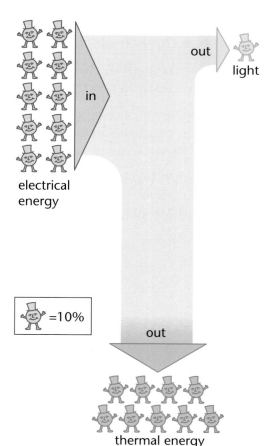

2   Copy and complete the following.

Energy transferred TO the light bulb	Energy transferred FROM the light bulb
electricity	light + thermal energy
100%	____% + ____%
	total: 100%

So:

      energy IN = energy OUT

■ Energy transfers in a car engine

The diagram shows what happens to the energy transferred from petrol in a car engine.

3 Copy and complete the following.

Energy IN to engine	Energy OUT from engine
from fuel	kinetic + thermal + sound energy energy
100%	_____% + _____% + _____%
	total: 100%

So:

energy IN = energy OUT

Whenever we transfer energy, some is always transferred in ways we don't really want. This energy isn't lost, but it is **wasted** as far as we are concerned.

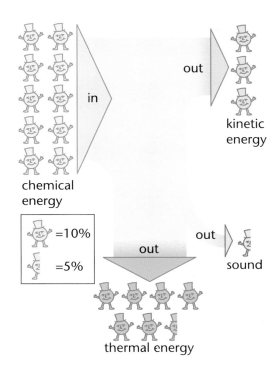

■ What a waste!

In fact, <u>all</u> the energy we transfer is wasted in the end. The diagram shows why.

4 What eventually happens to all the energy that a light bulb transfers to its surroundings?

Energy that is transferred to the surroundings gets very **spread out**. This means that it isn't easy to transfer it again.

Energy is transferred from a light bulb by light and as thermal energy. This energy is transferred to the things in the room. It makes everything in the room a tiny bit warmer.

WHAT YOU SHOULD KNOW (Copy and complete using the **key words**)

You don't only get what you want

When energy is transferred, it is _____ transferred in <u>some</u> way.
But some is transferred in ways we don't really want, so it is _____.

In the end, all transferred energy is wasted because it gets very _____ _____.

5.1 The Sun and the stars

People have watched the Sun for thousands of years. But it took a long time to work out what is really happening.

You can see the Sun move across the sky each day.

The diagram shows what you see on around March 21st each year. You see exactly the same thing on September 23rd each year too.

1 (a) Where does the Sun rise on these days?

(b) Where does the Sun set?

(c) When is the Sun at its highest point in the sky?

2 How many hours are there between sunrise and sunset on March 21st and September 23rd?

■ Watching the stars

People have also watched the stars for thousands of years.

A person in the UK looks towards the north on a clear night. The diagram shows the pattern of stars she can see in the sky. This pattern of stars is called the Plough.

3 (a) How do most of the stars seem to move?

(b) Which star doesn't seem to move?

WARNING!

You should never look directly at the Sun (not even if you're wearing sunglasses). You can badly damage your eyes.

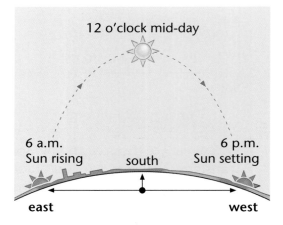

12 o'clock mid-day

6 a.m.
Sun rising

south

6 p.m.
Sun setting

east

west

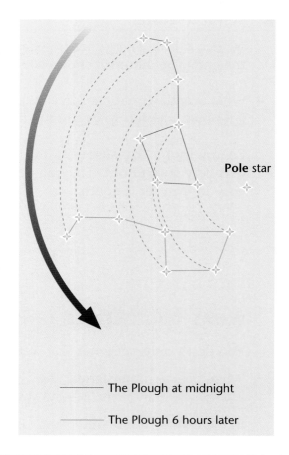

Pole star

——— The Plough at midnight

——— The Plough 6 hours later

■ Explaining what we can see

The Sun and the stars both seem to move across the sky. The diagrams show two ways of explaining this.

4 Copy and complete the sentences.

Either: The Sun and the stars move around the
_____ once every _____.

Or: The _____ and the stars stand still and the
_____ spins round once every _____.

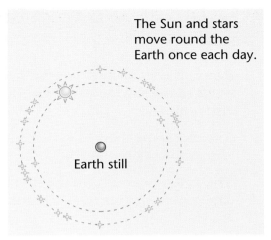

The Sun and stars move round the Earth once each day.

Earth still

What people used to think happens.

■ Which is the right explanation?

It doesn't seem like the Earth is spinning round all the time. So people used to think that the Sun and the stars move round the Earth.

Then some scientists started to say that the Earth is spinning. Most people found this very hard to believe.

5 Why did people find it hard to believe the Earth is spinning?

Today, most people do believe that the Earth **spins** round once a day. It doesn't seem like we're spinning because <u>everything</u> around us is also spinning at exactly the same speed.

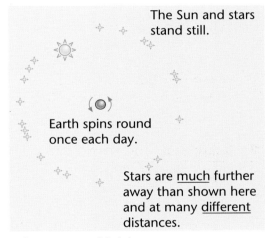

The Sun and stars stand still.

Earth spins round once each day.

Stars are <u>much</u> further away than shown here and at many <u>different</u> distances.

What we now think happens.

WHAT YOU SHOULD KNOW (Copy and complete using the **key words**)

The Sun and the stars

Every day the Sun seems to move across the sky from _____ to _____.

Every night the stars seem to go around the _____ star.

This is because the Earth _____ round once each day.

5.2 Why are the days longer in summer?

The Sun rises and sets every day. The Sun also stays in the sky longer in the summer than in the winter.

The diagrams show how the Sun seems to move across the sky in the UK.

The first diagram is for the middle of winter. The second diagram is for the middle of summer.

WARNING!

You should <u>never</u> look directly at the Sun. You can badly damage your eyes.

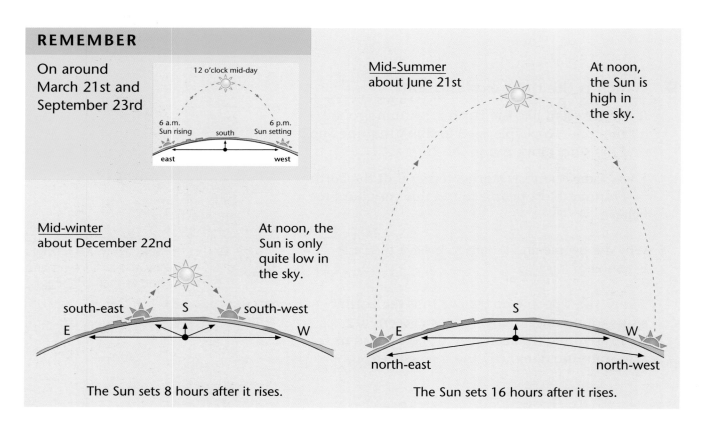

REMEMBER

On around March 21st and September 23rd

12 o'clock mid-day

6 a.m. Sun rising — south — 6 p.m. Sun setting

east — west

Mid-winter about December 22nd

At noon, the Sun is only quite low in the sky.

south-east — S — south-west

E — W

The Sun sets 8 hours after it rises.

Mid-Summer about June 21st

At noon, the Sun is high in the sky.

north-east — S — north-west

E — W

The Sun sets 16 hours after it rises.

1 Copy and complete the table.

Date	How high is the Sun at noon?	How many hours between sunrise and sunset?	What direction is sunrise?	What direction is sunset?
March 21st				
June 21st				
September 23rd				
December 22nd				

■ Explaining what we can see

The diagrams show why the days are **longer** in the summer than in the **winter**.

The Earth goes round the Sun once a **year**.

June ● ☀ ● December

The UK has:
- long days;
- short nights.

The UK has:
- short days;
- long nights.

North Pole

UK

South Pole

North Pole

UK

South Pole

The spinning Earth is **tilted**.

light from Sun

light from Sun

It is summer in the UK.

It is winter in the UK.

2 Copy and complete the sentences.

The Earth moves round the _____.
It does this once every _____.

The Earth also spins round once every _____.

But the Earth doesn't spin straight up.
The Earth is _____.

In June the north of the Earth is tilted _____ the Sun. The UK spends more time in the _____ than in the _____.
So it is summer in the UK.

In December the north of the Earth is tilted _____ the Sun. The UK spends more time in the _____ than in the _____.
So it is winter in the UK.

WHAT YOU SHOULD KNOW (Copy and complete using the **key words**)

Why are the days longer in summer?

The Earth moves around the Sun once each _____.

When it is summer in the UK, the north of the Earth is _____ towards the Sun.
This means that the days are _____ than the nights.

When the north of the Earth is tilted away from the Sun, it is _____ in the UK.
This means that the nights are _____ than the days.

5.3 Stars and planets

When you look at the sky at night, stars and planets look just the same as each other. They all look like tiny pin-pricks of light.

But if you look very carefully, you can spot the difference.

1 Look at the diagrams. How can you tell the difference between a planet and a star?

The word 'planet' means 'wanderer'. Stars stay in fixed places, but planets seem to wander about among the stars.

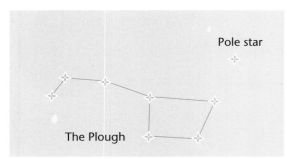

The Plough

Pole star

Stars stay in the same patterns. We call these constellations.

■ Looking through a telescope

If you look at stars and planets through a telescope, you can see another difference. The pictures show what this difference is.

2 (a) What difference can you see?

(b) How can you explain this difference?

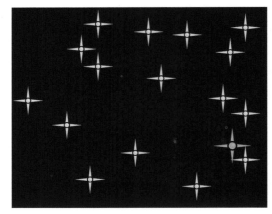

Part of the night sky.

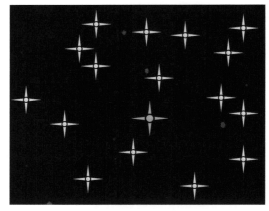

The __same__ part of the night sky a few weeks later. All the __stars__ are in the same places. But the __planet__ has moved.

 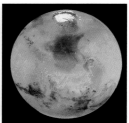

If you look at stars through a telescope, they still look exactly the same size. This is because they are so far away.

If you look at Mars through a telescope, it looks a lot bigger. This tells us that Mars isn't too far away from the Earth.

Stars

Stars are a <u>very</u> long way away. We can see them because they send out huge amounts of **light** energy, just like the **Sun**.

In fact, the Sun is a star. It is our nearest star.

Look at the diagram.

3 Which is the brightest star in the sky (not counting the Sun)?

4 How does Sirius compare with the Sun:

   (a) for size?

   (b) for the amount of light it sends out?

5 Why doesn't Sirius <u>look</u> as bright as the Sun?

Planets

Planets go round the Sun just like the Earth does. So the Earth is also a **planet**.

Planets are different from stars because they don't give out their own light.

6 Explain how we can see planets.

7 Why do planets seem to wander about among the stars?

> **REMEMBER**
>
> The Sun gives out huge amounts of light energy all the time.

Sirius is the brightest star in the sky. It is much bigger than the Sun and it sends out much more light. But it is a <u>lot</u> further away from Earth.

 Sirius

This diagram is <u>not</u> to scale.

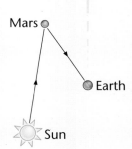

Mars

Earth

Sun

We see planets because they **reflect** light from the Sun. Planets, like the Earth, go round the Sun. So they seem to move among the stars.

WHAT YOU SHOULD KNOW (Copy and complete using the **key words**)

Stars and planets

All the stars except the _____ are a very long way away. Like the Sun, they give out their own _____.

The planets all go round the _____. They _____ light from the Sun.

The Earth is a _____.

5.4 The solar system

The planets look like stars, but they aren't stars. They don't give out their own light.

They also go round the Sun just like the Earth does. We say that they **orbit** the Sun.

We call the Sun and all its planets the **solar system**.

1 (a) Copy the table.

Planet	Average distance from Sun (millions of kilometres)
Mercury	58
Venus	108
Earth	150

(b) Then add the names of the other planets in order. Start with the planet nearest to the Sun.

(c) Next add the distance of each planet from the Sun.

■ How big are the planets?

The diagram below shows how big the planets are compared to each other and to the Sun.

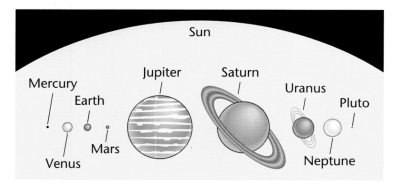

2 Write down the planets in order of size. Start with the biggest planet.

> Pluto has a very egg-shaped orbit. Usually it is a lot further away from the Sun than Neptune, but sometimes it is nearer.

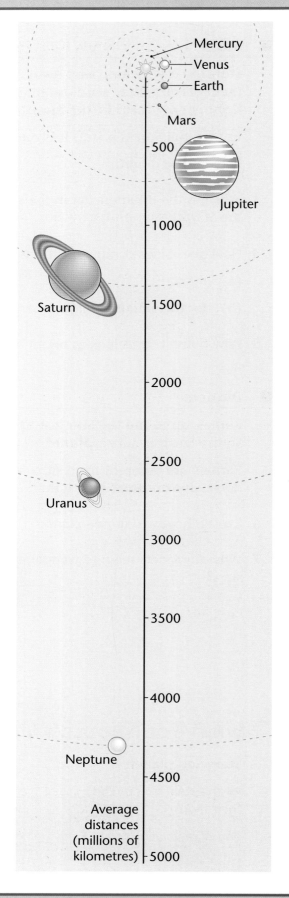

Average distances (millions of kilometres)

▪ Why do some planets look brighter than others?

You can sometimes see Mercury, Venus, Mars, Jupiter and Saturn without using a telescope. We say you can see them with your <u>naked eye</u>.

The main reason you can see these planets with your naked eye is because they are not too far away.

To see the other planets you need to use a telescope.

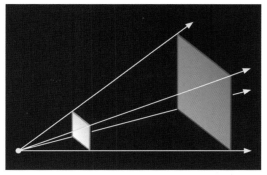

The further light travels, the more spread out it is. So it gets fainter and fainter.

3 You can't see Uranus, Neptune or Pluto with your naked eye. Why not?

4 Why is it difficult to see Pluto even with a telescope?

▪ Why does the same planet sometimes look brighter?

Mars looks much **brighter** at some times than it does at other times.

The diagrams show where Mars is when it looks bright and when it looks dim.

5 Where is Mars, in relation to Earth, when it looks bright?

6 Why does Mars look bright when it is in this position?

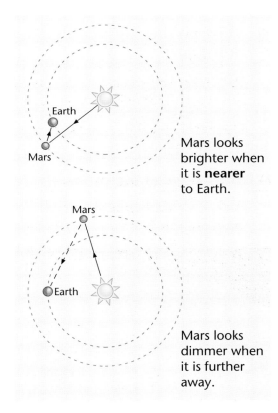

Mars looks brighter when it is **nearer** to Earth.

Mars looks dimmer when it is further away.

WHAT YOU SHOULD KNOW (Copy and complete using the **key words**)

The solar system

All the planets, including Earth, go round the Sun. We say they ＿＿＿＿＿＿ the Sun.

The Sun and all the planets make up the ＿＿＿＿＿ ＿＿＿＿＿.

We can see some planets more easily than others. This is mainly because they come ＿＿＿＿＿ to Earth. The nearer to Earth a planet is, the ＿＿＿＿＿ it looks.

5.5 Moons

The Earth moves in an orbit round the Sun.

The Moon moves in an orbit round the Earth.

The diagram shows the distances between the Sun, the Earth and the Moon.

1 (a) How far is the Earth from the Sun?

(b) How far is the Moon from the Earth?

(c) How many times further away from Earth is the Sun than the Moon?

■ Why do the Sun and the Moon look the same size?

The Sun is much bigger than the Moon. But from Earth they both look almost exactly the same size.

2 Why does the Moon look the same size as the Sun?

the setting Sun

the Moon in exactly the same direction at a different time

The Sun and the Moon look the same size.

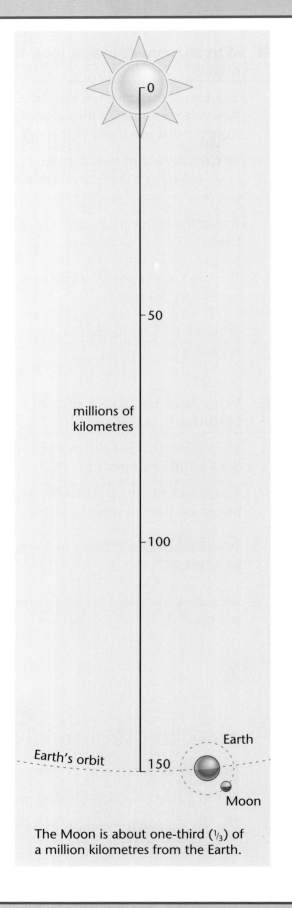

millions of kilometres

Earth's orbit

Earth

Moon

The Moon is about one-third (⅓) of a million kilometres from the Earth.

262

Other 'moons'

It isn't just the Earth that has a Moon. Most of the other **planets** have 'moons' too. The proper name for each of these 'moons' is a **satellite**.

Satellites of another planet were first discovered by Galileo about 400 years ago.

3 (a) Around which planet did Galileo discover satellites?

(b) How many satellites did Galileo discover orbiting this planet?

(c) How many satellites do we now think Jupiter has?

4 Sometimes you can only see <u>three</u> of Jupiter's four biggest satellites. Why do you think this is?

The telescope was invented in 1609. Galileo used a telescope to look at Jupiter.

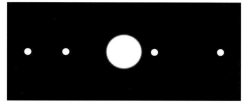

one night in 1610

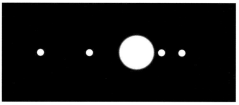

a few days later

12 more satellites of Jupiter were discovered later using more powerful telescopes.

Eclipses of the Moon

Sometimes the full Moon quickly goes dark. We call this an <u>eclipse</u> of the Moon. The diagrams show how this happens.

5 (a) Why can we normally see the Moon?

(b) Why is there sometimes an eclipse of the Moon?

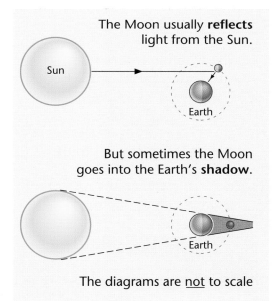

The Moon usually **reflects** light from the Sun.

But sometimes the Moon goes into the Earth's **shadow**.

The diagrams are <u>not</u> to scale

WHAT YOU SHOULD KNOW (Copy and complete using the **key words**)

Moons

The Moon is the Earth's _____.

Most of the other _____ also have satellites.

We can see the Moon because it _____ light from the Sun.

An eclipse of the Moon happens when the Moon moves into the Earth's _____.

5.6 Artificial satellites

The **Moon** is the Earth's satellite.

Satellites orbit most of the other planets in the solar system. These are called <u>natural</u> satellites.

We can also put **artificial** satellites into orbit around the Earth.

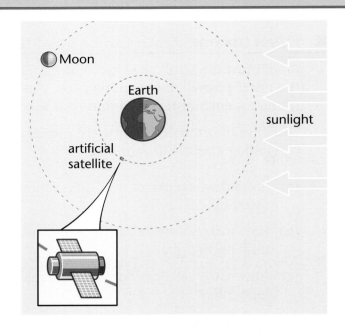

■ Using satellites to observe the stars

Astronomers often have problems trying to observe stars from Earth. The pictures show you why.

1 Why do astronomers have these problems?

Astronomers try to reduce their problems as much as they can.

2 Where on the Earth's surface can astronomers put their telescopes to do this? Give reasons for your answer.

The best place for observing stars is from <u>above</u> the Earth's atmosphere.

3 How can astronomers get their telescopes above the atmosphere?

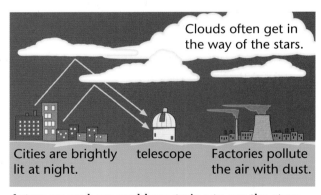

Astronomers have problems trying to see the stars.

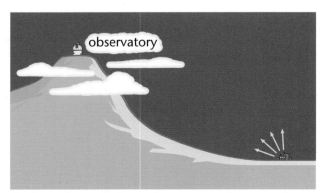

So they often put their telescopes on the tops of remote mountains.

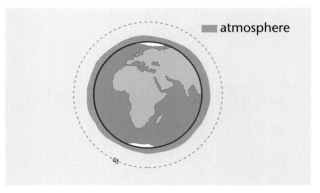

The best place to put a telescope is on a satellite.

Observing the Earth from a satellite

Satellites are useful for **observing** things on Earth as well as things in space. The pictures show some of the things on Earth we can observe from satellites.

4 Write down two of the things on Earth we can observe from satellites.

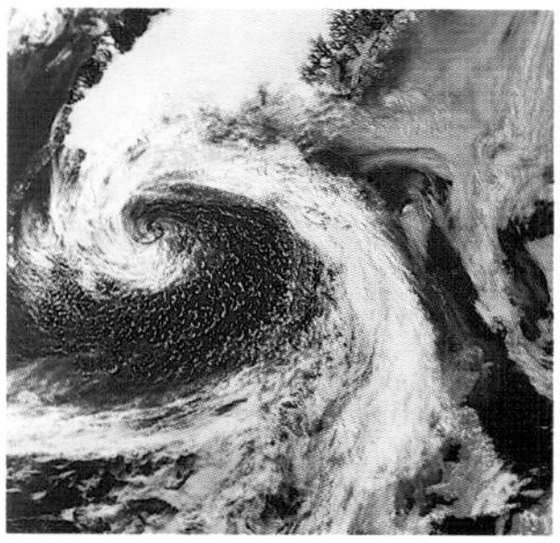

Satellite image of weather.

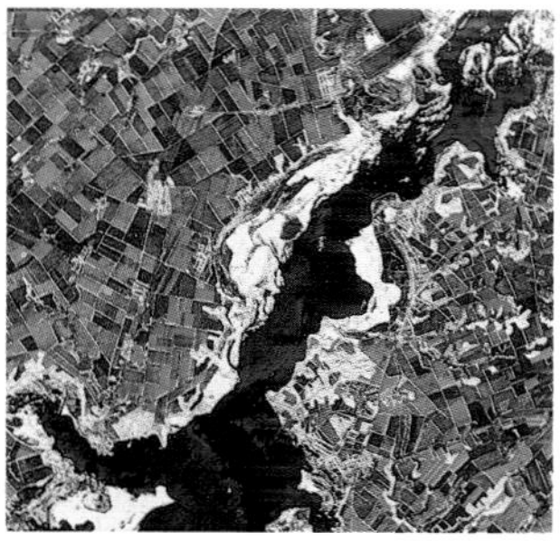

Satellite image of farm fields. You can see what crops are growing.

The orbit of an observation satellite

The diagram shows the kind of orbit that is often used for an observation satellite. This type of orbit is called a **polar** orbit.

5 Why is this type of orbit called a polar orbit?

As the satellite goes round its orbit, the Earth spins round underneath.

6 Look at the diagram. Then copy and complete the sentences.

The satellite takes __________ to make one orbit of the Earth. So it makes __________ orbits in a day.

The Earth spins round __________ ° each day.
So during one orbit of the satellite the Earth spins round __________ °.

During each 24-hour period, the satellite can observe everywhere on Earth.

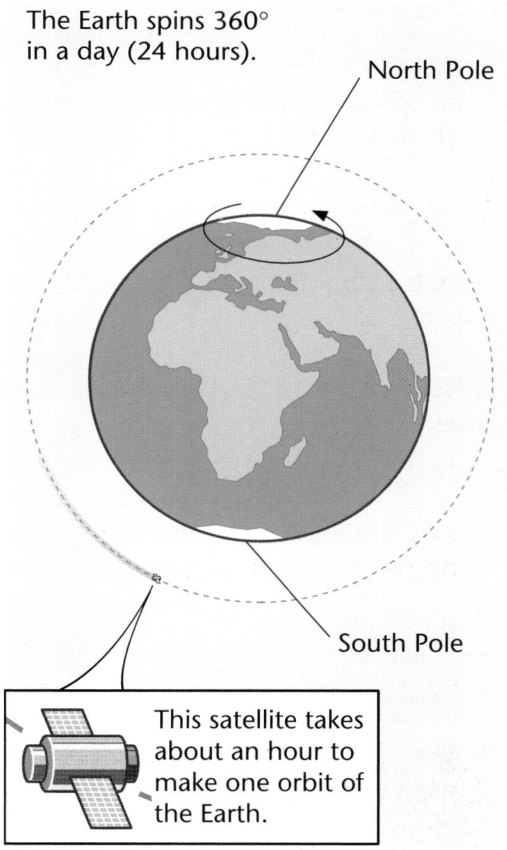

WHAT YOU SHOULD KNOW (Copy and complete using the **key words**)

Artificial satellites

The natural satellite of the Earth is called the ____________.

We can also put ____________ satellites into orbit around the Earth. These can be used by ____________ for observing stars.

Artificial satellites can also be used for ____________ things on Earth.
Observation satellites are usually put into a ____________ orbit.

5.7 What holds the solar system together?

The planets move in their orbits round the Sun, and satellites move in their orbits round planets.

All of this can happens because of the force of **gravity**.

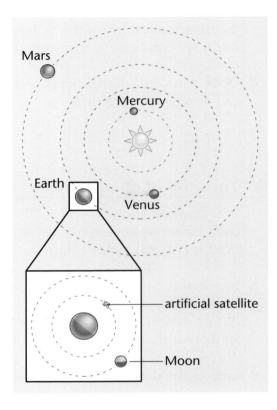

artificial satellite

Moon

■ What is gravity?

You have probably felt a <u>magnet</u> attracting a piece of steel or another magnet.

But <u>all</u> objects attract each other because of their **mass**. We say that there is a force of gravity between them.

The force of gravity between two small objects is very small. But if an object has a very large mass, it can produce large forces of gravity.

1 (a) Why is there only a very small force of gravity between two apples?

(b) Why is there a very much larger force of gravity between an apple and the Earth?

The force of gravity between two apples is <u>very</u> small. This is because they don't have much mass.

mass = 100g

The force of gravity between an apple and the Earth is quite large. This is because the Earth has a <u>very</u> large mass.

Earth

mass = billions of tonnes

■ Why do planets and satellites stay in their orbits?

Planets and satellites stay in their orbits because of two things:

- because they are **moving**;

- because of the force of gravity.

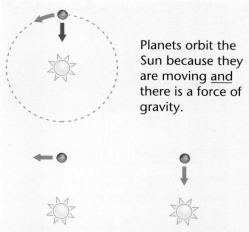

Planets orbit the Sun because they are moving <u>and</u> there is a force of gravity.

2 What would happen to planets and satellites if the force of gravity suddenly disappeared?

3 What would happen to planets and satellites if they suddenly stopped moving?

If there was no force of gravity, a moving planet would speed off into space.

If it wasn't moving, a planet would fall into the Sun.

■ Gravity acts both ways

The Earth attracts the Sun with exactly the **same** size of force as the Sun attracts the Earth.

But the Earth goes round the Sun because the Sun has a much bigger mass than the Earth.

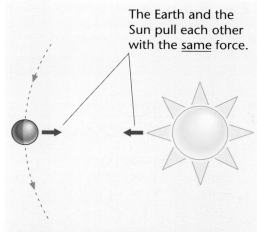

The Earth and the Sun pull each other with the <u>same</u> force.

4 Copy and complete the sentences.

A satellite attracts the Earth with the _____ force as the Earth attracts the _____.
But the satellite _____ the Earth because the Earth has a much bigger _____.

But the Earth **orbits** the Sun because the Earth has a much smaller mass.

WHAT YOU SHOULD KNOW (Copy and complete using the **key words**)

What holds the solar system together?

Planets and satellites stay in their orbits:

- because of the force of _____,

and ■ because they are _____.

The force of gravity between two objects is the _____ on both objects.
But a planet has a lot less _____ than the Sun, so the planet orbits the Sun.

A satellite has a lot less mass than a planet, so the satellite _____ the planet.

5.8 Why we need the Sun

light from the Sun

If the Sun stopped shining we would all soon die. All the other living things on Earth would die too.

Plants need **energy** from the Sun to make food. They use this food to grow.

■ Why do living things need the Sun?

Without the Sun, the Earth would be too cold for plants and animals to stay alive.

Even if they could keep warm, plants and animals couldn't live without the Sun. The diagram shows why.

Animals eat plants or other animals. They need the energy stored in this food to move and to grow.

1 Write down why plants need energy from the Sun.

2 A fox gets the energy it needs to move and to grow from the Sun. Explain how this happens.

Fossil fuels

Coal, gas and oil are fossil fuels. They were formed from the bodies of plants and animals which lived millions of years ago.

■ The Sun and other energy sources

Food isn't the only energy we get from the Sun.

We also depend on the Sun for most of the other energy we need at home, at work and for transport. Most of this other energy comes from burning coal, gas or oil.

3 How does the energy stored in coal, gas and oil depend on the Sun?

Energy from the Sun causes <u>all</u> our weather.

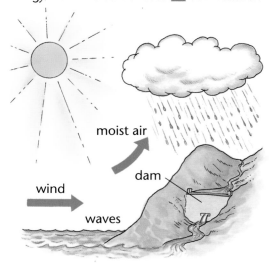

moist air

dam

wind

waves

We can also get energy from the wind, from the waves and from rainwater trapped behind dams.

4 Explain how these other energy sources also depend on the Sun.

You can read about these energy sources on pages 242–243.

How long has the Sun been shining?

Scientists think that the Sun formed about 5 **billion** years ago. Later, the Earth formed and then life on Earth began.

A billion years is a thousand million years.

5 Look at the time chart.

(a) About how long ago was the Earth formed?

(b) When did life on Earth begin?

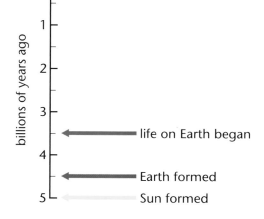

How can the Sun keep on shining for so long?

The Sun sends out HUGE amounts of energy all the time. Only a very small part of this energy reaches Earth.

The Sun isn't just burning like a fire. Otherwise it would have burnt out long ago. The Sun is more like a hydrogen bomb. This releases about a billion times more energy from each gram of hydrogen than just burning it.

Scientists think that the Sun has already used up about **half** of its nuclear fuel.

6 How many years more will the Sun keep on shining like it is now?

7 Copy and complete the sentences.

When the Sun stops shining like it is now:

■ it will first change into a _____ _____;

■ later it will become a _____ _____.

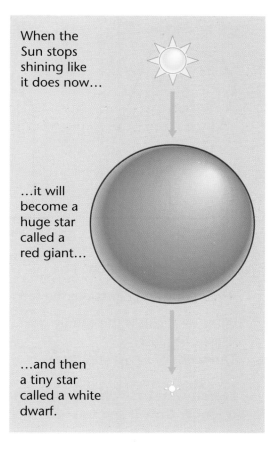

When the Sun stops shining like it does now…

…it will become a huge star called a red giant…

…and then a tiny star called a white dwarf.

WHAT YOU SHOULD KNOW (Copy and complete using the **key words**)

Why we need the Sun

All life on Earth depends on _____ from the Sun.

The Sun has been shining for about 5 _____ years. During that time it has used up about _____ of its nuclear fuel.

Investigating a candle burning

Science isn't just about what other people have found out. It is also about finding things out for yourself. As you read about how Seema investigates a candle burning you will learn about how to do science.

Seema puts a glass jar over a burning candle.

After six seconds the candle goes out.

Seema thinks that this happens because all the air has gone.

six seconds later

1 Read the "Information" box.

Then copy and complete the following.

After six seconds the candle goes _____.
This is because _____
(Answer as fully as you can.)

Seema wonders whether the candle will burn for a longer time if she uses a larger jar.

2 What do you think will happen?
Give a reason for your answer.

When you say what you think will happen you are making a **prediction**.

Scientists often make predictions.
Then they test their predictions to see if they are right.

INFORMATION

■ Candle wax needs oxygen to burn

■ About one-fifth of the air is oxygen

Planning an experiment

To find out whether her prediction is right, Seema must **plan** an experiment.

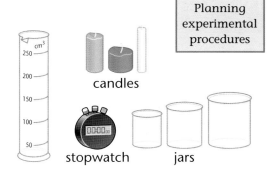

candles

stopwatch   jars

Planning
experimental
procedures

3 Copy the table. Then complete it to show what Seema should do. (Use the diagram of apparatus to help you.)

Problem	Plan
What can Seema use to measure the number of seconds the candle burns?	
What can Seema use to measure how much air there is in each jar (the volume)?	
How can Seema keep the experiment fair?	
The candle doesn't burn for very long.	
How can Seema get an accurate result for how long the candle burns?*	
How should Seema record her results?*	

[* Hint - if you don't know the answers to these questions look at the table below.]

Seema's results

The table shows the results of Seema's experiment.

Obtaining
evidence

Size of jar	How much air the jar holds (the volume in cm³)	How many seconds the candle burns				
		1st. try	2nd. try	3rd. try	4th. try	Average
small	250	2	3	3	4	3
medium	500	5	6	7	6	6
large	1000	13	12	14	13	13

What do Seema's results tell us?

Look carefully at Seema's results.

Analysing
evidence and
drawing
conclusions

4 Copy and complete the sentences.

When there is a bigger volume of air the candle burns for a _____ time.
This is/is not what I predicted would happen.

[continued on next page]

■ Drawing a graph

A graph is often a good way to show the measurements you make in an experiment.

You can then <u>see</u> what the results tell you.

5 Plot Seema's results on a graph.
[The diagram shows you how to do this.]
Then draw the graph line.

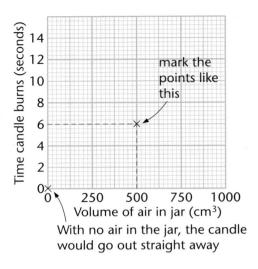

With no air in the jar, the candle would go out straight away

■ Testing another idea

Seema has another idea.

She predicts that a fat candle will go out quicker than a thin candle because it will use up the oxygen faster.

She tests her idea using a large jar.

Her results are underneath the diagram.

6 Was Seema's prediction correct?

7 Why do you think the results for the two candles are about the same?

8 Why does Seema get slightly different results even for the <u>same</u> candle?

Seema's teacher told her to cross out two of her measurements (the 0s and the 9s).

9 (a) Why should Seema should ignore these results?

(b) What do you think happened to give each of these bad measurements?

Time taken for candles to go out (s = seconds)	
Fat candle	Thin candle
24s	23s
25s	~~9s~~
24s	25s
~~0s~~	24s
25s	24s

Considering the strength of evidence

■ What else could Seema investigate?

Seema's teacher asks the class what other differences between candles might affect the results of the tests.

Here are some of the ideas the pupils come up with:

- ■ the height of the candles

- ■ the wicks of the candles
  (what they are made of, how fat they are)

- ■ the colour of the candles

Differences like these are often called **factors** or **variables**.

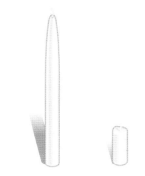

10 (a) For each of the factors mentioned by the pupils say whether or not you think it will affect how quickly the candle goes out under a jar.

(b) Give a reason for each of your answers.

11 You have made your predictions.
If you are a good scientist, what should you do next?

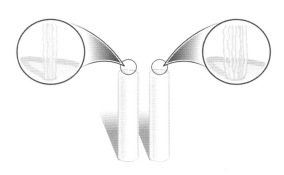

Biology

LIVING THINGS

1.1 What can living things do?

All animals:

- **move**, **sense** and **grow**;
- take in **food** and **oxygen**;
- get rid of **waste**;
- and **reproduce**.

We call these things **life processes**.

1.2 Is it alive?

Some things have never been **alive**. We say they are **non-living**.

They sometimes show some of the life processes, but they don't show **all** of them.

1.3 Plants are alive

Plants, like animals, are living things. They **reproduce**, **grow**, **sense**, **move** and get rid of **waste**.

Plants make their own food using **energy** from sunlight and **nutrients** from the soil and air.

Different parts of a plant do different **jobs**. The different parts of a plant are called **organs**.

1.4 Important parts of your body

The different parts of your body are called **organs**. These work together in groups called organ **systems**.

Some organ systems in your body

Organ system	What it does
circulatory system	carries food, oxygen and wastes around your body
nervous system	tells you what's happening around you
digestive system	breaks down food so your body can use it

1.5 The smallest parts of animals and plants

All plants and animals are made up of tiny bits called cells.

All cells have:

- a **nucleus** which controls what happens in a cell;
- **cytoplasm** where most chemical reactions take place;
- a **cell membrane** which controls what goes in and out of a cell.

Plant cells also have a cell **wall** and a **vacuole**.

1.6 Microbes

Microbes are everywhere. They are so **small** we need a **microscope** to see them.

Some microbes are useful. For example, they can break down **sewage**.

Other microbes are harmful. They can cause **diseases** in animals and plants.

1.7 Sorting out living things

We sort out all living things into **groups**. Plants and animals are two main groups.

Some living things, including **microbes**, do not fit into these two groups.

1.8 What is it?

We can use a key to sort living things into groups and then into **smaller groups**.

If we want to identify flowering plants, we use a **key** which is just for them.

1.9 Sorting animals with bones

Type of vertebrate	What it is like	Examples
fish	has scales, breathes through gills, lays eggs	cod
amphibians	moist smooth skin, lives on land and in water, lays eggs	frog
mammals	hair covers the body, young feed on mother's milk	cat
reptiles	dry scaly skin, eggs have tough leathery shell	crocodile
birds	have wings, feathers cover the body, eggs have hard shell	seagull

1.10 Sorting animals that don't have bones

Invertebrates
arthropods
have tentacles and stinging cells: **jellyfish**
flat body: **flatworms**
round body in segments: **true worms**
some hard parts: **molluscs**

2 pairs of antennae, 5 pairs of legs: **crustaceans**
3 pairs of legs, 2 pairs of wings: **insects**
no antennae, 4 pairs of legs: **spiders**
many segments with legs on: **many legs**

KEEPING HEALTHY

2.1 Healthy eating

To stay healthy we should eat plenty of **vitamins**, **minerals** and **fibre**, but not too much **fat**, **sugar** and **salt**.

2.2 Born to exercise

Your heart **pumps** blood to your lungs and to the rest of your body. The **ventricles** do this by squeezing the blood. Your heart has **valves** to stop the blood flowing the wrong way.

2.3 Where does blood travel?

Blood circulates around your body, from the heart to the **arteries** to the capillaries to the **veins** and back to the heart.

Blood carries substances such as glucose and **oxygen** to all the cells of your body.

2.4 Your lungs

When you **breathe**, you take air in and out of your **lungs**.

2.5 Breathing and asthma

In your lungs, **oxygen** passes into your blood and **carbon dioxide** passes into the air. We call this **gas exchange**.

2.6 How do we catch diseases?

Some bacteria and viruses can make you ill. Different microbes cause different diseases. For example, **bacteria** cause tuberculosis (TB) and Salmonella food poisoning. **Viruses** cause influenza and chicken pox.

2.7 Harmful chemicals

Drugs can **harm** you. They affect your mind and body. Even legal drugs like **tobacco** and **alcohol** are harmful.

2.8 Long-term effects of drugs

You can become addicted to **nicotine**, **alcohol** and other drugs.

Drugs can damage your body. For example, alcohol damages your **brain** and your **liver**.

2.9 Your skeleton

- supports your body;
- **protects** organs like your brain;

Your bones:

- give **muscles** something to pull on;
- have bone **marrow** to make new blood cells.

2.10 Joints

Bones let you move. Places where two bones meet are called **joints**.

When a muscle **contracts**, it pulls on a bone and moves it.

ENERGY FOR LIFE

3.1 Fuel and energy

We need energy for **moving**, **growing** and keeping warm. We get this energy from **food**. Food is our fuel.

3.2 Food for humans

Our food gives us the **energy** and the **materials** we need to live and to grow.
It comes from **plants** or from **animals** which ate plants.

3.3 What most of your food is made of

You need the right amount and types of food to stay **healthy**. You also need to drink **water**.

Most food is made of **carbohydrates**, **fats**, **proteins**, **fibre** and **water**.

Biology

3.4 What else must there be in your food?

To stay healthy you need to eat foods that contain **vitamins** and **minerals**.

3.6 Digesting your food

In your digestive system, you break large food molecules down into **smaller**, soluble molecules. This is called **digestion**.

These small molecules can pass into your **blood**. This is called **absorption**.

3.7 Absorbing and using food

Your **blood** transports small molecules of food to your **cells**.

Your cells use some of these molecules, together with oxygen, to give them **energy**. We say they **respire**.

Your food also gives cells the **materials** they need to grow.

3.8 How do plants grow?

Leaves use energy from sunlight, **carbon dioxide** and **water** to make food. We call this process **photosynthesis**.

Root **hairs** take in water.

3.9 Minerals for plant growth

Plants need chemical **elements** such as nitrogen for growth.
They take them in as **minerals** such as nitrates.

3.10 How plants take in what they need

Plant leaves make **food**.

Leaves which are **thin** and **flat** are best for taking in the sunlight and carbon dioxide the plant needs.

The water and minerals a plant needs go into it through its **root hairs**.
They pass in special tubes through the root and stem to the leaves.

Roots also **anchor** plants in the soil.

DEVELOPMENT AND CHANGE

4.1 Making babies

	Male	Female
Name of sex cells	**sperm**	**ova**
Where the sex cells are made	**testes**	**ovaries**
Opening to the outside	a tube through the **penis**	**vagina**
Other organs	**penis** to put the sperm in the woman's vagina	**uterus** where the baby grows

4.2 Growing and changing

4.3 Growing pains

Our bodies **change** as we grow. Sometimes it is hard to adapt to these changes.

Boys and girls start to make sex cells at the time of **puberty**. Girls start their **menstrual cycle** and they have a period (of bleeding) about once a month.

4.4 A new plant life

The life cycle of a flowering plant

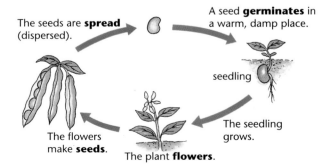

4.5 Looking at a plant's sex organs

Flower part	What it does
anther	Pollen is made here.
filament	This supports the anther.
style	This supports the stigma.
ovary	Ovules are made here.

4.6 Making seeds

Flowering plants grow from **seeds**. Seeds are made inside the flower.

First, **pollen** is moved from an anther to a stigma. We call this **pollination**.

The male sex cell nucleus inside the pollen joins with the female sex cell nucleus inside an **ovule**. We call this **fertilisation**.

4.7 What is a species?

A species is one kind of living thing. It differs from other **species** and it cannot **interbreed** with them to produce **fertile** offspring.

4.8 We are all different

Members of a species can be different in many ways. We say they **vary** or they have different **characteristics**. But they are still members of the same species if they can **interbreed**.

All humans belong to the same **species**.

SURVIVAL

5.1 Night-time and day-time animals

Some animals are **adapted** for feeding during the day. Other animals feed at night when it is **cool** and **dark**.

5.2 How animals and plants survive the winter

The different parts of the year are called **seasons**.

In winter there is less light and it can be very **cold**.

Plants and animals are **adapted** in different ways to survive the winter.

5.3 Town and country

The place where a plant or animal lives is called its **habitat**.
A habitat must provide **shelter** and a source of **food**.

5.4 Different bodies for different habitats

Different plants and animals live in different **habitats**.

Plants and animals have **features** which suit them to the places they live.
We say that they are **adapted** to their habitats.

5.5 Surviving in a garden

Plants and animals have **features** which suit them to the places they live and for what they do. We say they are **adapted** to their habitats and their way of life.

5.6 Feeding on plants

Food chains start with **green plants**. The rest of each food chain shows what **animals** eat.

In a food chain, A → B → C means that A is **eaten** by B and B is eaten by C. We use the arrows to show the direction in which the food goes.

5.7 Growing plants for food

Animals which eat the plants we grow for food are called **pests**.
We can kill them with chemicals called **pesticides**.

We can also encourage other animals to eat them. These animals are called **predators**.

5.8 Predators, harmful and useful

Animals which kill and eat other animals are called **predators**.
The animals they eat are called their **prey**.

If the number of prey increases, the number of predators also **increases**.
As the number of predators **increases**, the number of prey **decreases**.

5.9 Garden food webs

In a habitat, plants and animals belong to more than one **food chain**. This is why a **food web** is better for showing what eats what in a particular **habitat**.

5.10 Competition

Animals **compete** with each other for **space** and **food**.

Plants compete with each other for **space**, **water**, **nutrients** and **light**.

Chemistry

EVERYDAY MATERIALS

1.1 The right one for the job

The things that make a material good for a particular job, like how hard it is, are called its **properties**.

Materials you can see through are **transparent**.

All metals let electricity pass through them. They are called **conductors**.
Materials that do not let electricity through are called **insulators**.

1.2 Solid, liquid and gas

Solids have their own **shape**. Liquids and gases can **change** shape. A gas spreads out to fill any **space**.

Gases and liquids will **flow** through pipes.

Solids and liquids are heavier substances than gases; we say they are **denser**.

Something floats on a liquid if it is **less dense** than the liquid.
A lump of iron **sinks** in water because it is a denser substance than water.

1.3 Explaining the way things are

Solids, liquids and gases are all made of **particles**.

In solids, the particles hold each other together **strongly**. They cannot change places, but they can **vibrate**.

In liquids, the particles stay close together but they can **change places** with each other. This means you can **pour** a liquid.

In a gas there is a lot of space between the particles. The particles **move** around at high speed.

You can squash a gas because the particles are **far apart**. It is hard to squash a liquid or a solid because the particles are **close together**.

1.4 Mixing solids and liquids

When a solid dissolves in a liquid we get a **solution**.

Solids often dissolve better when the liquid is **hot**.

The liquid that the solid goes into is called the **solvent**. The solid is called the **solute**.

1.5 Melting and boiling

Many solids have a temperature at which they will melt. This is called the **melting point** of the solid.

The temperature at which a liquid boils is called the **boiling point**. As a liquid boils, it changes into a **gas**.

Boiling point temperatures are always **higher** than melting point temperatures.

1.6 Heat in, heat out

When we boil a liquid, we give **energy** to the liquid.

When an ice cube is melted we **transfer** heat to the ice.

The change from liquid to gas is called **evaporation**.

We can make evaporation happen more quickly by **heating** the liquid, and by **blowing** on the liquid surface.

Evaporation makes things get **colder**.

1.7 Other effects of heating and cooling

If a solid or liquid or gas is heated, it will **expand**.

If we cool the solid or liquid or gas down, then it will **contract**.

Expanding materials produce **push** forces. Contracting materials produce **pull** forces. These forces can be very large and cause lots of damage.

1.8 Looking at change

When things change, the **mass** doesn't change.

Changes which don't produce new substances are called **physical** changes.

Physical changes are usually easy to **reverse**.

CHEMICAL SUBSTANCES

2.1 Mixtures

Air and sea-water are both **mixtures**.

Air is a mixture of gases. The two main gases in the air are **nitrogen** and **oxygen**.

The sea is a mixture of water, **salt** and lots of other things.

Mixtures can be **split** up into their different parts. For example, you can get the salt out of sea-water by **evaporating** the water.

You can change the **amounts** of different things in a mixture.

2.2 Taking out the bits

Filter paper acts like a very fine **sieve**.

We can **separate** a mixture of liquid and particles of solid using filter paper. We call this **filtering**.

The **solid** left behind in the filter paper is called the residue.
The liquid that goes through the filter paper is called the **filtrate**.

2.3 Getting the liquid back

When a solid dissolves in water we can get the water back by **distillation**.

This works because the water **boils** and turns into steam.

The steam is cooled to **condense** it.

The **solids** get left behind.

The water we get at the end is pure. It is called **distilled** water.

2.4 What's in a colour?

Chromatography is used to split up a mixture of substances that **dissolve** in the same liquid.

The substances spread out through the paper at different **speeds**.

The pattern you get is called a **chromatogram**.

2.5 Elements

An element is a substance that cannot be split into anything **simpler**.

Water is made from the two elements **hydrogen** and **oxygen**.

Altogether there are about 90 **elements** that make up everything else.

2.6 Shorthand for elements

Every element has **a symbol**. This is either one or two letters.

The first letter is always a **capital** letter.

2.7 Putting elements together

A substance which contains more than one element joined together is called a **compound**.

Compounds have different **properties** from the elements they contain.

Many compounds are formed by **chemical** reactions between elements.

2.8 Useful compounds

The best-known liquid in the world is **water**.

A solid compound used to make lots of other substances is **salt**.

Air contains small amounts of **carbon** dioxide gas.

Water, salt and carbon dioxide are all very important **compounds**.

METALS AND NON-METALS

3.1 Looking at metals

Metals are normally shiny and **hard**.

Metals conduct **electricity**.

Metals **conduct** heat.

Iron and steel are **magnetic**.

3.2 Non-metals

Elements that are not metals are called **non-metals**.

Non-metals can be solids, liquids, or **gases**.

If we know an element is a **gas**, then we also know that it is a non-metal.

Most non-metals do not **conduct** heat or electricity.

Solid non-metals are **brittle**.

3.3 Where do we find non-metals?

Most of the things around us are made from **non-metals**.

Life is based on a non-metal called **carbon**.

We need to breathe a non-metal called **oxygen**.

Oxygen is also needed for **burning**.

Chemistry

3.4 Elements of Thar

An element is a metal or a **non-metal**.

Any element that is a **gas** must be a non-metal.

We can test to see if an element is a metal or a non-metal. Metals conduct **heat** and **electricity**. Most non-metals do not conduct.

3.5 Metals reacting with oxygen

A few metals burn very easily in the air's **oxygen**.

Metals that burn brightest are the most **reactive**.

3.6 Metals reacting with water

Some metals, for example magnesium:
- react slowly with **water**;
- react more quickly with **steam**.

A few metals react quickly with water, for example **sodium**.

All these reactions make a gas called **hydrogen**.

Some metals do not react with water, for example **copper**.

3.7 Which metals push hardest?

A reactive metal has a bigger **push** than a less reactive metal.

A reactive metal **displaces** a less reactive metal. We call this a **displacement** reaction.

3.8 Which metals react best?

We can list metals in order of **reactivity**. This list is called the **reactivity series**.

We put the most reactive at the **top** of the list, and the least reactive at the **bottom**.

The reactivity series is useful for **predicting** how a metal will react.

CHEMICAL REACTIONS

4.1 Chemical changes

Chemical changes always make **new** substances.

Life itself involves **chemical** changes.

4.2 Acids

Acids are substances that taste **sour**.

Some acids, like sulphuric acid, are dangerous because they are **corrosive**.

4.3 How can we tell whether something is an acid?

Indicators are special **dyes**. They change **colour** when mixed with acids or alkalis.

Universal indicator helps us to measure a substance's **pH**.

Alkalis have a pH of **more** than 7.

Acids have a pH of **less** than 7.

Neutral substances have a pH **equal** to 7.

4.4 Getting rid of an acid with an alkali

When we mix an alkali with an acid, we get a reaction called **neutralisation**.

Neutralisation reactions make two new substances, a **salt** and **water**.

To help us know when neutralisation is finished, we use an **indicator**.

4.5 Using neutralisation reactions

We can neutralise an acid with an **alkali**.

We can also neutralise acids by using sodium bicarbonate or a **carbonate**. These react with the acid to give the gas **carbon dioxide**.

4.6 How do metals react with acids?

Metals react with dilute acids to make a **salt**.

Metals push **hydrogen** out of the acid.

4.7 Salt and salts

We know sodium chloride as common **salt**.

There are **hundreds** of different salts.

A salt usually contains a metal element joined to at least one **non-metal**.

Salts form **crystals**.

Most salts dissolve in **water**.

4.8 Other kinds of chemical reaction

A chemical reaction that joins oxygen to a substance is called **oxidation**.

Examples of oxidation are rusting, respiration and **combustion**.

If we heat a substance and it breaks down, we call this thermal **decomposition**.

4.9 Writing down chemical reactions

Chemical reactions make **new** substances.

We show what happens in chemical reactions by writing word **equations**.

We put what we start with on the **left**.

We put what we finish with on the **right**.

EARTH CHEMISTRY

5.1 Different types of rock

Carbon dioxide gas is produced when acid is put on **calcium carbonate**.

Hot liquid rock deep in the Earth is called **magma**.

Rocks made from magma are called **igneous** rocks. Examples of igneous rocks are **basalt** and **granite**.

5.2 Getting new rocks from old

New rocks made under the sea from the bits that wear off the old rocks are called **sedimentary** rocks. These rocks are formed over **millions** of years.

Rocks can also be made from other rocks by **heat** and **pressure**. For example, heat changes limestone into **marble**, and pressure changes mudstone into **slate**.

Because marble and slate are both made by changing other rocks, we call them **metamorphic** rocks.

5.3 The rock cycle

The substances that make up rocks shift around over **millions** of years.
We call this shift the **rock cycle**.

5.4 How the weather breaks up rocks

When rocks are worn away by the weather, we call it **weathering**.

Changes in temperature from hot to cold can make cracks in the surface of a rock. Water gets in **cracks** and makes them bigger. This happens because water **expands** when it freezes.

Sometimes freezing water makes bits of rock **break** off.

Rocks and building materials are also worn away by bits blown in the **wind**. This is called **erosion**.

5.5 Acids in the air

Air contains **carbon dioxide**. This gas dissolves in rain water to make a very weak **acid**. This attacks building stone such as **limestone**. We call this process **chemical** weathering.

When we burn fuels we also make gases such as sulphur **dioxide** and nitrogen **oxides**. These are much more acidic and cause chemical weathering much **faster**.

5.6 Things we can do with limestone

Chemical **reactions** are used to make useful materials.

If you heat limestone, you make it into a useful substance called **calcium oxide**. The other name for calcium oxide is **quicklime**.

If you add water to quicklime, you get another useful substance called **slaked** lime. The other name for slaked lime is **calcium hydroxide**.

Lime water is made by dissolving calcium hydroxide in water. Lime water turns milky when **carbon dioxide** is bubbled through it.

5.7 Getting metals from rocks

You can find some metals like gold, silver and copper as lumps in the ground. These are called **native** metals.

Most metals come from rocks called **ores**.

Iron ore contains oxygen joined with **iron**.

We get the iron from the ore by taking away the **oxygen**. This is done by heating it in a **blast** furnace.

We have to use electricity to extract **aluminium** from aluminium oxide. This process is called **electrolysis**.

5.8 A problem with metals

Rusting is a chemical **reaction**.

Iron only rusts when in both air and water **together**.

Metals such as bronze do not rust. But they do **corrode**.

Polluted air causes much faster corrosion of **metals**.

5.9 Why do we keep on polluting the air?

Something that we can burn easily and safely is called a **fuel**. When fuels burn, they release **energy**.

Car engines make harmful gases called **nitrogen oxides**.

Power stations produce some sulphur **dioxide**. This makes **acid rain**.

Physics

FORCES

1.1 How to make things move

To start something moving, to speed it up or to change its direction, you must make a **force** act on it. This force must be in the same **direction** as you want the thing to move.

If you want to slow something down, the force must be in the **opposite** direction to the way it is moving.

1.2 Why do things slow down?

Moving things slow down because of **friction** forces. Friction forces act in the **opposite** direction to the way an object is moving.

There is friction between things which **slide** over each other.

There is also friction when things move through the air. This is called air resistance or **drag**.

1.3 How to reduce friction

You can reduce sliding friction between hubs and spindles:

■ by using **smooth** surfaces;
■ by using ball **bearings**;
■ by lubricating moving parts with **oil**.

You can reduce air resistance by giving things a **streamlined** shape.

1.4 Making good use of friction

Between tyres and the road there must be a lot of **friction**.
If there isn't, the tyre might **skid**.

You slow down cars and bicycles by using the **brakes**. These use **sliding** friction to slow the wheels down.

A parachute uses **air resistance** to slow the parachutist down.

1.5 Balanced forces

A force doesn't always change the way something moves.
This is because the force may be **balanced** by another force.

To change the way something moves, you need an **unbalanced** force.

1.6 How hard is it pressing?

If you spread out a force over a big area, it will only produce a small **pressure**.

To get a big pressure, you must make a force act on a small **area**.

1.7 Using forces to make things turn

Forces can make things turn around a **pivot** point.

If a force makes something turn clockwise, the opposite force will make it turn **anti-clockwise**.

If a clockwise turning force is the same as an anti-clockwise turning force, the forces **balance**.

1.8 How fast is it moving?

The distance something travels in a certain time is called its **speed**.

You can work out speed like this: speed = **distance** travelled ÷ **time** taken

Many things don't move at the same speed all the time. So the speed we work out is their **average** speed.

1.9 Working out the pressure

The pressure of a force depends on the **area** it acts on.

Forces are measured in **newtons** (N for short).

You can work out pressure like this: pressure = **force** ÷ area

LIGHT AND SOUND

2.1 How you see things

You can only see when there is some **light**.
The things you see either give out light or **reflect** light into your eyes.

Light travels in **straight lines**. So it can't go round **corners**.

When light can't pass through something, it makes a **shadow**.

2.2 Reflecting light

We can see some things because they give out **light**. We can see other things because they **reflect** light into our eyes.

Most things reflect light in all **directions**.

Shiny surfaces, such as mirrors, reflect light at the same **angle** as the light strikes them.

2.3 Using mirrors

When light is reflected from a mirror, angles X and Y are **equal**.

2.4 Colours of the rainbow

Light from the Sun is **white**.

When white light is split up by drops of rain, we get a **rainbow**.

We can split up white light into colours using a **prism** made of clear plastic.
We call the colours a **spectrum**.

We can also make coloured light from white light by using **filters**.
Filters let some colours pass through but **absorb** other colours.

2.5 Why do things look coloured?

Things look coloured in white light because they **reflect** some colours of light but **absorb** other colours.

White things and grey things don't look coloured because they reflect the same amount of **all** the colours of the spectrum.

Things which reflect hardly any light at all look **black**.

2.6 Comparing light and sound

We see when **light** enters our eyes. We hear when **sound** enters our ears.

Light travels **faster** than sound through the air.

The further light and sound travel, the **fainter** they get.

Light, but not sound, can travel through **empty space**.

Light can be different **colours**. Sounds can have a **different pitch**.

2.7 Making and hearing sounds

Sounds are made when things **vibrate**.
These vibrations then travel through the **air** to your ears.

Sounds can also travel through **solids** and **liquids**.

When sounds enter your ear, they strike your **eardrum** and make it vibrate.

2.8 Different sounds

Sounds can be different in two ways:
- one sound can be **louder** than another;
- the sounds can have a different **pitch**.

Loud sounds are caused by large **vibrations**. We say that these vibrations have a big **amplitude**.

The pitch of a sound depends on **how many** vibrations there are each second. This is called the **frequency** of the sound.

A frequency of 200 **hertz** (Hz for short) means 200 vibrations each second.

2.9 How to bend light

Light bends when it passes across the **boundary** between two different substances.
We say that the light is **refracted**.

A line at 90° to a boundary is called a **normal**.

When light passes from glass or water into air, it is refracted **away from** the normal.

When light passes from air into glass or water, it is refracted **towards** the normal.

When light crosses a boundary at **right angles**, it is not refracted.

ELECTRICITY

3.1 Making electricity by rubbing

If you rub an object with a different material, it becomes **charged** with electricity. The electrical charge stays where it is, so we call it **static** electricity.

A charged object will **attract** other things such as bits of dust or paper.

Physics

3.2 Two sorts of charges

Electrical charges can be **positive** (+) or **negative** (–).

A positive charge and a negative charge **attract** each other.

Two charges that are the same **repel** each other.

3.3 Electric currents

You can get a safe electric current from a **cell**.

Two or more cells joined together is called a **battery**.

A current will only flow if there is a **complete** circuit of **conductors**.

To stop a current flowing you must make a **break** in the circuit. You usually do this using a **switch**.

3.4 Other things that attract and repel

Some rocks attract things made of **iron** or steel. We say that the rocks are **magnetised**.

If a magnetised rock or a magnet is free to move, one end will point **north** and the other end will point south. The ends of a magnet are called the **poles**.

The north pole of one magnet will **attract** the south pole of another magnet.
Two poles that are the same **repel** each other.

3.5 Magnetic fields

The area around a magnet is called a magnetic **field**.

You can explore a magnetic field using iron **filings** or a small magnetic **compass**.

The lines on a magnetic field are called lines of magnetic **force**.

The arrows show the direction that the **north** pole of a compass needle will point.

The magnetic field around a **bar** magnet.

3.6 Using an electric current to make a magnet

You can make a magnet by passing an electric current through a **coil** of wire.
This is called an **electromagnet**.
The magnet works better with an iron **core** inside the coil.

The magnetic field of the electromagnet is the same shape as for a **bar** magnet.

An electromagnet is very useful because you can **switch** it off.

3.7 Building up circuits

If a current flows through one bulb and then through another, we say that the bulbs are connected in **series**.

If two bulbs are connected separately to a cell or a power supply, we say that they are connected in **parallel**.

We can draw circuits using special **symbols** for cells, bulbs, and switches.
Circuits drawn with these symbols are called **circuit diagrams**.

3.8 Using series and parallel circuits

You must put a switch in **series** with the bulb that you want to switch on or off.
If two bulbs are in series, the switch will turn off the current to **both** of them.

A bulb with a broken filament is just like a **switch** which is off.
In a series circuit, if one bulb breaks, the other bulb **doesn't light**.
In a parallel circuit, if one bulb breaks, the other bulb **stays on**.

3.9 Using electromagnets

Electromagnets are very useful because you can easily **switch** them on and off.

ENERGY

4.1 Switch on for energy

We need energy for light, for sound, to make things hot and to make things **move**.

We transfer energy to a light bulb by **electricity**. The bulb then **transfers** energy to its surroundings by light.

When something becomes hotter, it has more **thermal** energy.

4.2 Energy from fuels

We sometimes get the energy we need by burning **fuels**.
The energy stored in fuels is called **chemical** energy.

When we burn fuels, energy is transferred to the surroundings as **thermal** energy.
For fuels to burn, **oxygen** is also needed.

4.3 Using fuels to make electricity

Electricity is **generated** in power stations. The main energy sources used are all **fuels**.

In a power station:

4.4 Some other ways of generating electricity

To generate electricity we need an energy **source**.

Some of the energy sources we can use, besides fuels, are **wind**, **water trapped behind dams**, **waves**, **tides**, **potential** and **geo-thermal** energy.

4.5 Thank you, Sun!

Most of our energy sources depend on energy from the **Sun**.

Energy sources which don't depend on the Sun are **nuclear fuel**, **tides** and **geo-thermal energy**.

4.6 Will our energy sources last for ever?

Some energy sources will last for ever because the energy is constantly being **replaced**. We say that these energy sources are **renewable**.

Some energy sources will eventually run out. We say they are **non-renewable** energy sources.

4.7 Energy for your body

Your body gets the energy it needs from **foods**.

Food stores **chemical** energy. Your body transfers the energy from food mainly as **thermal** energy and **kinetic** energy.

When you lift something up, you give it more **potential** energy.

4.8 Ways of storing energy

You can store energy as **chemical** energy, **gravitational** potential energy or **elastic** potential energy.

Electricity is great for **transferring** energy, but you can't **store** electricity.
Batteries store energy as **chemical** energy.

4.9 You don't only get what you want

When energy is transferred, it is **all** transferred in some way.
But some is transferred in ways we don't really want, so it is **wasted**.

In the end, all transferred energy is wasted because it gets very **spread out**.

THE EARTH AND BEYOND

5.1 The Sun and the stars

Every day the Sun seems to move across the sky from **east** to **west**.
Every night the stars seem to go around the **Pole** star.
This is because the Earth **spins** round once each day.

5.2 Why are the days longer in summer?

The Earth moves around the Sun once each **year**.

When it is summer in the UK, the north of the Earth is **tilted** towards the Sun.
This means that the days are **longer** than the nights.

When the north of the Earth is tilted away from the Sun, it is **winter** in the UK.
This means that the nights are **longer** than the days.

5.3 Stars and planets

All the stars except the **Sun** are a very long way away. Like the Sun, they give out their own **light**.

The planets all go round the **Sun**. They **reflect** light from the Sun. The Earth is a **planet**.

5.4 The solar system

All the planets, including Earth, go round the Sun. We say they **orbit** the Sun.

The Sun and all the planets make up the **solar system**.

We can see some planets more easily than others. This is mainly because they come **nearer** to Earth. The nearer to Earth a planet is, the **brighter** it looks.

285

Physics

5.5 Moons

The Moon is the Earth's **satellite**.
Most of the other **planets** also have satellites.

We can see the Moon because it **reflects** light from the Sun.

An eclipse of the Moon happens when the Moon moves into the Earth's **shadow**.

5.6 Artificial satellites

The natural satellite of the Earth is called the **Moon**.

We can also put **artificial** satellites into orbit around the Earth. These can be used by **astronomers** for observing stars.

Artificial satellites can also be used for **observing** things on Earth.
Observation satellites are usually put into a **polar** orbit.

5.7 What holds the solar system together?

Planets and satellites stay in their orbits:
- because of the force of **gravity**,
and - because they are **moving**.

The force of gravity between two objects is the **same** on both objects.
But a planet has a lot less **mass** than the Sun, so the planet orbits the Sun.
A satellite has a lot less mass than a planet, so the satellite **orbits** the planet.

5.8 Why we need the Sun

All life on Earth depends on **energy** from the Sun.

The Sun has been shining for about 5 **billion** years. During that time it has used up about **half** of its nuclear fuel.

Glossary/index

A few words that occur very often such as <u>force</u>, <u>energy</u>, <u>animal</u>, <u>plant</u>, <u>electricity</u>, <u>chemical</u> and <u>reaction</u> are not included. Some of these words are the headings of the 15 topics in the book. Words in *italics* appear elsewhere in the glossary.

A

absorb, absorption: 1. when something 'soaks up' light rather than reflecting it or letting it pass through   207–209

2. when living cells or blood take in *dissolved* food or oxygen   53–54, 56, 60

acid rain: rain that is *acidic* because it has *sulphur dioxide* or *nitrogen oxides* dissolved in it   155, 181

acids, acidic: *solutions* that react with many *metals* to produce *hydrogen*, and that react with *alkalis* to produce *salts*   146, 148–157, 172–173

adapted, adaptation: when plants or animals have *characteristics* or *features* that make them suitable for where they live   79–80, 84, 86–87

addiction: when a person can't do without a *drug*   36–37

adolescent: a person who is no longer a child, but not yet an adult   65

air: a *mixture* of *gases*, mainly *nitrogen* and *oxygen*, that surrounds us   114, 135

air pollution: harmful *gases* such as *sulphur dioxide* or *nitrogen oxides* in the *air*   172–173, 180–181

air resistance: the *friction* force on something moving through *air*; also called <u>drag</u>   185, 187–188, 191

air sacs: small, roundish spaces at the ends of the air tubes in the *lungs*   28, 31

alcohol: a chemical that is used as a *drug*   34, 36–37

alkalis: the opposite of *acids*; they react with acids to produce *salts*   150–155

aluminium: a *metal* that you get from its *ore* using electricity   177

amino acids: *carbon compounds* that *proteins* are built from   52, 54

amplitude: the size of the *vibrations* that produce sound; a large amplitude produces a loud sound   214

anther: part of a flower that makes *pollen*   70–73

anti-clockwise: the opposite of *clockwise*

anus: the opening at the end of the *digestive system*   8, 51, 53

arteries: tubes that carry blood away from the *heart*   9, 26–27

asthma: a *disorder* of the tubes to the *lungs* that makes it difficult to *breathe*   30–31

atria: the two upper chambers of the *heart*; one is called an <u>atrium</u>   25

attract, attraction: things pulling towards each other   220–221, 225, 266–267

B

bacteria: *microbes* that are *cells* without a true *nucleus*; one is called a <u>bacterium</u>   12–13, 32–33

balanced forces: forces that are the same size but act in opposite directions   190–191

battery: made from two or more electrical *cells* joined together   222

boiling point: the temperature that a *liquid* boils at   106–107

brakes: used to slow down bicycles and other vehicles   188

breathe, breathing: taking *air* into and out of the *lungs*   2, 28–31, 55

burning: when substances react with *oxygen* and transfer *thermal energy*; also called <u>combustion</u>   127, 146, 160

Glossary/index

combustion: another word for *burning*

compass: see *magnetic compass*

compete, competition: when several plants and animals are all trying to get the same things **96–97**

complete circuit: an unbroken chain of things that *conduct* electricity **222–223, 230–233**

compound: a substance made from two, or more, different *elements* joined together **126–129, 163**

condense, condensation: changing a *gas* to a *liquid* by cooling it **113, 118–119**

conduct, conduction: an electric *current* or *thermal energy* passing through a material **99, 130**

conductor (electrical): a substance that an electric *current* will pass through **99, 130**

conductor (thermal): a substance that *thermal energy* will pass through **130**

contract: get shorter

1. muscles do this to produce movement **40**

2. *solids*, *liquids* and *gases* do this when they cool **110–111**

copper: a not very reactive *metal element* **139–141**

current: electric *charges* flowing round a *complete circuit* **222–223, 230–233**

cytoplasm: the contents of a living *cell* except for the *nucleus* **11**

D

decomposition: splitting up a *compound* into simpler substances **161**

dense: what we call a substance when a small *volume* of the substance has a large *mass* **101**

diaphragm: a sheet of muscle that separates your chest from your lower body **28–29**

diet: all the food that you eat **22–23, 46**

digest, digestion: the breakdown of large, *insoluble* food *molecules* into small *soluble* ones that can be *absorbed* **47, 52–54**

digestive juices: juices, made by *glands* in the *digestive system*, that help to *digest* food **50–51, 53**

digestive system: all the *organs* that are used to *digest* and *absorb* food **8, 50, 52–54**

disease, disorder: when some part of a plant or animal isn't working properly **13, 32–33, 90**

disperse, dispersal: the spreading of seeds away from the parent plant **69**

displace, displacement: when one *element* pushes another element out of one of its *compounds* **142–143**

dissolve: when a *solid* completely mixes with a *liquid* to make a clear *solution* **104–105, 146**

distil, distillation: *evaporating* a *liquid* and then *condensing* it again to get a pure liquid **113, 119**

drag: another word for *air resistance*

drug: a substance that can change the way your body works **34–37**

E

eardrum: the part of your ear that picks up sound *vibrations* from the air **213**

egest: get rid of undigested waste (*faeces*) through the *anus* **53**

egg cells, eggs: female *sex cells*; also called <u>ova</u> **62–67**

egg tube: the tube that carries an *egg cell* from an *ovary* to the *uterus* (*womb*) **62–63**

electromagnet: a magnet made by passing an electric *current* through a coil of wire; it usually has an *iron* core **228–229, 234–235**

element: a substance that can't be split up into anything simpler **122–125**

embryo: 1. a baby in the *uterus* (*womb*) before all its *organs* have started to grow **64**

2. the tiny plant inside a seed **68**

Glossary/index

enzymes: *protein* substances made in living *cells* which speed up chemical reactions without being used up   52

evaporate, evaporation: when a *liquid* changes into a *gas*   109, 115, 118–119

expand, expansion: when things get bigger, usually because they are hotter   110–111, 170

F

faeces: undigested waste that passes out through the *anus*   51, 53

fat: part of food that we use for energy   22–23, 43, 46, 52, 54

fatty acids: one of the building blocks of *fats*   52, 54

features: another word for *characteristics*   76, 84, 86

fertile: able to *reproduce*   75–76

fertilise, fertilisation: when a male *sex cell* joins with a female sex cell to start a new plant or animal   63–64, 67, 73

fertiliser: you add this to soil to provide the *minerals* that plants need to *grow*   58

fetus: a baby in the *uterus* (*womb*) whose *organs* are all growing   64

fibre: the indigestible part of our food; it is also called <u>roughage</u>   22, 46–47, 53

filament: the stalk of a *stamen* in a flower   70–71, 73

filter: 1. a thin piece of coloured glass or plastic that only some colours of light can pass through   207

2. separating a *liquid* (the *filtrate*) from a *solid* (the *residue*) by passing it through small holes, usually in paper   116–117

filtrate: the *liquid* that passes through a *filter*   116

food chain: a diagram showing what an animal eats and what eats it   88–89, 92, 94–95

food web: diagram that is made up of lots of *food chains* joined together to show what eats what in a *habitat*   94–95

fossil fuels: *fuels* formed from the remains of plants or animals that lived millions of years ago   244, 268

frequency: the number of *vibrations* in a second; this gives a sound its particular *pitch*   215

friction: a force that acts in the opposite direction that something moves or is trying to move; there are two types – *sliding friction* and *air resistance*   184–189, 191

fuels: substances that are *burned*; stored *chemical energy* is transferred as *thermal energy*   180, 238–241, 246, 250

fungi: 'plants' that do not make their own food but break down dead bodies of plants and animals and other waste; one is called a <u>fungus</u>   90

fungicide: a chemical that kills *fungi*   90

G

gas exchange: taking useful *gases* into a body or a living *cell* and getting rid of waste gases   31

gases: substances that spread out to fill all the space they can; they can be squeezed into a smaller *volume*   100, 102–103

generator: produces electricity when it is supplied with *kinetic energy*   241–243

geothermal energy: the energy stored by hot rocks in the Earth's crust   243, 245, 247

germinate: to begin to grow, for example a plant from the *embryo* in a seed   69

gills: *organs* for *gas exchange* in some animals that live in water   18–19

gland: an *organ* that produces a liquid, for example digestive glands produce *digestive juices* **50–51, 53**

glucose: a *carbohydrate* made of small, *soluble molecules*; a sugar **54–56**

glycerol: one of the building blocks of *fats* **52, 54**

granite: a type of *igneous* rock **164–165**

gravity: the force of *attraction* between two objects because of their *mass* **266–267**

grow, growth: to become bigger and more complicated **2, 4–6, 14, 42–43, 45–47, 55–59, 64–69, 83**

gullet: the tube that goes from the mouth to the *stomach*; another name for the <u>oesophagus</u> **8, 50–51, 53**

H

habitat: the place where a plant or animal lives **82–87, 89, 94**

heart: an *organ* that pumps blood **9, 24–28, 37, 46**

herbicide: weedkiller **90**

hertz (Hz): the unit of *frequency* **215**

hibernate: go into a deep sleep through the winter **80**

hydroelectricity: electricity produced by transferring the *potential energy* of water trapped behind a dam **242–243, 245, 250, 268**

hydrogen: 1. a *non-metal element*; it is a *gas* that *burns* to make *water* **123, 141, 156–157**

2. test for hydrogen **156**

I

igneous rocks: these are made when molten rock from inside the Earth cools down **165**

indicator: a substance that can change colour and tell you if a *solution* is an *acid* or an *alkali* **150–151**

infertile: not able to *reproduce* **75**

insoluble: opposite of *soluble*

insulator: a substance that will not let an electric *current* pass through it **99, 223**

interbreed: breed with each other **75–76**

invertebrates: animals that do <u>not</u> have a bony skeleton inside **16, 20–21**

iron: 1. a *metal element* that is attracted by a magnet; steel is made mainly from iron **130–131, 138–139, 177**

2. a *mineral nutrient* that is needed by living things **49, 54**

J

joints: the places where bones meet **40–41**

joule (J): the unit of energy **43**

K

kilojoule (kJ): **1000** *joules* **43**

kinetic energy: the energy something has because it is moving **240–243, 248–249**

L

large intestine: the wide part of the intestine between the *small intestine* and the *anus* **8, 50–51, 53**

life processes: what living things can do; for example move, *respire, sense, grow, reproduce,* feed and get rid of waste **3–6**

limestone: a *sedimentary rock* made from *calcium carbonate* **164, 167, 172–175**

limewater: a solution of *calcium hydroxide* in *water*; it goes cloudy when *carbon dioxide* passes through it **175**

lines of magnetic force: these tell you which way a *magnetic compass* will point in a *magnetic field* **226–227, 229**

liquids: substances that have a fixed *volume* but take the shape of the container that you put them in **100, 102–103**

liver: large *organ* in the lower part of your body, just under you *diaphragm* **34, 37, 51, 53**

loud: see *amplitude*

Glossary/index

lungs: the *organs* you use for *gas exchange* between your blood and the air 18, 24–25, 28–31, 34, 55

M

magnesium: a reactive *metal element* that *burns* brightly 127, 139–140, 146, 156

magnetic compass: a magnet that is free to pivot; it comes to rest with one end pointing to the north and the other end to the south 224–227

magnetic field: the area around a magnet where it *attracts* or *repels* 226–227, 229

marble: a *metamorphic rock* made from *limestone* 164, 167

mass: the amount of stuff in an object; it is measured in grams (g) or kilograms (kg) 112

melt: changing a *solid* into a *liquid* by heating it 106, 108

melting point: the temperature that a *solid melts* at 106

menstrual cycle: the monthly cycle of changes in the human female *reproductive system* 67

mercury: the only *metal element* that is a *liquid* at ordinary room temperatures 130

metals: substances that *conduct* electricity; they are usually shiny and often hard 130–131

metamorphic rocks: these are made when other rocks are changed by heat and pressure 167

microbes: microscopic living things; also called micro-organisms 12–13, 16, 20, 32–33

micro-organisms: another word for *microbes*

migrate, migration: what animals do when they move to different places in different *seasons* 80

minerals: simple chemicals that living things need in small amounts to stay healthy 7, 22, 48–49, 54, 58–61, 87, 97

mixture: different substances that are mixed, but not joined, together 114–115

molecule: the smallest part of a chemical *compound* 52–55

monthly period: the 'bleeding' when a woman loses the lining of her *uterus* (*womb*) about once a month 66–67

Moon: the natural *satellite* of the Earth 262–263

mucus: the sticky fluid made by some *cells*, for example in the air tubes of the *lungs* to trap *microbes* and dirt 34

N

native metals: these are found in the Earth's crust as the metal itself rather than as a *compound* 176

negative: one of the two types of electric *charge*; the other type is called *positive* 220–221

nervous system: the *organ system* that coordinates the activities of the body 8

neutral: what we call a *solution* that is neither an *acid* nor an *alkali* 150–151

neutralisation: a reaction between an *acid* and an *alkali* that produces a *neutral solution* of a *salt*. 152–155

newton (N): the unit that we use to measure forces 199

nicotine: a *drug* in tobacco to which people can become *addicted* 34, 36

nitrogen: the main *gas* in the *air*; it is unreactive 114, 135

nitrogen oxides: *acidic gases* produced when *fuels burn* 173, 180

nocturnal: the word used to describe animals that feed at night 78

non-metals: what we call *elements* that aren't *metals* 132–135

non-renewables: energy sources, such as *fossil fuels*, that are not replaced and will eventually be used up **246–247**

normal: a line drawn at **90°** (right angles) to a boundary **216–217**

north pole: the end of a magnet that points north when the magnet is free to move **224–227**

nuclear fuel: a fuel, such as uranium, used in nuclear power stations **241, 245**

nucleus: the part of a living *cell* that controls what happens in the cell **11**

nutrients: the foods needed by animals or the *minerals* needed by plants **7, 97**

O

oesophagus: another word for *gullet*

orbit: the path of a *satellite* as it moves round a *planet*, or of a planet as it moves round the *Sun* **260–267**

ores: *compounds* of *metal* and *non-metal elements* that are found in the Earth's crust **176–177**

organ: a structure in a plant or animal, for example *ovary*, *heart* or *lungs* **7–8, 34**

organ system: a group of *organs* that work together to do a particular job **9**

ova: another word for *egg cells*; one is called an ovum

ovaries: where *egg cells* (*ova*) are made **62, 65–67, 70–71**

ovules: these contain the female *sex cells* (*ova*) of a flowering plant **71, 73**

oxidation: reactions such as *burning* and *rusting*; *oxygen* joining with other *elements* to make *compounds* called *oxides* **160–161**

oxides: *compounds* of *oxygen* and other *elements* **127, 138–139**

oxygen: one of the two main *gases* in the *air*; it is needed for things to *burn* **114, 135, 138–139, 160–161**; it is also needed for *respiration* **2, 4–6, 9, 18, 26, 30–31, 55, 86**

P

pancreas: an *organ* that makes a digestive juice **51, 53**

parachute: this uses *air resistance* to slow down things falling through the air **188, 191**

parallel: a way of connecting bulbs etc. to a cell or a power supply so that a *current* can flow through them separately **230–233**

particles: the very small bits that everything is made from **102–103**

penis: an *organ* of the human male *reproductive system*; it is used to place *sperm* inside a woman's *vagina* **62–63, 66**

periscope: this is used to see over the top of things **205**

pesticide: a chemical that kills *pests* **90–91, 93**

pests: animals that are a nuisance to us, such as those that eat our plants **90–92, 94–95**

pH: a scale of numbers that tells you how strong an *acid* or an *alkali* is **151**

photosynthesis: the process in which plants use light energy to make *glucose* from *carbon dioxide* and *water* **57**

physical change: a change such as *melting* or *dissolving* that doesn't produce new substances; it is usually easy to reverse **112–113**

pitch: one of the ways that sounds are different from each other; a squeak has a higher pitch than a growl **211, 215**

planets: very large objects, including the Earth, that move in *orbits* around the *Sun* **258–261, 263, 266–267**

pollen: contains the male *sex cell* of a flowering plant **71–73**

pollen sacs: the parts on an *anther* where pollen is made **71**

pollinate, pollination: the transfer of *pollen* from an *anther* of a flower to a *stigma* of a flower of the same *species* **72–73**

Glossary/index

positive: one of the two types of electric *charge*; the other type is called *negative* **220–221**

potassium: a *metal element* that has *properties* and *compounds* similar to *sodium* **150, 153**

potential energy: the energy that is stored in something because it is high up (gravitational) or because it is bent or stretched (elastic) **242–243, 249–251**

predator: an animal that kills and eats other animals (its *prey*) **87, 91–93**

pressure: how much force there is on a certain area **192–193, 198–199**

prey: an animal that is killed and eaten by another animal (its *predator*) **87, 92–93**

prism: a triangular block of clear glass or plastic **206**

properties: what a material is like, for example whether it *burns* or *conducts* electricity **98–101**

protein: the part of food needed for *growth* and repair **43, 46–47, 52, 56, 59**

puberty: when boys and girls first start to release *sex cells* so that they are able to *reproduce* **66–67**

pulse: the stretching of an *artery* each time your *heart* beats **27**

R

rainbow: a *spectrum* of the colours in sunlight made by raindrops **206**

ray: a narrow beam of light **203**

reactivity series: a list of *metals* in order of how quickly they react with *oxygen*, *water* or *acids* **144–145**

recovery time: the time it takes for your *pulse* to go back to normal after exercise **27**

rectum: the last part of your *large intestine* **8, 51, 53**

reflect, reflection: light, or sound, bouncing off whatever it strikes **200–205, 208–209**

refract, refraction: light bending when it passes from one substance into another **216–217**

relax (muscle): become longer and thinner; the opposite of *contract* **40**

relay: a *switch* that works using an *electromagnet* **234**

renewables: energy sources that are constantly replaced and won't get used up **246–247**

repel: when things push each other away **220–221, 224–225**

reproduce, reproduction: when living things produce young of the same kind as themselves **3–7, 12, 14, 62, 70**

reproductive system: the *organs* in plants or animals that are used for *reproduction* **62–63, 70–71**

residue: the bits of *solid* that are trapped by a *filter* **116**

respire, respiration: the reaction between food and *oxygen* in living things; the reaction releases energy and produces *carbon dioxide* **55, 160**

rock cycle: the way that the material that rocks are made from is constantly moved around and changed **168–169**

root hairs: plant roots *absorb water* and *minerals* mainly through these **56, 60–61**

roughage: another word for *fibre*

rusting: *iron* joining with *oxygen* to produce iron oxide **160, 178–179**

S

saliva: a digestive juice made by the *salivary glands* **50, 53**

salivary glands: glands in the mouth that produce *saliva* **50–51, 53**

salt: a *compound* that is produced when an *acid* reacts with a *metal* or with an *alkali*; common salt, or *sodium chloride*, is just one sort of salt **128, 153, 157–159**

satellite: an object that *orbits a planet* **263–265**

scurvy: a *disorder* caused by lack of *vitamin C* in the *diet* **48**

seasons: the different parts of each year (spring, summer, autumn, winter) **80**

sedimentary rocks: these are made from small bits which settle on the bottom of lakes and seas **166**

sense: living things do this when they detect changes in their surroundings **2, 4–6, 14, 78–79**

series: a way of connecting bulbs etc. to an electric *cell* or a power supply so that an electric *current* has to flow through each of them in turn **230–233**

sex cells: special *cells* from males and females that are used for *reproduction* **62–64, 71, 73**

shadow: the dark area behind an object that light can't pass through **201**

sliding friction: the *friction* force between two solid surfaces which slide, or try to slide, across each other **184, 186, 188–189**

small intestine: the narrow part of the intestine between the *stomach* and the *large intestine*; *digestion* finishes and *absorption* takes place here **8, 50–51, 53**

sodium: a *metal element* that is soft and very reactive **126, 141**

sodium chloride: common *salt*; a *compound* of *sodium* and *chlorine* **126, 128, 152–153, 158**

sodium hydroxide: a *compound* that *dissolves* in water to make an *alkali* **150**

solar cells: these produce electricity when energy is transferred to them by light **244**

solar system: the *Sun* and all the *planets* that *orbit* the Sun **260–263, 266–267**

solids: substances that stay in a definite shape **100, 102–103**

soluble: able to *dissolve* **52, 104–105**

solute: what we call a *solid* that *dissolves* in a *liquid* **105**

solution: what you get when a *solid dissolves* in a *liquid* **104–105**

solvent: a *liquid* that *dissolves* a *solid*; some solvents are *drugs* **34, 37, 105**

south pole: the end of a magnet that points south when the magnet is free to move **224–227**

species: plants or animals that can breed with each other (*interbreed*) belong to the same species **74–77**

spectrum: the coloured bands produced by splitting up white light **206**

speed: how fast something moves; the distance that it moves in a certain time **196–197**

sperm: male *sex cell* in humans and other animals **62–64, 66**

stamens: male parts of a flower **73**

stars: distant 'suns' that give out their own light **254–255, 258–259**

static electricity: electric *charges* that are standing still on an object **218–221**

stigma: the part of a flower that *pollen* must land on for *pollination* to happen **70–73**

stomach: an *organ* in the *digestive system* **8, 13, 37, 50–51, 53**

streamlined: a shape that has very little *air resistance* or *drag* **187**

style: the part between the *stigma* and the *ovary* of a flower **70–71, 73**

sulphur dioxide: a *gas* that is produced when many *fuels burn*; it *dissolves* in *water* and makes it *acid* **173, 181**

Sun: the *star* at the centre of the *solar system* **254–257, 259–263, 266–269**

Glossary/index

switch: this is used to break an electric circuit **223, 230–233**

symbol: 1. a shorthand way of writing *elements*, e.g. O for *oxygen* and Ca for *calcium* **124–125**

2. a simple way of showing bulbs, *cells* etc. in an electrical *circuit diagram* **231–232**

T

territory: the space that an animal defends against other animals of the same kind **96**

testes: where *sperm* (male *sex cells*) are made in humans and other animals **62, 66**

thermal energy: the energy something has because it is hot **237–241, 248, 252–253**

tides: a *renewable* energy source caused mainly by the *Moon's gravity* **243, 245, 247**

transparent: what we call substances that light can pass through **99**

turbine: this turns round when you transfer *kinetic energy* to it from air, or water, or steam that is moving **241–243**

U

urine: a liquid containing *water, salts* and urea produced by the kidneys **3, 96**

uterus: where a baby develops until it is born; also called the <u>womb</u> **62–64, 67**

V

vacuole: a space, filled with *cell sap*, in the *cytoplasm* of a plant *cell* **11**

vagina: the opening of the human female *reproductive system* **62–63, 66**

valves: these stop blood from flowing the wrong way in the *heart* and in *veins* **25–26**

veins: blood vessels that carry blood towards the *heart* **9, 26**

ventricles: the two thick-walled lower chambers of the *heart* **25**

vertebrates: animals with skeletons made of bone inside their bodies **16, 18–20**

vibrations: to-and-fro movements that produce sounds **212–215**

virus: a *microbe* that can only live inside another *cell*; viruses cause *diseases* **13, 32–33**

vitamins: substances in food that we need in small amounts to stay healthy **22, 48–49, 54**

volume: the amount of space that something takes up; it is measured in cubic centimetres (cm^3) or millilitres (ml) **100–102**

W

water: a *neutral liquid*; a *compound* made from the *elements hydrogen* and *oxygen* **123, 140–141**

waves: a *renewable* energy source produced by the wind blowing over the sea **243, 245, 247, 268**

weathering: the ways that the weather gradually breaks up and wears away rocks **170–171**

wind: moving air; a *renewable* energy source **242, 245, 247, 268**

windpipe: the breathing tube between your throat and the smaller tubes inside your *lungs* **28**

womb: another word for *uterus*

word equation: a quick way of writing down what happens in a chemical reaction **162–163**